Back from 44 –
The Sacrifice and Courage of a Few

A Story of Heroism in the Skies Over Western Europe.

NICK CRESSY

BACK FROM 44 – THE SACRIFICE AND COURAGE OF A FEW

This book is written to provide information and motivation to readers. Its purpose is not to render any type of psychological, legal, or professional advice of any kind. The content is the sole opinion and expression of the author, and not necessarily that of the publisher.

Copyright © 2019 by Nick Cressy

All rights reserved. No part of this book may be reproduced, transmitted, or distributed in any form by any means, including, but not limited to, recording, photocopying, or taking screenshots of parts of the book, without prior written permission from the author or the publisher. Brief quotations for noncommercial purposes, such as book reviews, permitted by Fair Use of the U.S. Copyright Law, are allowed without written permissions, as long as such quotations do not cause damage to the book's commercial value. For permissions, write to the publisher, whose address is stated below.

Printed in the United States of America.

ISBN   978-1-64552-015-3   (Paperback)
ISBN   978-1-64552-016-0   (Digital)

Lettra Press books may be ordered through booksellers or by contacting:

Lettra Press LLC
18229 E 52nd Ave.
Denver City, CO 80249
1 303 586 1431 | info@lettrapress.com
www.lettrapress.com

CONTENTS

Dedication vii
Prologue ix

Chapter 1:   Situation Normal 1
Chapter 2:   Back to Reality 27
Chapter 3:   What Next? 65
Chapter 4:   Allies Moving On 95
Chapter 5:   Moving Again 118
Chapter 6:   Getting Settled 143
Chapter 7:   Battle of the Bulge 167
Chapter 8:   "Rainbow Leader, Zero Eight" 191

Epilogue 215
Acknowledgements 223
Bibliography 229
320th Bomb Group History 233
About the Author 235

DEDICATION

This book is dedicated to the servicemen assigned to the 320th Bomb Group, April 1942 through December 1945, who fought in the Mediterranean and European Theaters of Operations. For those who did not come home alive, their sacrifice was not in vain. Never forget past, current or future war veterans defending this nation and the freedom for which it represents in this dangerous world.

PROLOGUE

Prime Minister Sir Winston Churchill: "
It is probable that future war will be conducted by a
special class, the Air Force, as it was by the armored
knights of the Middle Ages."

This is a story of courage and sacrifice in the face of overwhelming odds against worldwide enemies during World War II in the skies over Europe and the Mediterranean. Dedicated military servicemen and women performed superbly to liberate our nation and our allies to live in freedom to enjoy the rewards of honest toil.

Aircrew chances of survival were one in three. Combat crew rotation policy varied. The 8th Air Force in the European Theater of Operations initially set the mission limit at 25 in the beginning of its daytime bombing campaign for its heavy bombers, B-17's and B-24's. As the war went on the U.S. Army Air Force (USAAF) determined that it was not feasible to release crews due to manpower limitations, required training time for replacement crews, and maintaining adequate personnel in battle areas. The number of missions crept up incrementally as determined by Army Air Force leadership and eventually, in most cases, for the duration of the war. Many crewmembers ended the war with over 70 missions and some over 100, the exception being the very first aircrews in combat.

Allied bomber crews were rotated out of the combat theater for a number of reasons. There was considerable discussion early on and into late 1944 on how crews would be relieved after completing specific requirements. How much could an aircrew member take under combat conditions? There were several scenarios and factors that determined whether a person would rotate back to the U.S. to train new recruits or be released from active duty. Those factors included the types of aircraft flown (i.e., fighters, heavy or medium bombers, transport, rescue aircraft), the number of hours flown, missions completed and medical conditions both physical and mental. As the war progressed it was obviously advantageous to use the skills and experience of combat veterans to teach or continue to lead the war effort in the combat theater. Point systems, number of missions and often a commander's recommendation were used as the justification for being rotated back to the Zone of the Interior (ZI), the United States. Missions completed was the standard for most of the major commands, 65 was the mission number for the Mediterranean and later in Europe.

Threats to missions and aircrew survivability in the European and Mediterranean Theaters of Operation included German anti-aircraft fire from *Flak*" The 88-millimeter and 105-millimeter cannons were adapted as flak guns from their original design use as a tank cannon or mobile artillery supporting ground combat with a range of over 15,000 feet. They were accurate, mobile and deadly in the hands of experienced gunners; radar also assisted aiming. The word "*flak*" comes from the German word "***FL**ieger**A**bwehr**K**anone*" translated as *flier defense gun* German Flak guns appeared in other various types and calibers both in a fixed position located in towers or more mobile towed versions with lower altitude ranges from 6,000 to 8,000 feet.

Other threats included the German Air Force (Luftwaffe) effective and feared Messerschmitt (Bf) 109 and Focke-Wulf (Fw) 190 fighters. The Bf 109 (a.k.a. Me 109) through constant development remained competitive with the latest Allied fighter aircraft until the end of the war. The Fw 190 underwent improvements as well, which made it effective at high altitude enabling it to maintain relative parity with its Allied opponents.

USAAF fighters that protected bomb groups in Europe were primarily the P-47 Thunderbolt and the P-51 Mustang. The P-47 was effective as a short-to-medium range escort fighter in high-altitude air-to-air combat and when unleashed as a fighter-bomber, proved especially adept at ground attack. The P-51 Mustang possessed excellent range and maneuverability operating primarily as a long-range escort fighter and also as a ground attack fighter-bomber. The P-38 Lightning was also utilized because of its long-range capability and provided excellent bomber escort. It had a good combat record depending on who provides an opinion; the P-38 was not highly regarded in the European Theater of Operations. It had problems related to its engine due to the low quality of European fuels. The fuel problems were resolved with the introduction of an upgraded P-38 "J" model; eventually, P-38 fighter groups transitioned to the new P-51 Mustang by late 1944. When available, British Spitfires also escorted American bombers. Other threats included bad weather, mid-air collisions, friendly fire and unforeseen mechanical problems experienced in-flight that could not be resolved resulting in aircraft and crew losses.

The U.S. Army Air Forces' 320th Bomb Group and its organic squadrons, the 441st, 442nd, 443rd, and 444th, operated out of Dijon-Longvic Airfield France from mid-November 1944 to March 1945 flying the Martin B-26 Marauder. This airfield offered a long concrete runway; it was a former German Luftwaffe base. The airfield had sustained bomb damage since the beginning of the war from allied bombing with buildings and destroyed aircraft wreckage scattered about. This airfield, often referred to as an aerodrome, provided a large base of operations for the 42nd Air Wing, 17th Bomb Group and the 320th Bomb Group inclusively designated as the First Tactical Air Force (Provisional). Also located on this airfield were units of the French Air Force, a P-47 squadron and various Army supporting units. Bombing missions flown out of Dijon-Longvic supported the American Third and Seventh Armies and the French First Army advancing towards Germany through the Alsace-Lorraine region of eastern France.

Severe cold and snowy weather limited operations for the 320th Bomb Group during December 1944 into January 1945. Every effort was made to keep aircraft ready to fly in these cold weather extremes. December was particularly terrible; it was the hardest winter civilians had seen in decades

December 16th 1944 brought the news of a significant breakthrough of German forces in the Ardennes Forest region of Belgium. The battle, known as *"The Battle of the Bulge"*, eventually focused on a strategic road junction at Bastogne, Belgium about 250 miles north of Dijon-Longvic's Airfield. German forces quickly surrounded Bastogne, held by the American 101 ᵗ Airborne and 10th Armored Divisions

The bad weather experienced during December meant that the 320th Bomb Group was prevented from responding in an all out effort to support allied ground forces. There were few days that aircraft could get off the ground to attack targets; crews were on standby more often than in the air conducting bombing missions. A few days after the start of The Battle of the Bulge, a German Panzer tank breakthrough at Hagenau France was of great concern. Hagenau was only 225 miles northeast of Dijon-Longvic Airfield, not a long distance for an unimpeded fast moving German force.

Snow and fog prevented the groups from getting in the air to support offensive operations in and around Colmar and Biche France, known as the "Colmar Pocket", also near Dijon-Longvic Airfield. The Colmar Pocket area was a closer distance of approximately 140 miles north- northeast. If the Allies could not hold off German forces in this area, evacuation would be ordered. The order for evacuation was given however it was reversed as quickly as it was known. American and French forces eventually cleared the Colmar Pocket and continued advancing through the Vosges Mountains in the Alsace-Lorraine region of France into Germany by the end of January 1945. Further north, the Battle of the Bulge was turning toward victory closing the "bulge" to its pre December 16th battle front lines and beyond eventually reaching into German territory.

For the Germans the Battle of the Ardennes, as they called it, was costly with roughly 120,000 soldiers and 600 tanks lost that at this late date of their war effort could not be replaced. Persistent allied day and night strategic bombing of German war assembly and parts plants was devastating. In support of the allied war effort, production of war material in the United States had reached milestones that seemed impossible in the late 1930's. Manufacture of aircraft, tanks, munitions, and other support supplies far exceeded the combined efforts of Germany and Japan by late 1943. Continued allied air superiority advancements prevented German aircraft supporting combined combat operations against allied ground forces. Surviving and demoralized German troops from their Battle of the Ardennes retreated home to defensive positions in western Germany.

The 320th's first assignment was in the Mediterranean Theater of Operations arriving in early 1943 conducting bombing missions against German and Italian forces. Combat operations were conducted out of bases located at Tafaraoui, Algeria, Montesquieu Algeria, Massicault Tunisia and El Bathan/Djedeida Tunisia. The group eventually moved off the African continent setting up operations at Decimomannu Sardinia, and then Alto Corsica. The bomb group participated in the invasions of Italy and Sicily during 1943 and into 1944. As the bomb group moved closer to the southern coastline of France, they were ordered into the European Theater of Operations supporting the consolidated effort to defeat Germany after two major invasion force landings in June and August 1944.

The D-Day invasion at Normandy, Operation Overlord, on June 6th 1944 was a success and put the Germans on a path to defeat. The invasion of southern France, Operation Dragoon, on August 15th 1944 where the 320th was an active participant in bombing pre-invasion and invasion force landing targets was a success as well. The southern invasion of France and the continued allied efforts pushing German forces out of France facilitated the movement of the 320th to France from its base at Alto, Corsica.

Conducting missions from Dijon-Longvic was the groups' first opportunity at bombing targets in German territory. The 320th would end the war with the record of having bombed more countries with the B-26 Marauder Medium Bomber in continuous combat longer than any other bomb group.

A total of 5,266 B-26's were built at two factories one in Baltimore, Maryland and the other Omaha, Nebraska. Newly assembled B-26's were flown to the Army Air Force (AAF) modification center at Offutt Army

Airfield in Nebraska for airframe and equipment changes directed by the Army Air Force. All changes to the originally produced aircraft from the factory were implemented based on field recommendations that were designed to better equip the aircraft. After completion and flight tests, they were flown to New Castle Army Airfield in Maryland where they were further inspected and certified as operationally ready for assignment.

Aircrews delivering B-26's to the European and Mediterranean combat theater of operations from mid-1944 to the end of the war for the 320th Bomb Group were ferried from the United States typically starting from Morrison Field in West Palm Beach, Florida or Lake Charles Army Air Field in Louisiana. Aircraft were primarily routed through a southern route. A northern route was used for other B-26 units located in England and northern France, however either course was used depending on weather and logistical considerations.

The southern route's first stop out of the continental Unites States was Boringuen, Puerto Rico. Subsequent stops included Kinso Field, British Guiana, Belem Field, Brazil and then the long crossing over the Atlantic to Ascencion Island. Taking off from Ascencion Island to the next stop at Marrakech, French Morocco and then the final stop to Decimomannu Sardinia commonly referred to as "Decimo". Ferrying flights to Sardinia changed as the 320th moved on to Corsica and then into France. The southern route stops provided time for refueling, repairing aircraft problems noted during flight, crew rest and recreation. Each stop also provided a unique observation of different countries, cultures, terrain, and climate.

Depending on re-organizations, aircraft were also transferred to and from other B-26 units within the theater of operations. Replacement crew personnel not ferrying aircraft arrived in the theater of operations on board troop ships leaving from an east coast port, Hampton Roads, Virginia, Charleston, South Carolina or New York, New York with a port destination in England or the Mediterranean area.

Training and preparing for combat in B-26's was demanding for pilots and crewmembers. Pilots were trained in single engine aircraft of the day, the Stearman PT-13 Trainer mainly, and then on to more advanced aircraft and pilot selections to fighter planes, bombers or transports. Twin-engine training aircraft like the Beechcraft AT-10, Cessna AT-17, or the Curtiss AT-9 Jeep transitioned pilots to multi-engine operations.

Ground support personnel and aircrews were trained in basic aircraft maintenance tasks. Advanced training for aircrews was more specific to their aircraft assignment and specialties (radio, navigation, bombardier, flight engineering); they received gunnery training on the ground and in the air. After training and certification, crews were formed and assigned to a bomb group at a base located in the United States or designated as replacements and placed wherever they were needed overseas

Each crewmember generally knew where they were being assigned before leaving the United States. If an overseas assignment was not known, replacement organizations in theater were setup to coordinate matching unit requirements with personnel arrivals.

Aircrews typically flew with the same crew as much as possible. Assignments were later determined on who was available and what skill they possessed to fill a need for a mission. Newer crewmembers were assigned to veteran crewmembers with more experience to get a good lesson on duties and responsibilities. When a newly assigned aircrew arrived in theater, they were given familiarization training on gunnery and other standard operating procedures. This training also included flying practice missions before being assigned to an actual combat mission. The feeling from any crewmember was that experience and ongoing familiarization training would get you farther than luck, however when your number came up, it was up.

The B-26 Marauder was nicknamed the *Widow Maker"*, among many other not so nice phrases or derogatory names, and known for not being forgiving to inexperienced pilots. It had a higher landing speed than most bombers and demanded the utmost attention to the airspeed indicator on final approach and landing. Because of the location of a main training base in proximity of Tampa Bay, Florida an unofficial adage cited on a regular basis was *One A Day in Tampa Bay"* This adage referred to dumping a B-26 in Tampa Bay on landing approach or take-off sometimes resulting in crew being killed or severely injured not to mention the destruction of a valuable aircraft

All of that changed over time as training was upgraded to provide trainee pilots with more training time and knowledge of aircraft handling and engine performance anomalies. Aerodynamic modifications increased wingspan along with larger fin and rudder modifications that gave better take off and handling performance. Once the initial problems were resolved, the bomber gained a reputation for reliability and performance. General Doolittle was involved in those changes. He was active in lobbying for the B-26 to strengthen the case for keeping it in production when Congress was considering cancelling the aircraft. Senator Truman, before becoming the Vice President, led the effort in Congress (known as the Truman Committee tasked with investigating defense production) to cancel production having great concern over the number of crashes. Doolittle proved the B-26 was a formidable aircraft and that it just needed upgraded training and slight airframe corrections. Doolittle's efforts included the demonstration of a B-26 flying on one engine maneuvering as if both engines were operating. The demonstration pilot working for Doolittle showed how the B-26 could be handled safely. The plane was taken off the congressional hit list and production and modifications were completed by February 1943.

The operational loss rate for the B-26 throughout the war was 0.422%, a credible record and the best for any bomber in World War II. The last B-26 ever built first flew on April 18th 1945 from the Glen L. Martin's Middle River airfield in Baltimore; it never reached an overseas combat unit and was broken up in the United States after the war. Its name was "Tail End Charlie", "30" serial number 44-68254.

Many B-26's flew in over 100 missions; one plane completed 207 missions. That B-26 was *Flak Bait*" of the 449th Squadron, 322nd Bomb Group based in England. Only a portion of the aircraft is displayed at the Smithsonian National Air and Space Museum. The cockpit section is the portion displayed in the museum; the remainder of the aircraft is in storage locally and could be joined with the front end in the future if desired

The known existence of other B-26's at this writing includes the following:

The *Chino Marauder"* owned by Kermit Weeks based at the Fantasy of Flight facility, Polk City, Florida. This aircraft is a pre-A Model B-26 (1940) and was found in Alaska; it was lost on a flight to Alaska in 1942. *It is the only known flyable B-26*

A former French Air Force aircraft used in training aircraft mechanics and the subject of a negotiated transfer to the U.S. Air Force Museum at Dayton, Ohio was restored to a static condition for display at the U.S. Air Force Museum.

A different former French Air Force aircraft that was parked for many years in a dormant condition at Le Bourget was restored to a static display condition. It is now on permanent display at the Musee de l'Air et de l'Espace, Le Bourget, Paris, France. A B-26 by David Tallichet (using three airframes) is being restored to static display condition by the Empire State Aerosciences Museum at Schenectady, New York.

A B-26 is being restored by the Military Aircraft Preservation Society (MAPS) of Akron, Ohio using leftovers from airframes found by David Tallichet.

Hill Aerospace Museum located on Hill Air Force Base (AFB) Utah is working on restoring a recent acquisition of a B-26 fuselage recovered by the Aerospace Heritage Foundation of Utah in 2000

The Utah Beach Museum (Musee du Debarguement Utah Beach) France currently has a static display of "Dinah Might" (41-31576 "131576") representing the 553rd Bomb Squadron. It shows the D-Day invasion paint scheme and was originally manufactured as 44-68219

In a speech by Sir Winston Churchill on August 20th 1940, Churchill was encouraging a nation in siege and praising the ongoing efforts of Royal Air Force pilots fighting the Battle of Britain during 1940. In that speech, the following quote appropriately praises Royal Air Force pilots' efforts. It can also be applied to the future efforts of allied aircrews in the Pacific, European and Mediterranean Theaters of Operations.

"Never in the field of human conflict has so much been owed by so many to so few."

320th Bomb Group Bombing Mission over Italy

CHAPTER 1

SITUATION NORMAL

General George S. Patton, Jr.:
"There is a time to take counsel of your fears,
and there is a time to never listen to any fear."

Fresh snow on the ground, calm and bone chilling cold on this pre dawn winter morning. The snowfall of the last three days seems to have taken a break; it has been colder than usual with plenty of snow over the last two months. A routine but distinctive sound of the cold crunch of snow under warm military issue boots as Staff Sergeant Buijak heads out of his squadron operations office and headquarters into the squadron tent area to wake up aircrews for today's mission. The squadron operations officer Captain O'Mahony is waking up the officers.

New day and another mission, maybe. Sleeping comfortably in my bunk I am starting to wake up on my own for some reason. I hear the snow crunching footsteps of someone approaching my tent door. The door opens letting in cold air and some snowflakes and a familiar figure approaches with his flashlight shining in my direction.

"Bentas... get up... mission briefing at 0900 hours... mission take-off at 1300, pass it on," barked Buijak.

"Get Ken and Ed up too... come on."

"OK... OK... I'm up... I guess the mission is on?" I asked rubbing the sleep out of my eyes and slowly sitting up in my bunk. "Come on... get that flashlight out of my face."

"Sorry... yea... looks like it's on, weather is sketchy but looks good enough... so far."

"Base Weather thinks it will clear before it snows again tomorrow."

"See you later... hot coffee waiting for me in the office."

Buijak in a hurry turns around to head back to a warm pot of coffee and then stops to look back, "You guys are my last wake up tent... better get moving for hot breakfast and a fresh brewed cup of "Joe"... everybody's betting on real eggs this morning."

"Yea... right, not betting on it," I said feeling the cold of the tent and standing up to get the rest of my uniform on watching Buijak rush out the door for his cup of "Joe".

It was zero three hundred. I woke Ken, my tent mate and friend from Detroit, and got Ed aroused to get up so we can catch the chow when it's nice and hot and plentiful. "Come on guys get up... mission today and the food's getting cold... get cleaned up... come on... move." Peeking outside my tent on January 19th 1945 the cold and snow making our jobs difficult and miserable... the snowfall has stopped. Sure wish the temperature would break.

Another mission to my credit, number forty-four if not called back; if the mission is scrubbed with no bomb drop and no presence over enemy territory, no credit. France has been cold, colder than any memory of most of my fellow airmen and any that I can remember having grown up in Michigan around the Detroit area. I took many a hunting trip to the northern part of the Lower Peninsula of Michigan with my dog "Duke" and several close friends from school. We prepared well for cold and wet weather, but we had opportunities to get in lodges and diners to get warm whenever we felt the need. The cold seems to penetrate my bones; I never seem to get warm.

Since our arrival here in November recreational activities and Red Cross clubs like the "Scrub House" were set up in the city of Dijon about twelve miles from our tent area around the "Chateau de Longecourt" in Longecourt. Movie theaters and other shops and approved cabaret clubs were available to socialize during off-duty; "G.I. Joe's Rendezvous" is a favorite. Dijon is about three miles from our airfield at Dijon-Longvic, a former Luftwaffe base. Dijon is a major French city with a population of about one hundred thousand. Going to the Scrub House and other places when we are not on mission gets us out of the cold and helps us forget where we are and offers a nice break in the routine.

Dijon at times had been placed off limits by Military Police for good reason. There was an off limits notice on December 15th; an angry crowd lynched a Nazi collaborator, the city's mayor. He was more interested in keeping Nazi occupiers happy than the city residents. Having had enough of him, the citizens of Dijon took the opportunity to seek their form of justice. It is hard to understand the anger, but when you hear and see the results of the occupation you understand. The crowd took the mayor to the jail, hanged him and then dragged his body through the streets.

Other incidents of revenge occurred when the townspeople identified certain young women of Dijon who had lived and slept with Germans during the occupation; they shaved their heads when caught, humiliating them in a public forum. Situations like these are best left alone, none of us want to get in the middle of anything that might get us in jail, hurt or killed. We all understand the anger from the Nazi occupation; it doesn't do us any good to be around any of this, we have enough to deal with on missions and getting back in one piece.

Headquarters for our bomb group is located in the Chateau de Longecourt next to our tent area and has nice rooms, warm fireplaces, and a definite taste of luxury in this region of France. Our squadron, the 441st, is in Longecourt along with the 442nd in smaller chateaus. The 443rd and 444th squadrons are in the village of Bessey Les Citeaux southeast of Longecourt about two miles. All of the enlisted are housed in tents, with a few exceptions; officers got the chateau rooms and some are billeted in villagers' homes if available. Sleeping in tents with wood stoves in this weather is annoying having to constantly keep track of firewood and restocking that firewood to stay warm. There is a constant effort to find firewood to keep the stove stoked; the villagers are getting a little upset by our scavenging for wood throughout Longecourt. I sleep in my uniform most of the time with heavy socks and gloves; it is miserable to shave, clean up, and sleep. Cleaning up is a chore and takes more time than those nice warmer days on Sardinia and Corsica… part of the extra time we have to get ready for briefings and pre flight checks in this weather. The extra time also gave us the opportunity to check out gear and equipment for potential problems.

Venturing outside in the dark cold chills my bones. After we got cleaned up Ken, Ed and I head over to the bomb group headquarters to check the mission assignment posting; Buijak was still working on it when I hit the sack last night. It seems a little calmer and maybe more snow will hold off until tomorrow. Buijak did tell me last night that most of us were on the board so we could expect a wake up call this morning.

"What do you think about flying today?" I said.

Ken looked around at the dreary looking dark sky and snow-covered area surrounding our tents, "I think it's too cold and I would love to get back in bed by our warm stove."

"I am definitely getting tired with maybe going out on mission and sitting in our planes on the ground… can't get my mission count and this war over with sitting in my tent."

I agreed, "Got that right… this weather has been too damn cold, don't like not being on a mission."

"Ed… are you awake?" Ken asked.

"Yea… sure would like to sleep in today," Ed said groggily.

We continue walking towards our squadron and group headquarters office building and enter the busy doorway and head to the operations board for the mission-posting sheet.

We know when we will fly on missions the day before when the operations staff post missions on the Squadron Operations Board, that is if it was posted before we hit the sack for the night. Sometimes you can get snagged as replacement crew on the same day; you will get a flashlight in your face and a wake up shout without warning if that happens. Looking at the mission assignments on the board and scanning through the listing, other crewmembers are mulling around the operations board looking for their assignment.

"Ken… Ed, look," I said pointing at today's mission posting, "I am on "My Gal II" battle number "08"… replacement plane."

"Lieutenants' (Lt.) McCurdy and Cudworth are pilot and co-pilot, John Hill bombardier, Henry "Bud" Tothammer tail gunner, Lloyd Rahl radio operator and waist gunner and me in the turret."

"Um… guess the ground crew got that newer B-26 that arrived recently from the States ready to go," I said amazed that a new "My Gal" was ready to go so quickly.

The previous "My Gal" was hit by flak on December 23rd, the plane's 114th mission. I watched the aircraft breaking apart and tumbling in flight to the ground. Not much to say when you see close friends die in front of you, just shock and delayed grief. I know this has happened before; it doesn't make it any easier to take or get used to. Yes, it is war; you tend to cling to friends anyway even though you or they may not return from the next mission. I need to, like the rest of us, make time to grieve. I need to focus on the mission and getting back alive.

Staring at the board I tell Ken, "John I know well… haven't flown much with Tothammer or Rahl or either of the pilots."

"McCurdy was the co-pilot on my first mission flying out of Sardinia in July and pilot for the January 2nd mission two weeks ago and co-pilot on the December 30th mission… um… never flew with Cudworth."

Ken finds his and Ed's assignment, "Looks like both of us are on "04"… good plane."

"Captain O'Mahony… pilot."

"I've flown with him several times," Ken said, Ed is still groggy and silently rubbing the sleep out of his eyes.

"OK… good plane, I really need some coffee," Ed slurred.

Ken shook his head and grinned at Ed, "Rumor has him as the next 44^t Commanding Officer when Major Smith moves on, he likes flying "04"… that's his favorite."

"I think that is also Major Smith's favorite plane," I said.

Ken continues to comment, "Yea… "04" is a good plane."

"He's been around a long time… as operations officer he pulls his rank to get "04" for his missions."

"Good for him… makes him feel comfortable and that's a good thing for a pilot and crew."

"He likes "14" too… but I think he favors "04"… absolutely."

"Don't see Major Smith on the mission today."

"Yea… I heard that rumor too… good guy, he came over just before I did in June last year," I said and commented on both planes.

"I flew on "14" several times… and "04" once last October."

"O'Mahony has been my co-pilot on just a few missions… don't know him real well."

"Too bad we don't have a choice on what plane we ride on for missions… some are better than others."

"Yea… some are just full of problems, others are great planes," Ken commented. Ed shook his head up and down. Ken and I think he will fall asleep sitting at the chow hall table.

Ken and I were engineer gunners so we never flew on the same aircraft during missions; we compared notes many times about aircraft problems we found and what we did to resolve those problems during missions. Ed was a radio operator and gunner; we've flown on several missions. Ed was part of my original crew. We shared notes on pilots and co-pilots. Earlier this month a close friend, Gene Fulk also an engineer gunner, rotated back to the states after sixty-six missions, sure miss his companionship. Gene, Ken, Ed and I spent a lot of time together between missions in Sardinia and Corsica.

"Ken… come on let's get over to the chow hall for a hot breakfast, maybe we'll have something new… like real eggs," I jokingly said.

"Yea… maybe it will be sixty degrees tomorrow," Ken responds with a grin and tone of sarcasm.

"I don't think we'll see eggs today," Ed said.

"Oh… are you finally waking up?" Ken asked sarcastically, trying to get a rise out of a sleepy-headed Ed.

"Yea… I'm up… I was sleeping so good, too."

"Just get me to the coffee."

Breakfast for this morning is powdered eggs made to taste like real eggs, toast, pancakes, and coffee; sometimes ketchup on the eggs makes them taste really good or makes them taste like something else. It seems like a distant memory of what a real egg tastes like, hope the chow hall supply sergeant can get some real eggs for all of us to enjoy. To give credit to the supply sergeant we did get some eggs the first week we got to France and a few times since. The food in this chow hall is somewhat palatable but better than it has been for a while. What is so nice is to have real plates to eat from and French waitresses serving our food, better food and service with a French accent. No Kitchen Patrol (KP) required since Italian prisoners of war did all the kitchen chores. Topics of discussion for this morning include the cold weather, a subject we seem not to ignore or stop complaining about, the rumors of the war effort and the mission for today.

Since January 7th the Germans have been retreating but we all wonder if they will reconstitute their forces, turn around and come back into France in our direction. The Battle of The Bulge started on December 16th and it has been nerving since. German forces have been real close to us and we couldn't even get up on most days to support ground forces because of bad weather. Just before Christmas Day, I think on the 2^{t}, a German Panzer tank force broke through at Hagenau, which is way too close for comfort. Rumor had it that we were going to get our B-26's out of here with only a pilot and co-pilot on board and the rest of us would stay behind, destroy the planes that could not fly and fight as infantry. We got the evacuation order to get out but it was recalled just as quickly as it was issued; glad we missed that bullet

Over the last several weeks we held out in or near our planes waiting to take off, hoping that maybe the weather would clear and get planes up for a mission. We even slept in our plane to be ready to get off the ground on a moments notice. There were a few times we would actually take off on these damn icy runways with our bomb load of four thousand pounds, fly around in the cloud cover for over an hour and land with bombs still on board and no credit for a mission

The last mission I flew was January 2nd and I must have had four or five missions cancelled since because of weather. Missions getting cancelled can be a blessing and you were glad to stay on the ground because of particularly bad flying weather or the reputation of the target area being damn dangerous with heavy flak or fighter threat. We endured the cold and we were bundled up in our flight suits with the heaters on as much as possible.

We also are getting used to an occasional night alert because of German night fighter aircraft intruding our airspace. We ignore the sound of alerts and ponder whether or not we need to run to a bomb shelter. It is too cold and our cots with our new sleeping bags and the warmth they provide makes us think of staying to keep warm or freeze on the way to the shelter. The shelter is cold as the outdoors and so as soon as we think this through their planes are gone.

God bless the maintenance crews, despite the severe cold they ready all assigned aircraft, engines working, fuel tanks filled, bombs loaded, defensive machine guns operable with ammunition loads in place. Sometimes I think I don't have it as bad when I think of those guys on the flight line maintaining the aircraft day and night; they really do have living conditions worse than the rest of us. The intense cold makes maintaining the aircraft a tough job, even routine tasks such as spark plug changes and minor adjustments are painful and numbing to their hands. Skinned knuckles, cracked flesh from the freezing metal and the raw gasoline, noses running and short tempers are the norm. They have been inventive in creating shelters out of nothing to keep them out of the weather in that open exposed airfield. Crappy duty but someone has to do it

Ken, Ed and I finish up eating at the chow hall and head to the briefing room for today's mission. Pilots, Co-Pilots and crews assemble for briefings on routes to target, weather, navigation points and intelligence.

We all took our seats in the briefing room, everyone is in their own conversation and then the chatter of small talk breaks with the shout of "Ten Hut", everyone stops and stands up at attention. The Deputy Group Commander, Major Hayward, enters and heads to the front of the briefing room. He stops turning around and then in his authoritative loud voice, "At ease, take your seats."

He looks around the audience and begins a short speech standing at ease with his hands behind his back in his usual good military form. He began his combat flying career with the Royal Canadian Air Force (RCAF) and then transferred to the Army Air Forces and has flown combat missions in Tunisia, Sicily, Italy, France, and now Germany. Highly regarded and popular, great officer and leader, he should be pinning on Lieutenant Colonel silver oak leaves soon.

"We have been weather restricted most of the last month and this month from getting off the ground to support combat ground operations and destroying enemy supply and support targets, but today that will change… we will be flying a mission today."

"I will be flying today as the main force commander."

"Mission lead names and details will be briefed by the Group Operations Officer… Major Evans."

"Major… it's all yours," Looking over to the major he nods and hands over the mission brief

With pointer in hand Major Evans begins, "Today's mission is the Achern Marshalling Yards east of Strasbourg France in German territory."

The Operations Sergeant for the 441st Squadron Staff Sergeant Buijak is assisting the major today and takes the cover off the map board revealing the details of the routes to and from the primary and secondary target. He also uncovers the flight schedule timetable board.

Major Evans points to the board.

"Aircraft stations at 1215."

"Engine start at 1220."

"Taxi for first take off and lead aircraft is 1250."

"Take off 1300… following aircraft at thirty-second intervals."

"Because of the cold weather… engine start up is planned for 30 minutes versus 20 minutes before taxi and initial take off."

He continues with emphasis on safety and visual verification, "Make sure you can see the take off of the planes in front of you then proceed… be on time and safe."

"Begin form up over Dijon at 1315."

"Proceed to Luneville for a planned 1400 hours rendezvous with escort fighters... P-47's."

"Grid reference is WV-0800."

"Standard operating procedure for take off and climb."

"Climb out at 175 to 190 mph up to 1000 feet before your first turn."

"Form up over Dijon at 3000 feet and proceed to Luneville reaching a flight altitude of 8000 feet."

"Flight leads have discretion for climb to that altitude."

"Cloud cover and visibility will determine altitude adjustments for the bomb run from the operations order."

He continues with the latest weather report, "Weather reports indicate stratocumulus clouds at eight to ten thousand feet."

"Scattered multilayered thin stratus up to eight thousand feet over northeastern France and the western German border defined by the Rhine River."

He pauses and then elaborates further, "I know we've been screwed by bad weather and wasted time in reconnaissance flights... weather shouldn't be too much of a concern."

"But... anything can change, stay sharp."

"Base Weather says that another snow front may move in tomorrow."

He pauses and continues the brief with conviction having been frustrated from previously cancelled missions due to weather, "The weather is not going to stop us from today's mission, scattered reports have clearing and overcast conditions fluctuating so there may be a decision enroute to change the primary target area to the secondary."

"Be ready if that happens."

Moving to the map and pointing at the detail he continues, "We will attack the German troop marshalling area near Achern with two flights to target... a decoy flight and a main force."

"The secondary target is the Lahr Barracks and Supply area, Germany."

"Two flights one decoy the other main force for the secondary as well."

He continues shuffling through pages of the published operations order, "The Mission Commander, designated "Bingo One", is Captain Cahan."

"Decoy flight lead pilot, designated "Rainbow Leader", is Captain O'Mahony."

"The main force flight commander is Major Hayward designated "Jigsaw"… with Lt. Rolling as flight lead pilot."

"Additional aircraft in support of this mission include P-47 escort fighters and… two in-flight spares for this mission, Lieutenants' McCurdy and Robinson."

Adding a quip, "Lt. McCurdy… your aircraft is "Tail End Charlie"."

Lt. McCurdy responds with a smile, "Yes sir… tail end spare, that's me."

After a short audience chuckle, Major Evans continues, "Intelligence reports indicating enemy preparations to deploy fighters… our little friends will be our cover."

"The Germans are probably just as prepared as we are for this break in weather."

"They will be looking for our bombers along their border… keep your eyes peeled."

"There are still German fighter pilots hungry for a fight… especially as we bomb their homeland at will."

"There have been reports of German fighter pilots being trained to ram bombers."

"Watch out… this hasn't happened since P-51 and B-24 crews reported ramming incidents in early 1944," he continued, "The result of a ramming, as you might think, is catastrophic… and it can happen real fast."

"They may start this again in desperation… it's effective but stupid."

"We think part of their training for ramming is also to survive it… they may have a way to approach and ram… then the pilot will attempt to jump out of the way, if possible."

"Gunner's be alert and knock these guys out… they will get in close and fast."

Major Evans continues with operations order in hand and looking up, "Take off noted earlier is 1300 hours."

"Rendezvous with P-47 escorts over Luneville scheduled for 1400 hours… from Luneville proceed to Schirmech One checkpoint."

"Grid reference for Schirmech… WV-6287."

Putting down the operations order on the briefing table, he takes his pointer and points to the map at Luneville north of Dijon then drawing a line with his pointer to the Schirmech checkpoint east of Luneville not quite in German territory south of Strasbourg near the Rhine River. Continuing on he points out and circles the map location for the primary target, Achern.

He then points out the secondary target route to Luneville, Schirmech and crossing the Rhine River to Lahr in German territory, "Decision change to the secondary target will be made at the best possible time to allow navigation to adjust the Initial Point to the Bomb Run on Lahr."

"Lead Navigator will brief pilots and co-pilots on alternate flight routes and details for the Initial Point to the target Bomb Run… that includes of course the primary and secondary targets for decoy and main force."

He continues with a warning, "As I said earlier, we will have two flights for this mission today… let me be clear and I mean crystal clear… the 17th and 320th Bomb Groups will not fly over Switzerland… let me repeat that, do not fly over Switzerland."

Then in a firm and authoritative voice, "There will be no mistakes on targets and no mistaking when you are over neutral territory, remember last month's misguided mission… the brass got their asses chewed big time… serious stuff and the shit rolls down hill right at you."

"Also… do not land in Switzerland by mistake or on purpose."

"You all know what that means… so don't do it."

Switzerland being a neutral country will get you the assistance needed if your plane was severely damaged but you would be interned for the duration of the war. The war effort needs everyone to get back to home base

"Watch your navigation and check in with Sector Control for correct steer back to base… don't be embarrassed if you have doubts and need an assist."

"The weather and instrument malfunction can, as you all know, get in the way of navigation… ask and be careful."

We are located close to the German, Switzerland and French borders, you can get disoriented and fly over neutral territory if you are not paying attention. There was a recent incident of mistaking a target location for German territory no civilians were killed. That incident was last month; there was a bomb drop mistake over Switzerland. A lot of civilians could have been killed and they would not have known what hit them. No one was hurt but it initiated an investigation from the top Allied brass, General Eisenhower even showed up to talk with bomb group leadership. It was determined that it was not a lack of leadership but an unfortunate mistake of target identification.

Major Evans continued referencing the operations order intelligence report, "Intelligence reports and other ground observations indicate a high concentration of flak guns not in the target areas but outside each area along the German border, the Rhine River."

"According to the last reconnaissance flight there were not as many gun positions located in and around the target area."

"Photos were taken and can be viewed in the Intelligence Office at group HQ, they are classified."

There is an assumption that flak would be a problem even as the Germans may be retreating in this area, but they are in their own country and building up their defensive capability along the border. They may not have had time to build up the target areas for our mission today, too bad intelligence is not more precise.

Continuing on, "Radio calls signs for the 320th is "Shorty", Control Center Voice Call Sign is "Baggage" on Channel "C"."

"The fighter escort Voice Call Sign is "Cobra", the cancellation Code Word is "Meatball", questions so far?"

"Captain… do you have any input for this brief?" None heard from an officer talking low to another officer in an unnecessary conversation. He continued, "Call Sign for Sector Control is "Boxcar" on Channel "B"."

"Tower control call sign remains "No Room"."

"Taxi flare signal is Red."

"Take off flare signal is Green."

More detail is briefed and questions asked regarding ground intelligence for both target areas as to what and how much is located at each target area, troops, trucks, supplies and civilian locations to avoid. The concern is the flak gun locations that may be hidden throughout the target areas that have not been reported. These marshalling areas by their nature are heavily defended; maybe the Germans have not had the opportunity to build up in their retreat. Collateral damage in civilian areas too often is unavoidable and certainly unintentional, we try to steer clear of it as much as possible.

Our bomb group has an excellent reputation of being accurate on target, Patton himself asked for our group to support his efforts based on our reputation and his observation of missions in support of his forces since our arrival in France. The briefing for the navigational details for pilots, co-pilots and navigators continues as the rest of us are dismissed. After briefings, depending on the end of the briefing and take off time, I give my gear a second and third look over to check on condition. Got my .45 pistol and holster, flight suit with warmer, boots, chute harness, gloves, hat and scarf. I have my ID bracelet from my wife that my gloves and suit arms cover but it is Mary's gift to me, it says affectionately on the reverse,

This man belongs to me, Mary"

She sure does, can't wait to get this war over with and get home to her. Seems like forever since I held her in my arms. Looking around for anything I may have missed but I think I am ready to get this mission over with, we should be back around 1530 or 1600. I need to write a letter home when I get back; Mary is always on my mind.

"Ken, is our ride here?" I said.

"Yea… let's go, the faster we get there we can get the heaters going in our suits, damn it's cold." Ken, Ed and I grabbed our equipment and headed toward the back of the truck. Hopping in the back on the cold metal floor wasn't pleasant, the floor had snow and some hard mud clumps scattered around.

Our ride to the airfield and our plane is about 20 minutes. We all cram in the six-by-six deuce-and-a-half GI trucks with tent canopy overhead and cold wood bench seats. The driver is taking it slow to avoid skidding off the roads in this weather, ice forms quickly since it has snowed and sleeted off and on throughout the last three days.

As we get to the airfield it is amazing how much snow the ground crews have moved out of the way to keep the runway and taxiways clear. When the Group Commander directs missions all kinds of equipment gets into the effort, turbine-fan motor-driven snowplows, bulldozers, and graders. Army engineers did not always keep the roads to and from our living quarters and the airfield open so we all get involved using shovels and brooms and other heavy equipment. I'm moving to a climate where there is no snow after the war; don't ever want to own a snow shovel

Finally arrived at our B-26 "My Gal II" tail number "08" newly painted tail number in the group's color yellow for our pre-flight. Frustration settles in as we arrive and notice the snow was all around the aircraft. We are going to have to shovel a path in front of the wheels, sweep snow off the wings then start our pre flight checks. The grumbling started, as I got ready to leap off the truck into the snow.

Waved at Ken and Ed, "See you all later… let's head into Dijon."

"Yea… sounds great." Ken smiled and waved his right hand in a friendly salute. Ed smiled and waved.

John, our bombardier, being more vocal than most of us shouted out as we approached our plane, "Are you kidding me… damn it!"

He continued and sounding even more pissed off, "Can we make this harder… what a FUBAR!"

We all felt the same way. FUBAR gets in the way a lot and gets to be a common adage when an unexpected frustrating situation arises. Don't know who started or made up the phrase "*F***ed p Beyond All Recognition*" but it makes you feel good to opine when something goes wrong

All of us looked around at the snow around the wheels and on the wings and complained that we really don't have time for this; Lt. McCurdy sternly looked at John and the rest of us and said, "Come on damn it, I don't like this either."

"Get it done."

We grumbled to ourselves as we worked to clear the path for our wheels and snow off the wings and plane body done as quickly as possible. We finished and went on to our checks avoiding dirty looks at the ground crew.

I checked engine cowlings installed and secure. Lloyd and Bud check fuel levels and caps secured. The pilots check the overall appearance of the aircraft, the landing gear for the leg irons and safety clamps off and the Pitot tube cover removed. They enter their compartment through the front nose gear hatch to start checklists. I enter the aircraft through the waist windows aft of the bomb bay, a little hard with all my gear.

Settling inside the aircraft I move forward with John to the bomb bay to check bomb racks secure and safety wires in place. I check the fuel tank valves in the bomb bay for "ON"... emergency flap and main landing gear cranks stowed... hydraulic fluid levels good... emergency bomb bay door opening pressure at 1,200 pounds per square inch... emergency air brake pressure at 1,000 pounds per square inch, all good. Parachute packs for each crew in place, emergency rescue and first aid packs, flak vests and helmet on board. Guns ready and ammunition cans ready.

During engine start I move forward to the pilot's compartment so I can look over the pilots shoulder at all of the gauges, all seems good to go. The ground crew stands by during engine start with fire extinguishers as always in case of fire. They signal McCurdy ready to start the left engine, the Number One, and then start Number Two on the right.

Lt. McCurdy begins the engine start checklist looking down at the list and at the instrument panel gauges and over to Lt. Cudworth as he verifies each step.

"Ignition switch to "Both" magnetos." "Both."

"Booster pumps to "ON"." "On."

"Engine primer "ON"." "On."

"Energizer switch hold to "Left" until inertia flywheel reaches maximum RPM." "Max... OK."

"Primer switch and starter switch "ON" and "Left"." "On… left." "Mixture control "AUTO RICH"." "Auto rich… check."

"Engine is firing, set throttle to 800 RPM until the oil pressure gets up… OK, increase RPM to 1000." "Roger… RPM's 800… pressure up… to 1000… check."

Everything looks good from my view for Number One. Starting Number Two McCurdy repeats the same steps; Number Two looks good.

McCurdy signals disconnect external ground power cable and confirms with the ground crew. He continues on with the final checks before we can move out to taxi and take off, "External power cable disconnected."

"Check hydraulic pressure… 800 to 1050 PSI." "PSI at 1020."

"Oil shutters as needed." "Roger… oil shutter."

"Carburetor air control levers at "COLD" position." "Cold position… check."

"Radios set."

"Lloyd, got the tower yet?"

Lloyd establishes communication with Baggage Control on Channel "C" and Boxcar on Channel "B". He hands over to Lt. McCurdy, "Sir… "No Room" is also on Channel "B"."

"Channel "C" is also open."

Lt. McCurdy confirms radio set with the tower, No Room, "Lloyd… thanks."

"Tower this is Zero Eight standing by for taxi flare and altimeter setting… over."

The tower controller verifies settings, "Hold for take off… wait for signal flare."

"Altimeter is seven two six feet, out."

"Roger, No Room… out," Lt. McCurdy confirms with the tower and sits relaxed watching the engines run up monitoring the gauges.

"Engines sound good… gauges OK."

"Hydraulic fluid levels good."

"Emergency air brake pressure and generators good to go," I confirmed with Lt. McCurdy.

Lt. McCurdy looks over to Cudworth, "Start the take off checklist… take off should be in about ten minutes."

"Time looks good… we should be on schedule."

From the checklist, McCurdy quickly reads, "All flight controls free to move."

"Supercharger controls to "LOW"." "Low… check."

"Carburetor air cold and control in neutral." "Neutral… check."

"Cowl flaps full open." "Full open."

"Oil cooler flaps open." "Flaps open."

"Mixture controls "AUTO RICH"." "Auto rich… check."

"Prop circuit breaker buttons in." "In."

"Prop selector switches to "AUTOMATIC"." "Automatic."

"Prop governor controls full forward to "HIGH RPM"." "Check… high RPM."

"Set prop and throttle locks." "Roger… locks set."

"Apply 3 degrees right rudder tab." "Three degrees… check."

"Wing flaps to one-half." "One-half… check."

"Booster pumps to "ON"." "Pumps on… check."

"Crew at stations… Bentas confirm all hatches, bomb doors closed and secured," I confirmed and Lt. Cudworth confirmed as each item was checked off

We wait till our direction to taxi from the tower; I can see the red flare for taxi. McCurdy confirms taxi flare and nods to Cudworth; McCurdy grabs the controls and slowly moves out for taxi to the runway.

As we taxi out to the runway, we can see snow blowing all around, looks like it is undoing the snow plowing efforts of the ground crews. In position between the pilots I continue to check all gauges and to observe the take off, I'll move back to my turret position once we are airborne. McCurdy brings the aircraft to our position in line for take off. The Green flare has gone off and planes start to take off. Our position is last as we watch each B-26 before us take off into some low clouds and ascend. We wait for our turn. The delay offers all of us the opportunity to double-check our checklists and equipment. Silence throughout the plane as we wait. The skies seem to be better for flying than it has been the last several weeks, even better than those hour long "we can bomb and find the target" reconnaissance rides that didn't give us any mission credit and wasted our time. Turning onto the runway the snow is still blowing like a small blizzard from the previous planes take off. I can still see the green flare burning off on our right side.

We are heavy for take off with four one thousand pounders, fuel, gear and crew, McCurdy brings the plane to full power and we accelerate. A little bumpy rolling down the runway, we pick up speed and lift off at 140 miles per hour. McCurdy releases the landing gear lock and pulling the landing gear lever to "UP". "Indicator showing full retraction… flaps "UP".

Cudworth confirms as the aircraft continues to pick up speed approaching 175 miles per hour and moving faster, "Roger… gear and flaps up… full retraction."

McCurdy acknowledges, "Roger, let's get this mission over with."

The airfield fades behind us. As we gain altitude we notice the clouds are low but can see some patches of blue sky as well and high clouds at about eight thousand feet. After ascending through low clouds and getting situated to form up with our planes we level off, I could see some of the rest of our aircraft through the clouds. McCurdy increases and then maintains airspeed at 190 miles per hour and continues climbing to an altitude of one thousand feet before our first turn. He and Cudworth listen for joining up directions, watching for visual confirmation and listening for navigation indications from the flight lead.

Everyone has their eyes peeled for other aircraft to avoid a mid-air collision. I can see our formation up ahead at about three thousand feet, still scattered clouds restricting some visual confirmations. Looks like all aircraft are in formation, it's tough with the cloud cover.

McCurdy and Cudworth have to watch and listen for any missteps in other aircraft flight paths. The German fighters have the same problem. They wouldn't want to attack in this kind of cloud cover; they would run into each other or directly at one of us without warning in an unwanted collision

I took one last look at the aircraft gauges in front of the pilots; all looks good turning around heading back to my gun turret position. It is always a struggle to fit into the turret gun position with all this cold weather gear on, but once I get situated in the seat I can see great. Turret movement works smoothly and the gun elevation switches are functioning. Spinning around to view 360 degrees of sky. "Sir... can we test fire our guns?"

Lt. McCurdy responds, "Yea... just a few rounds... watch out where."

"We are tail end so make sure you shoot aft and away from the formation."

"Just a few rounds... one burst... OK?"

"Roger sir."

Squeezing my trigger I fire one burst, maybe four rounds. Checking the belt feed, looks good. I hear the tail gunner, Bud, and John in the waist position below me fire off a few bursts. I smell that familiar odor of cordite in the turret

We gradually increase our altitude and air speed as the flight lead directs the formation to eight thousand feet towards Luneville. The formation is on track for rendezvous with our escort fighters over Luneville north of Dijon; flying time forty minutes. Cloud cover is scattered with multilayered stratus clouds; the occasional cumulus tops extend up to about ten thousand feet. The sight is beautiful. I can see breaks in the clouds and small blue patches of sky.

Looking down through the cloud gaps I can see the snow-covered French landscape. There are dark lines throughout showing roads, as well as the darker forest areas and what appears to be vehicle or tank tracks in open fields from German and Allied forces movements throughout the area. It looks dreary but the occasional sunshine breaks through to show the bright white of snow. No reports of German fighter threats so far and we are on our way to rendezvous with the P-47's; they will follow us over the Rhine to our target in Germany.

Listening to "Baggage" Control radio chatter, McCurdy hears "Meatball" for the primary target area, "Sounds like Achern is socked in for a bomb run... heading to the secondary."

Radio silence is resumed. McCurdy comments to Cudworth with some doubt as to getting to either target, "The weather must be moving in again."

"Lahr isn't too far south of the primary… maybe a no-go on the secondary too… maybe."

We divert our concentration to the secondary target area at Lahr Germany, no change in checkpoints for Initial Point locations briefed this morning. There is no chatter on the plane during missions, only when the situation requires responses or giving out warnings of enemy fighters and positions, no need to chitchat.

As we approach Luneville our escort fighters are not in sight; radio chatter has "Cobra" en route. We will need to make as many 360-degree turns as necessary adding flight time to our mission to allow our P-47 escorts time to rendezvous

Lt. Cudworth looking all around out the windshield says, "Escorts are late… hope they don't take too long to meet up."

McCurdy responds noting the flight lead turning the group formation in wide 360-degree turns as we wait for the escorts, "Yea… the flight lead is starting a 360 degree turn… keep a sharp eye out for fighters,"

"Theirs and ours."

Cudworth acknowledges, and the rest of the crew responds in unusual unison, "Roger."

"I think we are all listening… never heard a chorus of "Roger" before."

"Roger… roger… sir," Someone in the back responds in a quick quip of humor. A lighter moment in the mission, takes the edge off.

On the start of the third turn over Luneville I spotted our P-47's maneuvering around towards our formation in a protective cover position.

Lt. Cudworth scanning forward, right then left notices the escorts, "Look… 9 o'clock… P-47's."

McCurdy glances towards the 9 o'clock position, "Yea… good to see our little friends."

"John... arm the bombs, safety wires off," Lt. McCurdy directs John, as we maneuver to the Initial Point and Bomb Run on target. John removes the safety wires on the bomb fuses. He will move forward to the bombardier seat in the nose of the aircraft at the Initial Point (IP) just before the Bomb Run to toggle the bomb releases.

We turn east to reach our next checkpoint at Schirmech just west of the Rhine River, still over French territory. The silence starts again except for the humming sound of the engines and the rushing air outside the aircraft; it is getting colder as we gain a higher attack altitude, my warming element in my suit seems to be a little off. I can see from my gun turret position the cloud formations at different levels; there are a few small blue-sky patches but the ground looks clear enough to get a run at the secondary target location. Weather can change in what seems to be an instant; clear patches of sky can change to clouds in a short amount of time. I don't see any German fighter planes nor have I heard warnings over the intercom.

We are not expecting a lot of flak according to intelligence reports from the mission brief this morning; we have been surprised before with unexpected and accurate flak. When the flak from the German antiaircraft guns are active over the target area there is no fighter activity, only the exploding rounds shrapnel hitting our plane sometimes penetrating the outer skin causing minor to severe plane damage and wounds to crew that can be deadly. Flak is the worst anyone can imagine, small and large blasts around the plane. There have been missions where it literally seemed thick enough to walk on, the concussion of the blasts and the shrapnel make for a bumpy and dangerous ride.

Fighter attack is more frightening; you watch in nervous anticipation as the plane approaches with cannon tracer rounds streaking past you, some hitting the aircraft. The tracer rounds visible flashes are typically one in five rounds so there are a lot of rounds coming at you that you can't see. It's frantic with weapons firing in all directions. I have my twin .50 caliber machine guns in the top turret and I feel pretty damn good having the ability to fire back. Hearing the cannon rounds hitting the plane goes unnoticed with the adrenaline rush and noise. Minutes seem like hours, keeping track of all the shout outs over the intercom for fighter location in relationship to the aircraft and the visual scanning can be confusing. It is controlled confusion.

After almost two and a half combined years of training and combat flying you get to know the engine sounds and can sense the slightest rough running of the engines. I notice a rough running sound as we approach our checkpoint at Schirmech.

I got on my intercom telling Lt. McCurdy I was coming forward, "Sir… coming forward to check engine gauges."

"I hear something that doesn't sound right."

Lt. McCurdy responded, "OK… come on up."

I wiggle my way out of the turret seat and move forward through the bomb bay and past the radio and navigator seats to the pilots' compartment to talk with Lt. McCurdy on what he may have noticed.

I plugged in to the intercom connection in the pilot's compartment, looking at me then forward at the gauges McCurdy said, "I hear a slight roughness on Number Two… is that what you heard?"

"The temperature is rising for the oil on Number Two."

Looking over to Cudworth, "I'm noticing some slight aircraft handing in the controls… how about you?"

Cudworth responded, "I can feel a minor control problem… but it doesn't feel any different than usual in this weather and cloud turbulence."

I responded, "Yes sir… I noticed the sound about five minutes ago." I have seen this kind of engine problem during training and in other missions. The Pratt-Whitney engines in cold weather had a quirky action, especially newer engines, that would indicate an overheating situation on the oil temperature gauge. In this situation the pilot would instinctively open the oil cooler shutter when in actuality the oil had congealed and restricted the flow of oil; the shutter needed to be closed to clear, not open. If this is not resolved the engine may seize up and we will need to feather the prop and return to base with one engine. Since we have a heavy gross weight with four thousand pounds of bombs, fuel, crew and ammunition we will need to keep the good engine below wing level at about 5 degrees for better control if the engine seizes.

"Sir... we need to adjust the oil shutter."

"If this doesn't work the engine will freeze up, we will need to feather the prop," I said to Lt. McCurdy.

"Sir... if it gets worse I recommend shutting it down and feather the prop."

Controlling the aircraft is difficult on one engine, but it is possible with delicate handling of the aircraft from both pilots and their following proven procedure. The wing flight level of 5 degrees below level on the good engine gives lesser amount of rudder necessary to hold the aircraft straight, which in turn reduces the load and stress on the rudder and gives the pilot better control and keeps the aircraft in a straight controllable path.

Lt. McCurdy sounding a little nervous responded, "Let's see if we can resolve this oil shutter control, we'll follow the engine failure procedure if it happens."

He continued sounding anxious, "I'll contact Baggage Control on the situation, let's work this out."

McCurdy started the oil shutter control adjustment and said to Cudworth, "Grab the wheel tight I'll need help to hold control... just in case."

"I'm going to close the oil shutter all the way."

Cudworth nodded his acknowledgment with eye contact to McCurdy and then looked in my direction, I gave thumbs up.

I added a precaution, "Sir, the engine may seem to cut out, like a choking affect... do it slowly."

Both acknowledged and slowed and then stopped the adjustment. I hear a slight sputter then another and another. Looking out the co-pilot's window at Number Two I notice the propellers irregular appearance in its rotation. When you can see the blades of the prop in the rotation of the blades rather than one steady blurred image there's a problem with the engine not maintaining constant propeller speed. If we can't get a handle on this oil shutter and temperature problem, the oil will overheat and cause the engine to seize.

The best position for a dead engine is to feather the propeller blades edge-on to our direction of travel. If the propeller doesn't feather it will cause a windmill affect, a flat surface face-on into the airstream with high drag on the right side of the aircraft causing control problems. We can feather the propeller even after the engine quits that is if the propeller electric pitch change mechanism is not broke.

I noticed Lt. Cudworth grabbing the wheel even tighter and adjusting his sitting position in anticipation of helping McCurdy with what will be some difficult handling of the aircraft if the prop windmills.

The rest of the crew John, Bud, and Lloyd are aware of the problem we are experiencing; they notice the sounds and feel of the aircraft as much as the pilots and I. Don't need a FUBAR situation. We've all been around long enough to know we can get through this but it is nerving to have problems so soon into the mission. We haven't yet made it to the IP for the Bomb Run on target; we may not be bombing today. The B-26 is a sturdy plane, if we have to belly in it will be a bumpy but survivable ride. We could bail out if we had to or dump our bomb load and other heavy items for better control with less gross weight, regardless; we have options to get back safely.

Breaking radio silence Lt. McCurdy calls out on the radio, "Baggage, this is Zero Eight, my Number Two is runnin' rough… need to head for the barn."

The main force flight commander Major Hayward is listening, breaks in and answers before Baggage responds, "Roger, Zero Eight… switch to Channel "B" and contact Boxcar for steer to Dijon."

"No Room will direct you on low visibility approach to the field."

"Contact Rainbow Leader for his heads up… good luck… out."

19 January 1945 Mission Route

CHAPTER 2

BACK TO REALITY

General George S. Patton Jr.:
"If I do my full duty, the rest will take care of itself."

What is wrong with this engine? Why won't the oil shutter clear? Is there a generator problem my preflight checks missed? We can get through this. Did I get through training and missions on luck or skill? Was it skill with divine intervention? Thoughts of my entering the air corps and thinking about where it would lead me; I didn't know what to expect. Frustrating situations like this get on my nerves.

I remember my report date for final classification and basic military training; it began the day after Christmas 1942. Dreading the goodbyes to my sisters, mother, father, and Mary, my girlfriend. Taking it all in stride remembering the sights and sounds of home. My room, the kitchen, backyard, our garden, they are permanent picture memories. I can still smell the aroma throughout the house from Ma's cooking. When will I get back home? Where will I end up? Pacific or Europe? Both have risks, doesn't matter.

I will never forget the feel of Pa's stern hands cupping my face and his gaze into my eyes; he had a heavy Greek accent, "Nicholas… be careful."

"Do your best."

"Be best at what you do."

Then after a tear began to show in the corners of his eyes, "I love you… come back home."

Could not help getting tearful looking into his concerned eyes and starting to sense an awful empty feeling in my stomach. When I went to Greek school learning the language there are other variations of the use of father and mother "Pater", Greek for father and mother is "Mater". It is what the person means and feels so I use "Pa" and "Ma" for mother. He had served briefly during World War I as a draftee in the infantry. Fortunately for him the armistice occurred just as his troop ship, headed for France to join the American Expeditionary Force, was about half way across the Atlantic. His service ended shortly after returning to the United States, but his memory of friends leaving for overseas and some who were killed in action haunted him. He was a Greek immigrant and had just become an American citizen, and he was on his way overseas. He missed out on ground combat but the thought of his son going off to war was a great burden. He was an employee for the City of Detroit working on the street maintenance crews; he was employed during the depression. Ford Motor Company supported city workers to keep the city functioning.

Ma was more emotional, her accent more pronounced.

"Nicholas… I love you… miss you… be good." With a bear hug that I have not felt before; she seemed to not want to let go. She had emigrated from Greece to the United States with Pa. Her cooking was fantastic and her discipline appropriate throughout the childhood and teen years. We have a loving home atmosphere, and I will miss the affection, the food, friends and neighbors.

My sisters both had the biggest hugs and kisses for me as I was torn about leaving the house for the Military Induction Center at Fort Wayne south of Detroit. I am the oldest, my sister Dolly is next and Matina the youngest. We had our times of disagreement and sibling rivalry, but we get along otherwise. They seemed to always want my opinion on boys and disagreements with Pa and Ma. I was very protective of Dolly since she is closest in age and more prone for boys courting her. I have high standards and would definitely give an opinion of dissatisfaction without hesitation. They both had tears and faint goodbyes with their hugs and kisses.

Lastly, I looked into Mary's eyes, she was trying to hold back tears her lips quivering and then an outburst of tears and crying, her arms swung around my neck. How could I leave this? I have got to get going or I will never get to the induction center. Too much emotion at once, it is overwhelming. I can still smell her soft perfume and sense her soft touch.

"Mary," I said looking into her eyes and putting my hand over her right cheek, "I'll be back on leave as soon as I can."

"I'll write as often as I can."

It was understood between us that we would marry; I had not gotten around to ask

"I miss you so much already… please don't worry."

"I won't… I mean I'll try… well, I will worry," she said in a gentle voice that has never left my memory. Looking past her beautiful face I notice a car pulling up to the curb in front of our house. "Well… my ride is here… I have to leave," I said and started to walk through the front door off the porch of my home into a cold, calm, sunny winter day. Christmas decorations all around the neighborhood and my home, seems strange leaving during the holidays.

My good friend Ken was able to get his father to drive; there are four of us going to the induction center, Jeff, Ken, Rich and me. My father didn't have a car; he used the bus to get to work or caught a ride to work and home with a coworker occasionally. Stores were a close walking distance for food and the bus could get you anywhere to buy other items. Downtown Detroit shopping was not far away by city bus. Looking back at my family, Ma wiping tears away, my sisters also.

Pa looked sad but firm and in control of his emotions. Then Mary's look of sadness and tears as we pull away from the curb and on to Fort Wayne for induction processing.

All of us were at Fort Wayne 12 days ago to get sworn in and then placed in the Enlisted Reserve Corps. This was a temporary holding corps of all enlisted not yet fully classified. We were told of our obligations, were given initial tests and some basic medical exams for a few days. We were given orders to get back to be processed for more medical examinations and classification tests. All of us had tested well for classification to the air corps and qualified for a flying job. This could mean air cadet-pilot training or enlisted aircrew in radio communications, engineering maintenance and, of course, aerial gunnery. All of us went to Detroit's Cass Technical High School where you compete to get in; we all had good grades in math and physics. The air corps needed our skills.

"Well… here we are," Jeff said with some anxiety in his voice.

"I hope we don't need to stand in that medical exam line again," He recalled to all of us the line of recruits in underwear and the brilliant sarcastic joke and outburst of laughter. When the doctor told us to face forward, drop our shorts and spread our cheeks, one smart ass spread his face cheeks; we all had a hardy laugh. The doctor eventually burst out in laughter, it certainly eased the anxiety of the whole process of military production-line medical examinations.

"Yea… what a hoot," I said. I laughed again and Jeff, Ken, and Rich started, we couldn't stop. That moment really sticks in my mind.

Fort Wayne's buildings were built in the 1840's; it still had the old fort-style, star fortification walls and look of an old fort. Its origins date back to 1701. The ironic thing about its history is that it never fired a shot in anger against an enemy force. Most of the newer buildings were outside the old star fortification walls, all of them inside and out were used to some degree for inducting draftees and enlistment personnel. It was also building up to support distribution of war material. Fort Wayne was a focal point for the war effort and becoming the largest motor supply depot in the world. Detroit factories that produced tanks, trucks, jeeps, tires, or spare parts that were being sent to Fort Wayne and then forwarded on to where they were needed.

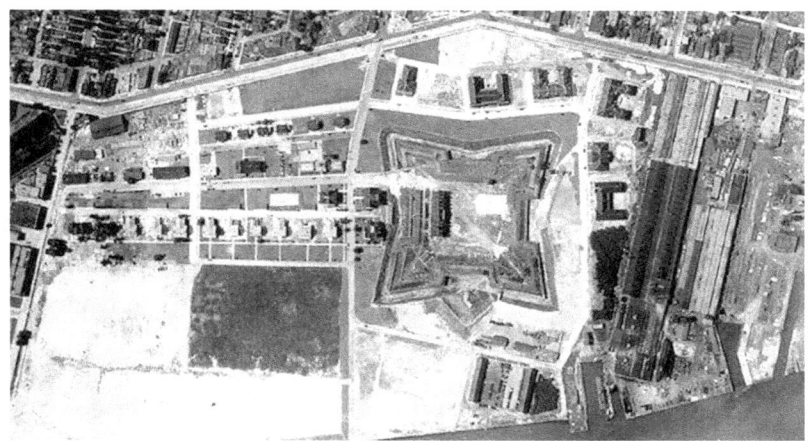

*The Build up for WWII * Fort Wayne Detroit Michigan Circa 1938*

After meeting our sergeant in charge we were assigned a bunk in an open bay area to spend the night and ship out the next morning for basic training at Sheppard Field, Wichita Falls, Texas. Texas was going to be home for 13 weeks. We continued to classify, more tests and waiting in lines for the rest of the day and then to bed for the long trip to basic training in the morning.

Got the first taste of a military wakeup in the morning. "Get up… get up… get cleaned up… get up," the sergeant was loud and ready to throw us out of our beds if we didn't get up fast enough. He had what looked like a drumstick banging against a shiny garbage can lid making loud un-tuned ear-piercing banging sounds on metal.

"Get up and get cleaned up for chow," he barked as he continued banging the lid.

"Hey… what was that?" I said and started to move out to the latrine to get cleaned up, wiping the sleep from my eyes stumbling in a fog. Everyone was alarmed looking around and shocked out of a deep sleep not knowing what or where to go next. I barely had my pants on holding them up as I walked quickly to the latrine.

As we were scattering around trying to get our bearings and wake up, the sergeant barked again, "Chow in 20 minutes… get packing and be ready with all your stuff."

"We are heading out to the bus in 10 minutes for chow."

"Move it," his final shout was louder and forceful and we were moving quick not knowing what to do first. It was mass confusion and looking back a little funny watching everyone trying to wake up and the same time cleaning up for the day.

We made it to the chow hall and all of us wondered what was that stuff being slopped on metal trays with divided compartments.

"What the hell is that?" Jeff said. Ken was standing in front of me and Rich so Jeff got the first look at "SOS".

We all looked at each other and thought if it tasted as bad as it looked

The cook serving the SOS said it was chipped beef with a very special sauce on slices of toast, known as "Shit On a Shingle." He smiled and said," You'll love this… better get used to it." And then slop!

"Better get some coffee and plenty of ketchup," Jeff said sarcastically.

We all pondered what this SOS would do to our stomachs.

When we sat down with our SOS and what ever else we could find that was edible for a variety of food for breakfast, the taste was surprisingly good. At least I thought it was OK. Rich agreed but Jeff and Ken gave me a strange look of disagreement.

"Guys… we better get used to it."

"I overheard a couple of sergeants talking and they said that this is the Army's gourmet dish favored all over the world and gets served often in chow halls."

Rich smiled and said, "Nick… they were pulling your leg."

"They knew you were listening to them."

"Ya… I know," I said knowing he was right.

"We better get used to it and get thick skinned."

"It's kind of like snipe hunting at night with flashlights," I said and got a chuckle out of Jeff, Ken and Rich. We finished breakfast and got ready for the long trip to Texas.

Thirteen weeks of basic training with seemingly endless military orientation classes, obstacle courses, physical training, weapons familiarization and marksmanship, close order and open order drill. Cannot forget that oh so loved task of "Kitchen Patrol" known as KP, all of it went by fast. The weather started out fine, then March came along and brought a sultry heat, you could change clothes several times a day to keep dry from sweating. Oh... and don't you ever forget to take your salt pills, oh no. Our favorite mess hall meal SOS, showed up quite often and we all got used to it. I was the only one who really didn't mind the taste. We looked sharp in our uniforms and couldn't wait to show off on leave.

All of us qualified for air corps but not pilot training. Good grades with math and basic physics got Ken and me an assignment for engineering duties. This was a satisfactory path for me in the Army Air Force (AAF); the AAF liked it too. Jeff and Rich were classified in radio communications. We would head to gunnery school after specialty schools and then aircrew training. "Got orders for... Sheppard Field."

Sheppard was also a training base for airplane mechanics, so Ken and I are staying here for another twenty or so weeks.

"What's your report date, Ken?"

"Um... it says... three weeks from today."

"Can we go on leave?" Ken said wondering if we could get a furlough at this early time in our military service.

"Don't know... I have the same report date on my order... same class." Then looking at Ken we both said in unison, "Home... Detroit... let's go!"

Jeff and Rich were not so lucky; they had to report in four days to a base somewhere in Arizona

"Sure wish we could join you guys," Jeff said looking at Ken and me. Rich didn't look too happy either.

"Well... leave will have to wait for a while," Rich said.

"Enjoy it... we'll get our time."

"We will... when do you ship out for Arizona?"

"Looks like tomorrow morning," Rich said looking at his order.

"Well... let's keep in touch, you know our home addresses... right?"

"Yea... I got yours and Ken's, we'll pass on our address when we get settled." Rich got out his address book to double check if the Detroit address was in the book

"Yea... got it."

"Well… let's get something to eat and say goodbye," Rich said, Jeff nodded and said, "Nick… are you going to have your mom make some SOS so you won't forget the taste?"

"No, don't think so… the Greek word for SOS is not pretty… it might ruin the taste." We all had a laugh and then off to the mess hall and USO to visit and then say goodbye for who knows how long.

The following morning Ken and I went over to the orderly room and put in paperwork for furloughs. The First Sergeant signed off on our papers. With paper in hand, we ran back to the barracks and threw everything we could think off in a suitcase, not thinking of how we would get to Detroit or getting back. Can't remember how much we spent for tickets but we got booked on a bus to Detroit; two long days on a bus with multiple stops.

Springtime in Detroit and Michigan can sometimes be a little chilly; nice break from the sultry Texas climate. Some rain up north in the Upper Peninsula and it can still snow a few inches, but it melts fast. Arriving at the downtown Detroit bus station late in the afternoon, we hurried off and ran to the nearest phone booth. Can't wait to see Mary, Pa, Ma, Dolly and Matina. I can smell the aroma of Ma's cooking already, I won't ask her to make any SOS.

Ken got us a ride home; his father is on his way to pick us up. On the phone I got a hold of Mary and was she surprised; she will head over to my parents house and wait. I put in another nickel and called home, Dolly answered and was ecstatic with the news I was on leave and headed to the house. She said Ma and Pa went to the corner market and should be back when I arrive later

"OK… we've got three weeks, let's plan on getting back early," I said. "I don't trust that bus ride back… we could be absent without leave (AWOL) if the bus breaks down."

Ken looking puzzled, "You're panicky… we'll get back OK."

"Oh no… cautious," I said.

"We cannot afford to have an AWOL on our records… let's be smart and not chance it… OK?"

After a short pause staring with a serious look I raised an eyebrow at Ken waiting for an answer, "Come on… humor me."

"OK… I got it," Ken reluctantly agreed and we bought our return tickets before we left the bus station to start leave

"Let's enjoy ourselves," Ken said looking around the downtown area around the bus station

"Still looks the same."

"Yea… seems a little busier," I said noticing people, cars and trolleys mingling throughout the streets.

Getting anxious and waiting out our rides arrival, then, "There's my dad… a sight for sore eyes." Ken smiled as his father's car approached the curb outside the bus station. Ken greeted his father, he opened the trunk and we threw our bags in. Off we went for the ride home and an anticipated relaxing leave away from military life.

Ken and I enjoyed being home. I went to the Detroit Zoo and park for picnics, visited family, church, Belle Isle Park on the Detroit River, and ate Ma's fantastic meals

The time went by fast; we headed back to the bus station to get back to Texas for airplane mechanics school. Sitting on the bus my thoughts wander back to home and Mary. Looking over to Ken I said, "Ken."

"Yea… what's up?" Ken responded as he was flipping through a Life Magazine he picked up at the last stop.

"I asked Mary to marry me… on my next leave."

"She said yes."

"Hey… that's great," Ken was not surprised.

"I knew that was coming."

"Yea… getting nervous already, I am not looking forward to the long absence when we head overseas, wherever that is," I said thinking hard about what lay ahead.

"Nick… we'll do our best and be the best at what we do," Ken said confidently and sure of his dedication. I was too.

Sitting on the bus and looking out the window I wonder when my next leave will be. Mary is planning for a wedding, just family not too big, can't afford a lot on my Army pay.

After entering the main gate we headed for the orderly room to sign in. Texas weather is getting sultrier; wish the Michigan springtime weather had followed us here. "You guys are not due back for another three days... what's up?" The orderly room sergeant asked, he has never seen anyone back early from leave. Usually it is a mad rush to get back and sign in just before the time limit. He had a look of disappointment on his face as if he was looking forward to putting someone on AWOL and disciplinary actions.

"Well, we didn't want to get caught in any delays with the bus stops, so we checked in early."

"We knew you would enjoy filling out AWOL paperwork," I said, the sergeant just snickered and grinned. We left the orderly room and headed off to the barracks to get settled and wait for class to start in a few days. "Class starts in 20 minutes... let's get going," I said getting ready in the barracks latrine. Twenty weeks of airplane mechanic classes, eight hours a day with lots of study and exams. There was time for relaxing at the USO club and a day or weekend pass. Occasionally Ken and I get into town but homesickness seems to be prominent in our mind when not in class or studying. Writing home and getting mail is the best part of any day.

"Nick... our orders are being cut for the Martin aircraft factory near Baltimore," Ken said finding out after talking with the training cadre. Both of us knew we would be headed to this place as the next stop if we were picked for flight engineer on B-26's.

"That's what we thought... that's the "Widow Maker"." It had a reputation for being fast and dangerous.

"Yea, but you and I know of the fixes for wing load, rudder refinements and pilot training," Ken and I both knew there was a big flap from Congress that the plane might be scrapped. This aircraft was fast and quick for a twin-engine medium bomber but required more training and aerodynamic adjustments. General Doolittle got involved with supporting the B-26 and proved it was formidable and capable; more training and airframe adjustments were needed. He saw a real fighter in the B-26 and convinced congress that it was a vital warplane. "I think we'll learn more when we get to Baltimore, but I think it's OK."

"At least for now then we can request transfers to other planes."

Ken quipped, "Yea… and its going to snow in Texas in June."

"Smart ass… it just might."

Then a short sharp punch to my upper arm as Ken ran to the orderly room to check the training squadron bulletin board postings for orders.

Baltimore was warm, busy with classes and intense study from the Martin Company's engineer and air corps cadre. We even got to fly in the plane to get to know the flight characteristics and how the supporting systems work together. This plane is fast; landing speed is about 150 miles per hour. That speed really pushes the pilots to be sharp to handle this plane on landing and take-off. Our first flight was exciting and yet scary, you've got to be on your best to handle this plane and get back safe. Twenty-five weeks of class left no time to think about leave, but we may have a chance to take leave before going to gunnery school in Harlingen, Texas hot and sultry Texas again.

"Ken… looks like no leave."

"I checked the bulletin board and our report date is in a week, just enough time to get ready and travel."

"I know… I ran into the personnel clerk and said the order is being cut for next week reporting… Oh well, maybe after we graduate from gunnery school," Ken said disappointed in the short window to report to Texas

"When's the wedding?"

"Well… it will have to be short notice, I've been writing back and forth with Mary on timing."

"School is only six weeks, so sometime after we can get out of Texas."

"Hey… get a Justice of the Peace and then a real wedding after the war… what do you think?"

"I'll think about it… good idea especially when all I have heard of is Justice of the Peace weddings because of the war footing."

"Yea… good idea."

"We'll make it happen, make sure you can be there for my best man and witness… what do you say?"

"My pleasure… proud to be there for you."

"Let's get some chow and relax a bit before we leave for that wonderful Texas sultry weather," Ken said sarcastically and pulling me off by the arm to get to the chow hall.

More days on a bus and train than I ever what to experience, finally made it to Harlingen Army Airfield. The sign above the main gate read,

Harlingen Army Airfield
9th Flying Wing
93rd Flexible Gunnery Training Group
AAF Eastern Central Training Command

Signed in and headed off to our barracks to settle in and report to class the following morning. Training was six weeks, on the ground and in the air gunnery. We started off shooting BB guns at fixed targets then moved on to skeet shooting with shotguns. After getting good scores the harder training and shooting started with rifles and then the .30 and .50 Caliber Browning machine guns. Everything so far was shooting at fixed targets; the next phase was going to be shooting at moving targets on tracks on a shooting range. The last phase was shooting from a flying platform at towed airborne targets; this was hard to track and get good scores.

"Nervous in the service?" I asked Ken as each of us stood in formation waiting to get in an AT-6 single engine training aircraft. Each plane had a .30 Caliber machine gun mount in the back for students to take shots at a towed target. This was our first training flight in the AT-6. "You bet… don't want to fall out… gives me the creeps," Ken said kind of shaky from what was to be.

"I hope I don't throw up that great Army breakfast… you know that SOS you like so much."

"OK… I feel the same way, got to keep it down."

"Make sure your safety strap is secure… you are my best man… OK?"

"OK… got it… let's get this over with."

"Hope the pilot knows what he's doing," Ken said as he was directed by the training sergeant to get on the next plane. Ken looks a little pale… my turn now I'm feeling nervous.

Our rounds are color coded so the evaluators can determine our percent of hits; 20 percent is passing. Flying in an open cockpit compartment aft of the pilot got easier. We got comfortable and passed with over 20 percent hits. Another training platform was a turret gun mounted on the flatbed of a converted pickup truck. We drove through fields and shot at random targets, this was probably the most realistic firing experience. Training was also conducted on a B-26 training aircraft with all of its gunnery positions in place to get familiar with its weapons stations. My position, as flight engineer, was routinely the top turret gun, but all crewmembers needed to be able to man a gun at any location on the aircraft. I sat in my rotating gun turret and got to know what it was like to fire twin 50's at targets. I would find out later it's much different shooting at real German fighter planes roaring past you with guns blazing. The experienced trainers who were in combat told us to lead the aircraft several plane lengths ahead or behind depending on which direction the fighter was headed in relation to the bomber heading. That type of training practice with a dummy aircraft or towed target we didn't get; he was right when the real thing came along.

*AT-6 Gunnery Training Planes * Gun Platform (left) and Towed Target (right)*

Ground Training Gun Turret Used In B-26's

We graduated and waited for orders to report for aircrew training in Louisiana or Florida. Graduation ceremony was longer than everyone wanted; the heat was oppressive. We were anxious but proud of our new gunner's wings on our uniform and our two stripes, corporal rank. After the ceremony we got packing, signed out and rushed to the bus station for the long trip out of southern Texas to Detroit. Time between gunnery school graduation and reporting for aircrew training gave us thirty day's worth of furlough, excited to get home to Detroit and getting married.

Mary had made arrangements for a quick wedding at church, Ma and Pa were satisfied, and we prepared for the wedding.

"I do," I said as I was asked to have and hold in sickness and health till death do us part.

Mary's soft response, "I do."

I looked deeply into her warm, loving eyes and we kissed as man and wife. Out we went to our small reception at my house with immediate family and some close friends and, of course, my best man Ken. Our first night together was at the Hotel Statler on Washington Boulevard across from Grand Circus Park. What a great place, it's close to movie theaters, shopping downtown and the famous Michigan Palace Supper Club. We spent more days there than planned, but we couldn't pull ourselves away from the atmosphere and privacy. We would live at Mary's house or my folk's house until after the war to settle into our own home

"Nick... I have something for you."

"What?" I asked wondering what surprise she may have as we sat for dinner at a romantically lit table in the hotel restaurant.

"Here... open it," she was excited but anxious; I couldn't wait to see what she had for me in this small beautifully wrapped package. Looking into the box pulling away the tissue covering... it is an identification bracelet. It is silver with linked chains and a clasp to hold on my wrist, it reads on the front,

Nick Bentas

On the back there is an inscription that reads,

This man belongs to me, Mary

"Thanks... so much... it's never coming off my wrist."

"I Love you... forever," I said as she returned, "I Love you so much." We both started to get teary eyed, but smiled and kissed.

We enjoyed getting together with families after our honeymoon stay at the Hotel Statler and just going wherever we wanted. Our travels took us around the Detroit area and an occasional trip to Windsor, Canada for dinner and shopping. I lost track of Ken as he went on his bachelor ways and visited his family. We needed to get back soon and report to Lake Charles, Louisiana for B-26 aircrew training. Leaving this time was harder than the first, being married and not knowing when I would see her again.

Saying Good Bye

Back on the bus again for the long ride to Lake Charles Army Air Field, Shreveport, Louisiana aircrew training and replacement assignment, we hope. We still don't know which theater of operations; we suspect the European or Mediterranean.

We waited for four weeks until we were assigned to crews to train with, time on our hands and nothing to do. However, being enlisted we got some trivial duties to perform to keep us busy. The officers, pilots and other officer crew didn't get any tasks but spent a lot of time in town and in the clubs. A drink once in a while was OK, but some of the officers and enlisted got out of hand, they paid for it hugging the porcelain throne. I can still remember a Coke machine at the end of the hallway on our first floor of the barracks; we used it with or without liquor. The Coca Cola Company made a bundle on filling that machine. The weather was not too bad, but it was getting warmer as spring approached summer. Louisiana's weather is as sultry as Texas and has just as many bugs around to annoy. You've never seen bigger cockroaches, I mean really big.

Finally... crew assignments and orders for replacement crew to the 320th Bomb Group currently located on Sardinia in the Mediterranean. Ken and I both received orders for the 320th Bomb Group, they have the nickname of "The Boomerangs"; they keep coming back from missions. Some combat casualties and lost planes to enemy action, but a strong reputation so far.

I finally got the names of my crewmates; I was hooked up with First Lieutenant Rich Cahan our pilot, Second Lieutenant John Miller the co-pilot, Corporal's John Hill as tail gunner, Ed Geronimos radio operator and gunner, Jed Vollmer bombardier and gunner, and me as flight engineer gunner in the top turret gun. The bombardier was typically an officer if we had a Norden bombsight installed, but we would know ahead of time if the aircraft were equipped with one. Jed's job was to watch the formation ahead of us from the nose position to toggle the bomb drop switch when he saw the lead bombardier drop his load over the target. Navigators were similar but we all needed to understand the duties in case we were to assist the pilot and co-pilot and communicate with the lead navigator. Most of the time we would not have a navigator; this was mission dependant.

"Sir... Corporal Bentas, flight engineer," I said and saluted approaching Lieutenant Cahan for our meeting location on the flight line by the hanger where we were told to gather for a quick meet and greet. He was tall with a boyish complexion; he looked like he just graduated from high school, confident and seemed to be a real straight shooter.

"Corporal... my pleasure, looks like you are the first one here," he returned my salute and then looked around wondering where the others were

"Seen or met anyone else on our crew?"

Looking around as if to catch a glimpse of the rest of the crew, "No sir... saw them at the chow hall this morning, don't know where they are."

"Haven't met Lieutenant Miller yet."

Just then coming around the corner of the hanger door the rest of the enlisted crew came over to greet the lieutenant; the co-pilot was running behind to catch up to the rest of them. We all got acquainted quickly; Lieutenant Cahan put us all at ease. He was experienced as any pilot having been an instructor for the B-26 before volunteering to take on a crew and go overseas for a combat assignment.

As the conversation slowed down and all of us were thinking about what to talk about not really knowing each other well Cahan gives us a little pep talk, "Gentlemen... glad to have you on this crew, I've had time to review your training records and they all seem impressive."

"However... your training and ability to work together to get this plane up and flying straight, do the mission and get back safely is yet to be seen."

"I have confidence we can get this done... if there is any doubt on what and where, do not hesitate to ask."

"We must watch out for each other to be successful."

"Roger?"

We all replied in unison, "Roger."

Lieutenant Cahan smiled and said, "Oh boy... a flying chorus."

We all seemed to relax and then went on to our classroom training for the day.

No drill or physical training, no formations, if we weren't flying we were in classrooms. Our day started at 0600 and ended no earlier than 1900 hours. The pilots and navigators always got a few more flights; flight engineers were usual crew additions to pilot only flights with pilot instructors. We started flying as a crew for practice bombing techniques, ground strafing and long-range navigation flights. All our training flights took us over the southern U.S. or over water in the Gulf of Mexico. Pilot's got more flying time to get navigation down and control techniques perfected. We got used to our crew in flight and in the classroom; we worked well and started to anticipate the others actions and responses the more we flew. If any crew could not work together and understand individual duties and teamwork, it would mean a failed mission

It was a Friday... a routine training flight for pilots and co-pilots only with a flight instructor; I was selected to be the flight engineer. We were at about 7,000 feet with the instructor pilot in the right seat, a flight officer in the left seat, one pilot standing between the pilot seats on the flight deck and one riding in the nose compartment bombardier seat. It was about two hours into the flight, I notified the instructor pilot that I needed to transfer fuel, "Sir... going to the bomb bay to transfer fuel."

He nodded and replied, "Roger… go ahead."

Headed back to the bomb bay where the fuel transfer switches were located. I needed to transfer fuel from the auxiliary tanks to the main tanks; the transfer required was from the right auxiliary tank to the left main tank

I turned and headed aft into the bomb bay to the transfer control selector. As I completed the transfer much to my surprise there was a sudden ceasing of engine noise.

"What the hell!" I shouted aloud to myself and headed forward to the pilots compartment pushing my way through the bomb bay. As I approached the pilot's compartment I heard the pilots laughing, they were attempting to shut down and then start a dead engine; practicing this without telling me. At the same time I noticed two pilots with a cigarette in their mouths, both engines were going to full power.

I shouted again, "What the hell are you doing with those cigarettes?"

"I'm transferring fuel… no smoking… damn it."

I was not happy and didn't care if I said "sir" before addressing the pilots; smoking while transferring fuel is a big no-no. I headed back to the bomb bay and to my horror the bomb bay floor was covered with fuel. I shut off the switches and with my heart pounding I rushed forward to the pilots compartment yelling, "Fuel sloshing in the bomb bay floor."

I swear I saw the cigarettes that were hanging from their mouths being swallowed. Their eyes had a sudden look of panic and shock. The pilot in the bombardier position in the nose shouted with a panic tone, "Should I open the bomb bay doors?"

"No," I shouted back quickly.

"The sparking of the steel sprocket and chain door linkage could set off the fumes."

The slipstream started to suck out the fuel through the seam crack of the bomb bay doors. I started to think, what the hell happened? The only thing that could cause this was that my hand must have flipped the selector switch valve to the bomb bay tank position by mistake as I pushed my way past the bomb bay moving forward. There was no bomb bay tank so the fuel emptied into the bomb bay. The odor of fuel was getting potent; I went aft to open both waist windows to get the fumes out of the plane. No one was smoking and no other incidents as we returned to base about an hour later

We landed safely and parked the aircraft. After shutting down I got out of the aircraft exiting from the waist windows onto the flight line. Captain Rodgers, the instructor pilot, came up to me as I started the post flight check of our B-26 and asked, "Corporal... what happened?"

Still a little pissed at the smoking incident but realizing my mistake, "Sir... I must have bumped the selector switch when I moved forward after starting the transfer."

"I know for sure I did not select the bomb bay tank."

Captain Rodgers looking concerned and scratching his head with his hat cocked to his right side said, "OK... won't write this up, the pilots should not have been smoking when fuel is being transferred either."

"I talked with them already... carry on."

"Yes sir... lesson learned," I responded with a salute and relief. I thought how easy it could be to screw up without thinking; this could have been a bad day. There was a vision in my head of a huge fireball in the sky, but as fate would have it a chance to learn from a huge mistake.

I had a long talk with Ken on what happened that day and he was surprised that nothing catastrophic occurred.

"Wow... did you fill your pants? Ken chuckled and then he said seriously, "Better learn now than when you can't recover from a mistake."

"Yea... still shaky, I think a stiff drink will calm my nerves," I said still somewhat wobbly.

Ken wide-eyed said, "OK... let's get cleaned up and head over to the club, I need one too."

"Oh... I thought you didn't drink?"

Looking at Ken and with a wink, "Only in emergencies."

Not all of my flights were mistakes and mishaps. On one of our five-hour navigation training flights with our crew, Lieutenant Cahan noticed off in the distance a lone B-17. The sky was clear with a few clouds above us no turbulence, a really smooth flight. We were about an hour into the training mission and had settled in for a routine flight.

The B-17 was big compared to us and much slower. Cahan decided to have some fun, "Pilot to crew… if you're getting bored I have an idea."

"I am going to shut down Number Two and feather the prop… there is a B-17 ahead at about our one o'clock."

"Watch as we pull up and pass her by," he and Lieutenant Miller shut down Number Two and followed the drill perfectly. They adjusted rudder and trim controls; we watched and waited as we gained on the Flying Fortress.

I had a great view from the top gun turret. As we moved closer to the Flying Fortress, quite impressive aircraft by the way, we eased up on her left side. Gaining on the B-17 and maneuvering closer our Number Two engine would appear on her left side; it would look like we didn't have any engine power. The illusion would have us going faster with no engine power as we passed by. You should have seen the pilot and co-pilot looking at us with mouths dropped to their floor.

"How's that fly boys… no match for the B-26," Cahan pronounced as we passed the big bomber.

"That was amazing," I said to the pilots, "Didn't know we could do that."

We all waved at the big bomber not getting a response only open eyed stares and open mouths, definitely one for the books. Lieutenant Cahan restarted the Number Two after we passed the B-17; we finished our navigation mission and headed for home base.

You always assume you will get back from a mission but our training provided other options in case we would ditch the plane in water or on land. We learned proper procedure and crash positions for a belly in situation on land, a controlled clean landing without wheels down. Another scarier training practice I did not like nor did I ever want to experience for real ever… the ditching facility at Lake Charles. The training scene was a large round pond with water of about five to six feet deep; a B-26 in the center partially sunk with its wing ends clipped, and a connecting dock. On the end of the left wing was a dinghy raft. This raft is part of the equipment of the B-26 when missions are flown over water; they are self-inflatable.

The control building adjacent to the pond had a training officer inside using a loud speaker; he began, "Get in your assigned mission positions."

"Get ready for the command to exit… you will have thirty seconds."

"You will hear the command to "get out" and then the alarm bell."

"Time starts when the alarm bell starts."

We entered the training aircraft and went to our positions to get ready for the command to exit. You are required to get out of the aircraft if you ditch in the water quickly, don't think about it just get out. Just outside the training plane were two sergeants standing ready to guide us out of the plane.

"Get… Out!" the loud speaker blared." Immediately after the exit command an alarm bell sounded and kept going until the training cadre shut it off. We moved out as quickly as possible bumping into each other clamoring to get out of the plane in the required time. Training was serious and you can just imagine what it would be like if you had to get out in the water. The reality of the training made me think of the ones who could not get out. What if you have wounded? What if you are wounded? Trapped in the airframe? Scary when the real thing happens, no one wants to drown, especially in a panic. We did this several times, not passing the thirty-second threshold until our tenth try. By that time it was getting easier and then finally… twenty-five seconds.

"Congratulations boys… twenty-five seconds… finally passed."

"Get your gear together and move out," the training instructor directed and motioned for the next crew. It seemed like we were there all day.

After a long training day in class and at the ditching facility Ken and I met at the barracks, "Ken… I think it's time to have a drink to settle down a bit."

"Water escape ditching training today was more than I expected."

"We did it more times than I want to think about… ten times," I said shaking my head and wiping my brow.

"I… I panicked more than I thought I would."

"All the shouting and confusion… we had the instructors yelling at us until we got it right."

Feeling a bit calmer I said, "Well… better learn now."

"Yea… that's what this is all about," Ken said in a reassuring voice.

"Our experience there was just as bad… seven tries."

"Still need that drink?"

"Yes… let's relax," I said and we headed over to the club for a quick drink and conversation about other things not military or training.

Lots of chatter in the club then silence as some serious looks and conversation broke a festive, relaxed atmosphere. Then some bad news began to circulate, a plane with its crew crashed north of Lake Charles. What could have happened? Ken and I knew vaguely some of the crew.

"Ken… that's that guy from Chicago… Jensen?

"Did you know anyone else? I started to think about whom but couldn't think of anyone.

"What happened?

"Nick… there's the safety officer," Just as Ken finished the safety officer began to get everyone's attention.

He started by making an announcement, "The bar and club are shut down by order of the base commander, Colonel Manson."

Looking around at each other we put down our drinks and started to move to the door then he continued, "At ease… don't leave yet… all personnel on flying status report to the base theater in Class A's, no exceptions… 0800 hours sharp… Colonel Manson's order."

Hard to get to sleep thinking about what happened and sad for those killed and their families. There had been some pilots doing low level buzzing passes, seemingly to impress or startle locals. This practice went on and some of the pilots got a kick out of it, I wonder if this is what happened. Cahan never did a buzzing while we were with him; he never bragged or talked about it if he did.

After a short night's sleep, we got ready in our Class A's and went to chow. The mood was somber, we finished and walked over to the theater and sat down in plenty of time… it was 0745. Lots of talk about what happened and other conversations.

"What do you think?

"This must have been pretty bad," Ken said to me as we waited for the colonel

"I don't know… I overheard someone say that they were buzzing a house in a small town where the pilot was from."

"Six guys dead."

Then breaking the silence a loud "Ten Hut! All of us snapped to attention as Colonel Manson entered and walked down the aisle to the front of the theater. He stopped and turned around facing the audience in a stern look, a perfect parade rest stance in a flawlessly groomed uniform. His stone cold silence made me nervous until in a low tone firm voice, "At ease… take your seats."

We sat wondering what was next as Colonel Manson stared at the audience and didn't talk for what seemed to be an eternity then he let loose with a firm lecture, "Last night one man committed suicide and five men were murdered."

"Last night one of our pilots decided to show the folks in his home town what a shit hot pilot he was, he buzzed Main Street and crashed."

"When I arrived at the scene their remains were still burning." The colonel's voice was never raised but his focus went right at you… we listened.

His eyes were like steel and if looks could paralyze he continued, "I am sick and tired of such appalling stupidity."

"I guarantee to each of you that if I catch anyone using my airplanes for buzzing and showing off, I will court martial your ass and send you to federal prison."

After his final statement he moved up the aisle and out of the theater… there was silence. We left the theater thinking about how stupid we can be without thinking about the consequences. Ken and I looked at each other and said nothing for now; we both knew how serious our training was and its element of danger. No time for goofing off no matter what, no time for foolish showing off.

"Ken… I hope I never run into a pilot that thinks he knows everything and conducts himself in a careless manner," stating the obvious but with anger to a senseless death of five guys who lost their lives for nothing but stupidity.

"Nick… I'm with you, we just have to speak up and say something."

"The more I think about it the more I get pissed off... let's go... class starts at 0900."

Training got more routine and comfortable as we learned to work together. We knew our jobs and stuck with it; combat missions would bring more stress. Everything seemed to be instinctive and we gained confidence in our abilities and survivability.

It was getting close to summer and the end of our time at Lake Charles... Lieutenant Cahan pulled us all together before our scheduled bombing practice flight. Little did we know it would be our last flight out of Lake Charles Army Air Field.

"Gentlemen... today's mission will be our last here so stay sharp."

"Heads up... we will be going to Florida to get our ship to ferry over the ocean... MacDill Field."

"While we are there we will have a little down time as we prepare to leave... there will be a flight of four planes going to the 320th Bomb Group," Cahan continued to give us instructions from an operations order he received this morning.

"We will be doing practice missions on our assigned plane so we can adjust whatever we need before we leave for the long trip over the ocean," "Any questions?"

I spoke up, "Sir... do you know how long we will be in Florida?" "About three weeks... weekends off... probably short days."

"We may be assisting maintenance personnel in any last minute modifications that were not installed at the facility in Nebraska or Baltimore."

"Timing of our stay is dependent on making sure modifications fit and work... and practice missions to check out plane functionality."

"We will make sure the aircraft is working perfectly... it's a long trip over the water," "Any more questions?"

John Hill our other gunner asked, "Sir... are we flying or taking a train or bus to Florida?"

"Good question... we will ferry this aircraft and a crew from MacDill will fly it back here... so pack accordingly," "Questions?"

We looked at each other with no more questions, "None heard… let's get the pre-flight done and on with this mission… let's go." Lieutenant Cahan smiled and went to the nose gear wheel well entry door to start his pre-flight in the pilots seat.

Our mission was a short two hours and as we broke up for the day I met Ken at the barracks, his crew got the same order.

"Nick… we are going to MacDill to pick up our plane and then on to Sardinia," Ken said as I entered our barracks room.

"Good news… me too."

"I'll try to make a phone call or telegram to Mary… maybe we can see each other before I leave."

"Hope so… better get word to her soon… we could be on our way to Florida in a few days," Ken responded knowing that time was short to get Mary down to Florida.

I headed to the orderly room to see if I could get a phone line to call Mary's home. I was able to get a hold of her and told her to pack her bags for Florida. I'll get a motel room close to the field when I get there. The most direct route to MacDill was over the Gulf of Mexico, more time to practice navigating over open water. Lieutenant Cahan said he has permission to do a multiple point navigation route to MacDill; our flight will be longer but should be smooth. The weather forecast for next week is clear over the gulf. Taking off from Lake Charles with all our baggage, it was early… 0600 hours.

Lieutenant Cahan over the intercom, "Pilot to crew… we are going to make two navigation points and then on to MacDill."

"Relax and enjoy the break… looks like a smooth flight so take it easy." Just as he finished we hit some hard turbulence and jolted the plane up and then down, "Ouch… what the hell? It was a quick thump, bumped my head on the bulkhead beam by the turret gun, just as I was getting relaxed and settled. The others got bumped around too. "Sorry guys… didn't see that one," Cahan said over the intercom.

John and Jed looked at me and we just rolled our eyes and rubbed our bumped heads and arms.

"MacDill tower… this is flight 9009… permission to land?" Cahan called the tower at MacDill for permission to land. We can see off in the distance the city outline of Tampa, Florida, Tampa Bay, and the airfield landing strip.

The tower responded, "Flight 9009… permission granted… winds 5 to 10 miles per hour… elevation fourteen feet… approach runway 22."

"Roger… tower… fourteen elevation… runway 22… out," Cahan confirms landing approach. He and Lieutenant Miller execute a perfect landing, the main gear touch down smoothly and then the nose gear. The weather is warm with a nice breeze off the gulf. We taxi to our parking spot, shut down, start post-flight checks and unload our baggage.

"Florida… first time here," John said.

"Yea… me too," I said.

The rest of us with the exception of Lieutenant Miller are first time visitors

"You'll love the beach… sun… girls… tanning… swimming," Lieutenant Miller said with a big smile on his face, he spent a lot of time in Florida as a kid and then college.

"Oh yea… spent a lot of time partying on the beach with my friends with lots of girls during college… wow… great to be back," Miller said with that huge smile permanently fixed on his face. Lieutenant Cahan, Corporals John Hill, Ed Geronimos and me are the only married crew, "Have fun guys… my wife will be down here soon for some beach time and sun," I said.

"OK guys… get your gear off and wait for the ride to our barracks… briefing at the training operations office at 0700 tomorrow… get up and get chow… be ready," Lieutenant Cahan said, "Don't forget to get all your gear off this aircraft… its leaving tomorrow morning for Lake Charles."

We got our ride in a G.I. six-by-six truck to our barracks, got settled in and waited for Ken to arrive. His crew's flight was the day after ours. I got unpacked and then got out to find a Western Union office on or off base and tell Mary to get her tickets to get down here. I found a motel; I'll wait for a good date to get a room for Mary and me.

The mood was relaxed, over time the "yes sirs" and officer versus enlisted courtesies were muddled, we got used to addressing ourselves by nicknames or first name. Lieutenant Cahan became "Skipper." Since his wife, John and Geronimos's wife and Mary were coming down to Florida we could hang out at the beach and dinner at nice restaurants on the Gulf of Mexico. We got acquainted and off-duty time was relaxing, flying became a synchronized blending of our talents and skills.

The sun was high in the sky, it was a weekend day off, Mary and I were at the beach relaxing and soaking in some sun.

"Nick… when are you leaving for overseas? Mary asked with a tone of concern, she was enjoying being together but knowing that a long absence of who knows how long was coming.

"Well… rumor has it at about a week," I told her but I knew I could not say anything for security reasons, "You know I can't tell you the exact date… you'll have to head back soon… let's enjoy the moment."

"OK… can't stop thinking about it… let's just enjoy ourselves and the beach and sun," she said changing her tone with a big smile putting off the thoughts of a long absence.

Our final night with the wives, time was closing for us to take our plane and leave for Sardinia. We had a crew dinner at this beach house restaurant outside Tampa; don't remember the name but it was really nice and not too pricy.

The Skipper interrupted the conversations and was going to give a toast, "Gentlemen, and ladies… I want to offer a toast to all of you… success in our mission and safe return," he paused and recognized our families and wives, "A toast as well to our wives, Mary, Jill, Doris, my sweetheart Ann… be safe and please pray for us daily." With that we drank, we all fell silent for a moment then, "We probably need to get back to our room's… I know the wives are leaving tomorrow morning… so good night and God bless." Standing up we all left to our own business and saying goodbye till who knows when.

The image of Mary's beautiful features, her green eyes, brown hair, and soft touch and voice… this is harder than I could have imagined…

but necessary. Got to get on with the war and our duty… struggling to switch my mind back to flying.

After getting back to base, the Skipper let us know that there would be a briefing at 0700 hours tomorrow. This was the beginning of our travels

First briefing, medical with the subject's malaria, venereal disease, insect control, personal hygiene, and other medical problems, we will be going over jungle, water and desert and might encounter these medical issues. Hope not, this took all morning. The afternoon briefings were dedicated to the travel route across the Atlantic. The squadron armorer issued all of us side arms, a .45 caliber 1911 pistol with ammo for three magazines pistol belt and flying harness. We will pick up our new aircraft, a B-26 G model tail number 574 at Morrison Field in West Palm Beach. Morrison Field is the main point of departure and ferrying point for aircraft and supplies going to Europe and Allied forces in the Asian theater. We will get a bus ride to the field when we leave on June 15th

At the end of the day we were briefed on the landing of Allied forces at Normandy, Operation Overlord that started early this morning, June 6, 1944. We are 6 hours behind in time zones so it has been a long day for those landing and parachuting into France. It was the largest assault ever put together; we all wondered if the war would be over by the time we get to Sardinia. I decided, don't know why now, to start a journal; I'll start it on the 15th. Looking forward to seeing the different countries on our way overseas. Our flight will take us over the Caribbean to Puerto Rico, French Guiana, Brazil and then a long crossing over the Atlantic. Once we make it over the ocean, North Africa stops and then on to Sardinia

Found a nice small journal book at the PX I can stuff in my jacket pocket and started my journal,

> *June 15 & 16: Left late for MacDill Field by bus to Morrison Field—Arrived late in the a.m. June 16th, processed in early, got orders and got paid $96—Pre-flight newer B-26 NICE aircraft!—Delayed to tomorrow morning (June 17) for take off at 0600 hours*

> *June 17: Took off on time flying to Puerto Rico airfield Boringuen (can't pronounce this one)—Nice flight beautiful*

blue water and lush green—Problem with gauges and engine temperature—Did post flight checks hit the sack late

June 18: We all slept in—Went to our B-26 gave up leaving found a few more problems—Went to PX and ate ice cream for dinner—Laid in the sack the rest of the evening—Weather hot and steamy—cool drink would be nice—Had a coconut, real hard to peel—John teased me as I tried to peel it apart

June 19: Another delay, weather—Did nothing all day long—Went to a movie and saw "So Proudly We Hail"—Good movie about MacArthur with Claudette Colbert, Paulette Goddard, Veronica Lake, George Reeves—Went to bed late, read the Yank and Stars and Stripes over and over

June 20: Waited all morning for status of take off—Gave up leaving went to lunch **Bad Food** *choking it down yuck—Wrote Mary and Ma & Pa, don't know where I can mail this??—Went to bed late too hot to sleep*

June 21: Finally—Ate breakfast (not too bad) went to plane pre-flight took off at 0600 hours—Islands very pretty, blue water—passing over more beautiful islands—Landed at Kinson field British Guiana—Landed at 1200 hours—Barracks with two-stories, mosquito netting—Jungle all around, natives nice—Watched a Cricket game then did a daily check on our B-26

June 22: Early to rise at 0300 hours, ate breakfast—Raining cats and dogs—Took off at 0600 hours—Lots of jungle below with low clouds—Crossed the Equator at 0945—Saw the Amazon River and several outlets to ocean—Landed at Belem Field Brazil—Lots of natives, rained really hard, bananas, trees, jungle—Had a beer (warm) with the rest of the crew, went to bed under my mosquito netted bunk

June 23: Up at 0430 hours did pre-flight took off at 0600 hours—Raining lightly for take off, nice weather the rest of the flight to Natal Brazil—Slept about an hour—Finally landed at 1100 hours, did post flight checks—Saw the rest of our four ship flight—Ken and his crew here, met for a drink went to chow (bad food again)—Visited with Ken and wrote a letter to Mary, base ops was able to mail out letters, had three to mail, Lt. Cahan censored per security reasons, OK and sent

June 24 & 25 & 26: Slept bad, tossed and turned—Inspected the plane all day and night, 25 hours—Beat slept in, tired—Delay for maintenance problems, minor but will take time—Got a truck and several of us went to the ocean, swam in the ocean, nice beach with natives selling ornaments, bought some to send home—Went to another movie "Once Upon a Time"—Went to bed late each night June 27: Woke up at 0400 hours for trip to Ascension Island— nervous, longer flight over water—Checked over aircraft real good, double checked everything—1,475 gallons of fuel on board—Tail end plane, flight of four—Took off at 0600 hours climbed to 8,000 feet, beautiful view ocean real blue—ETA 1300 hours spotted the island at 1250 hours—Glad to see the island and the airstrip—Landed and checked out the rest of the island with Ken, Ed and others from the other crews—Felt good to be this far, had a good nights sleep got chilly

June 28: Nice weather, cool morning—Ate breakfast and did pre flight on our plane—Took off at 0700 hours, cloud formations are beautiful, puffy looked like someone painted them on canvas—Ocean all the way over then a glimpse of Africa, we went to lower altitude 1,000 feet—our ETA 1140 hours—Beautiful green hills heading to Roberts Field, Cahan did an instrument flight the rest of the way about ten miles inland—Landed and checked in at operations and Great Chow! Finally! Nice beds but malaria—Goops (boys) natives took care of gassing up our plane—Here we are French West Africa—Monrovia, Liberia

June 29: Raining all day, field is closed—We fooled around all day, not much to do with the rain—Good chow and went to bed early, we heard natives chanting in the jungle, heard some funny birds, odd!

June 30: Got up at 0600 hours, ate chow and checked plane, did an engine run up for functional checks—All good to go—Took off at 0800 hours, saw a Firestone plantation and rubber trees, interesting—Saw a lot of tall trees and swamps—Weather bad most of the flight, bumpy flight—passed over Freetown and Portuguese Guiana—We saw the stronghold at Bay of Bakar and some sunken ships—Landed at Dakar, Senegal French West Africa, check plane post flight—Ate chow and had briefing for Algeria and Sardinia, general war information and updates—D-Day invasion progressing, talk of southern invasion of France—Went to bed late after writing a letter to Mary, tired

July 1: Next stop Marrakesh, French Morocco—Up at 0500 hours, raining like hell—Are we getting delayed? NO!—Went to chow and checked out the plane, took off at 0900 hours and headed out over the Sahara Desert—Really God awful hot!—Saw nothing but sand and hills, a few oasis passed by, more sand and hills— Approached mountains got through a pass at 14,000 feet, on O2— Cahan said we were at 350 mph on the down side of the mountains heading to Marrakesh—Tower directed us to land at Marrakesh versus on to Casablanca—Landed safely, kinda fast for a landing, Cahan is a really good pilot!—Gassed aircraft and checked it over good for the next leg—Went to bed hot and tired

July 2: 0600 hours wake up, ate a quick breakfast grabbed K & C rations for the flight—Took off at 0900 hours for Tunis—Flying over Atlas Mountains, beautiful site—Landed at 1430 hours—Lots of wrecked planes and ships, bullet holes everywhere—Rest then on to Sardinia—Tired fooled around and talked with Ken, Jed, Ed and some others from Ken's crew—Weather hot sticky with bugs, lots of flies—We all decided to go into town, got a pass saw some interesting stuff, markets, café's, bars, and Arabs, French, Italians etc., got to bed late

July 4: Finally the last leg to Decimo Field Sardinia, been interesting—Happy Fourth of July!!—Took off at 0900 hours, weather clear a little windy—Landed safely at Sardinia, Decimo field, wow 6 landing strips, did our post flight checks—Good ship over the ocean wish we could keep her, Goodbye 574!—Greeted by the operations officer for the 441 Squadron, 320th Bomb Group

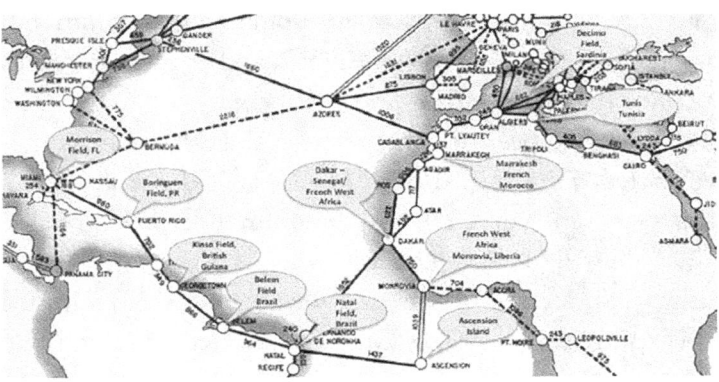

Flight Path to Sardinia via the Southern Transit Route

Sardinia's airfield, Decimomannu or "Decimo" for short was twenty miles north of the port city of Cagliari, was long and wide. All four aircraft landed safely and taxied to parking spots directed by two officers in a Jeep. Three G.I. six-by-six trucks showed up to transport all four ship's crew and bags. We all managed to arrive with no incidents, some planes had gone missing, got lost or had severe maintenance problems coming over from the U.S., we were fortunate. Got in the truck feeling like I really needed a bath or quick shower, weather hot and a little sultry with a dusty wind. We headed down a muddy road and turned into an olive grove to the 441st Squadron Headquarters and signed in.

Decimo was a Luftwaffe base and was heavily bombed by our planes during the battles to drive the Germans out. There were wrecked and abandoned remains of German planes strewn all through the olive groves that ringed the field.

Met the new squadron commander, just got the job a few days earlier, Captain Sydney "Snuffy" Smith, Snuffy after the funny papers character. He shook each of our hands with a smile and, "Welcome aboard, glad you made it in one piece," he said and motioned us over to a briefing area outside the squadron office. We got as comfortable as possible sitting on old chairs and stonewalls on an old open patio area of the building.

"You'll get your tent assignments… officers and enlisted… plenty of room… just want to take a few minutes to welcome you all."

"If you need anything… please use your chain of command… I'm here to make sure you are mission capable and that means taking care of your concerns, your training and well-being."

"The 320th has been on this airfield since November of '43, so we have gotten quite settled with our tents and barracks and other amenities and comforts… our group commander is Colonel Eugene Fletcher… you will meet him later."

Pausing and clearing his throat, "We are co-located with the 319th Bomb Group, the 17th Bomb Group is located at an airfield near Villacidro… rumor has it that the 319th will convert to B-25's, so good for them… B-26's are the best and fastest of the medium bombers."

"Our bomb group is part of the 42nd Bomb Wing under the authority of the 12th Air Force."

"When you get a chance… get the 12th Air Force patch for your Class A's… we don't wear our A's unless we have a ceremony of some kind."

Just as Captain Smith was finishing, three sergeants came over to greet the enlisted aircrew, "For the enlisted… follow Sergeant's Fulk, Jensen and Simmons, they will show you to your tent and get a schedule down for familiarization training… OK?" We all acknowledged and went on our way to our tent to settle in, "Carry on… glad to have you on board."

Sergeant Fulk in a relaxed voice with a smile, "Gentlemen… grab your gear and follow us… we'll show you to your resort hut… you are officially short-timers," joking of course, "Most of our huts, or casa's and buildings are not too bad… you'll get used to it." We did a quick introduction with the sergeants and moved out to our hut.

Sergeant Fulk showed us his hut and said, "Nick, you'll be here… you too Ken and Ed… the rest follow Jensen and Simmons."

I threw my bags in the door and looked for my bunk… picked the best before Ken got in the door, "Ah… great bed… nice net."

"OK guys… settle in, chow in thirty minutes… food is not too bad here," then he said, "Call me Gene… we're going to be tent-mates… by the way tomorrow at 0800 hours you'll get your first familiarization briefing… survival in the water."

"Oh yea… watch out for the rats and lizards… mosquitoes are big as birds so sleep under your net." Hunting rats became a past time event when not flying on a mission, we used our .45's.

"Something you need to get done today, unless you did this before you left the States, is taking your POW photos and papers filled out in case you get shot down and captured… very important before you start flying practice and real missions."

"See you all later… got some training stuff to attend to," Gene smiled and gave a friendly salute then headed out the door, "Catch you all later for chow and some cards… there might be a movie tonight."

We settled in to the routine, ground training on bomb group and squadron standard operating procedures, and gunnery tips from gunners who actually shot at German fighters. Ken found out from the personnel officer that Jeff took the long way over on a troop ship and should be here in within a week. Lucky turn of events that three of us from the same high school and neighborhood got assignments to the same bomb group and squadron. Rich got orders for England also on B-26's with the 322nd Bomb Group, 449th Squadron. England is not bad certainly better weather and living conditions than Sardinia. He missed the D-Day invasion but is getting combat flight time over northern France. It's been a few days since I made a journal entry,

> *July 13: Not ready for first combat mission—Flew three practice bombing missions with crew—Plane kind of beat up but flies great—Familiarization training for survival, SOP for bomb group, gunnery (in the air) practice—Food not too bad NO SOS! Miss it though—Jeff will get here in a few days—hired a "bat boy" when I arrived to do laundry and chores (make beds!!), 2 bucks a week, Deal!*

> *July 15: Operations certified me (and other new guys) ready for assignment on combat missions—Waiting for the first one—Jeff finally made it—Ken, Jeff and I had a great time getting back together—More interesting to have flown over, Jeff got sea sick quite often—Flew another practice mission—Gene has been a straight shooter, good mentor and trainer, he is a flight engineer, has some good stories and quick fixes he has learned—Gene was right about the rats and lizards we are having fun with target practice, medics don't like their disease so no one complains*

Today's mission, July 19th, was fierce according to some of the 44t crews returning from the mission; I am scheduled for tomorrow's mission. Most of the planes were from the 444th Squadron, the 442nd and 443rd are on stand down for a few days. Target was the Borgoforte Railroad Bridge and the alternate Piacenza, Italy, 33 total planes over target; all returned, one with a wounded turret gunner. Five German Me 109 fighters attacked the formation just before the bomb run; they were aggressive but made only one pass each. They attacked from 11 o'clock high, P-47 escort fighters went after them and observed shooting down one. Antiaircraft fire from flak guns was heavy during and after the bomb drop, five aircraft damaged. A top turret gunner from the 444th was badly wounded; medics didn't think he would make it. A 50-caliber German round hit him, it penetrated the right side of the aircraft leaving a one-inch hole going through the gunners chest and back and his left arm. This is real, so get ready.

"Get up… get up," Sergeant Buijak, the squadron operations sergeant woke me up and the rest of us for today's mission, July 20th my first. It was also Ed and Ken's first. I saw the posting sheet for the mission last night and noticed my regular crew was missing, flying with new guys and just meeting them the last few days. The target is the same today as it was yesterday; I better be ready for fighters and flak. Nervous this morning as I get ready for chow and briefings.

"Ken… you're on for today… right?" I knew the answer but I am still nervous

"Yea… you knew that… I'm nervous too," Ken said sounding a little short, "After today we won't be virgins anymore," his humor breaks the tense mood

"Ed… what plane are you on?" I asked.

""Number "23"… haven't met any of these guys yet," Ed responded. Ken, Ed and I head over to the briefing area at the group headquarters, there's a mix of 441st and 444th crew gathering. The posting had me on aircraft battle tail number "02" with Lieutenant's Asher as pilot, McCurdy co-pilot, Burger bombardier, Staff Sergeant's Dalton radio-gunner, Rahl gunner, Stife photo and me as flight engineer turret gunner.

The Group Commander, Colonel Fletcher enters the briefing area then the shout, "Ten… Hut!" We all stand at attention.

Colonel Fletcher begins, "Gentlemen… at ease take your seats… target today is the same as yesterday's… Borgoforte Railroad Bridge and the alternate Piacenza," the colonel has a firm stance when he talks and presents himself in a confident manner, he is getting close to 90 missions… the most of any B-26 pilot. His confidence, skill and leadership show, it gives the group and me confidence.

"I'll hand over to the flight commander, Captain Nunn… Captain your brief."

"Thank you sir… as the commander said our target is Borgoforte Railroad Bridge and the alternate Piacenza," the operations sergeant for the group uncovers the schedule board and map showing the same mission as yesterdays, "Take off at 1620 hours… colors for the day and time frame is Red and Red… taxi and take off."

"The enemy has been using smoke screens to obscure target areas… we are going after it anyway."

"We will alter our flight path from yesterdays… navigators and pilots will be briefed separately."

"Spares for this mission with the formation are Lieutenant's Sinn and Lazo… ground spares Madden and Lindale… don't expect to launch the ground spares… stay sharp."

Captain Nunn continued with the weather report and the intelligence report… navigators and pilots head off to their own brief and we are dismissed to get ready and head out to the flight line. Weather looks good today, should be clear with some scattered clouds at various altitudes... 4/10 to 6/10 coverage.

Odd being with a different crew; they all have some experience except the co-pilot, McCurdy, he's new in theater. The rest of the crew are experienced, talking with Gene this morning he said to do what you have been trained to do, "You'll be OK... you've got a good training record... concentrate and stay focused."

Took off on time; our plane is third from the end of the flying formation. Forming up for the flight over target, watching the engine gauges with the pilots, generator functioning properly. All looks good, "Sir... heading back to the turret gun."

"Roger... go ahead... everything looks good," Lieutenant Asher looked my way and gave me thumbs up. I disconnected my intercom gave a quick salute wave and headed back to my gun position.

> *July 20: First mission, nervous expected Me 109 fighters— Smoke screen coverage so we hit the alternate, a perfect hit, just a few strays—Flak was light not accurate, saw flak explosions on my right, a small piece of shrapnel hit my turret Plexiglas made a small crack, reported to ground crew, startled me when it hit—Heard over the intercom 2 possible enemy aircraft at our five o'clock low as we finished bomb run, P-47 escorts chased them, heard nothing else— All returned safe—Nerves intact!*

The primary target area turned out to be obscured with enemy smoke screen so we hit the alternate target, the railroad bridge at Piacenza. Scattered clouds at 5,000 feet, good bombing weather. Returned at 2120 hours, weather is dry 80 degrees and starting to cool down for the evening, I'll sleep well tonight.

CHAPTER 3

WHAT NEXT?

General George S. Patton, Jr.:
"If a man does his best, what else is there?"

Being of low rank, corporal, and one of the new guys in theater gave me the privilege of some special duties sanitizing the latrine. This duty was especially unpleasant for smell and visuals, and needed to be done for sanitation purposes. Why couldn't our "bat boys" get paid for this? I think its character building for the new guys. Each latrine out house had two seat holes for the occupants; you had to pour a small amount of gasoline in the catch barrel and then light it off to get rid of the contents. There were doors on the outside wall that were hinged at the top with a handle at the bottom with a latch to hold it open to pull the barrels out. Once a day this was done.

One fateful day at one of the officer latrines, an anxious let's get it done corporal put gasoline in both holes and then realized he forgot matches. Gas in the barrels and still in place under each seat hole, an unsuspecting captain walked over to the closest latrine to take care of business. Cigarette in mouth and the Stars and Stripes newspaper in hand he sat down and decided to get rid of his cigarette. He dropped it through the seat hole and then very much to his surprise a sudden whoosh of flames erupted that singed his cheeks. His new call sign, "Burnt Butt", he survived with minor burns and the flight surgeon gave him some salve to soothe his burnt cheeks. Word got out to watch out for new guys with gasoline and no matches. I only forgot matches once.

No mission assignments for over two weeks, only practice missions. Off duty time can be boring, and you looked for something constructive to do rather than drink or get into trouble. There was a comfortable beach house that was built by the water in Cagliari that was a favorite place if you wanted sun and surf to relax. A swim in the Mediterranean was nice once in awhile but not for me too much without Mary. There was a ball field for baseball with bleachers and dugouts for the teams, someone spent a lot of time getting this in place. The Special Services Squadron was always getting recreation activities for crews off missions. Keeps us busy. Finally mail from home and Mary, it always makes my day when mail call comes around and my name is called.

I spent time in getting comfortable and hanging out with Ken, Jeff, Ed, or Gene if they weren't on a mission. Ken and Jeff had the same break in mission assignment; Gene and Ed flew at least two in the last two weeks. On one day when Gene was around, we got the great Idea to sign out a Jeep from the transportation officer and head out to explore the island. We heard about a castle not far from here, took our side arms, water and rations in case we couldn't find a place to eat and headed off the airfield. The castle was not too far from base, and we all had noticed it from the air when we were flying around Sardinia. It did look like ruins and not an intact or occupied structure. We got to within a half-mile and stopped to get up there on foot and follow a path we saw that led up to the castle.

Gene was driving, he had been there before and thought it would be a good place to see, "Well... we need to park it here and climb up that small hill to a narrow path that takes you up to the castle."

"Wow... it looks pretty high up and steep," Jeff said, "I'll bet there are great views from up there."

We all climbed out of the Jeep and headed up the hill to the path. The path was rough with loose stones and gravel, lots of overgrowth of trees and bushes... then we finally reached the castle. A breathtaking view all around, you could see Decimo field off in the distance to the east and Cagliari off to the south and the blue waters of the Mediterranean. None of us brought a camera... we're going to have to make another trip. The view was spectacular. The castle walls were something to see with the large stones and height of the walls, makes you think of old times when this was built and how old it was.

Jeff was a history and literature buff and had read Dante Alghieri's *Divine Comedy*… he started to quote and give us some history. Didn't know he was such a literature buff. He started to give us a history lesson, "This is the castle Acquafredda… it was mentioned for the first time in 1215," he continued as if he had an old world history book in front of him, "This place gained fame because of a Pisan nobleman, the count of Donoratico, he was the governor of Sardinia in 1252."

We all looked at one another and then to Jeff who was just enamored with the place, "I didn't know you knew so much about this place," Ken said with a smirk, making fun of Jeff.

Jeff realized he was getting poked at, "Well… I do know and I love old world history… did you know that," Ken interrupted him and said, "OK… just kidding… really didn't know you were such a history buff. "This would be a great place to just relax and dream the day away,"

I said looking around and enjoying the view, it's great. We spent about four hours just relaxing and talking about home and sweethearts and dozing off every once in awhile, it was a peaceful day and the weather was perfect.

Headed down the path later in the day and climbed into the Jeep to drive back to the base, Gene somehow got lost as we took a different road than he did earlier. The road was muddy and got our Jeep stuck in a rough stretch, "I thought these Jeeps were mud proof," I said sarcastically.

"Well… I guess not," Gene responded with frustration and scratching his head wondering how he got off track and missed the road back to base

"OK guys… get out and push."

We climbed out jumping into the quagmire and swore the whole time until Gene managed to get the Jeep out.

"The 'bat boys' are going to need extra elbow grease to get the mud out of our uniforms," Jeff said as we all looked down at the mud covering our pant legs and boots.

"Climb in… I know where we are now… damn, let's get going," Gene said as he put the Jeep in gear. Scraping as much mud as possible off our boots and pant legs we climbed in and sped off avoiding the mud as much as possible. Finally made it back to base just before chow, just in time to change clothes and clean up.

Heading over to the orderly room to get a copy of Yank or Stars and Stripes to read before chow and I heard a familiar voice coming from behind

"Nick… Corporal," Lieutenant Cahan shouted motioning me to stop, he told me we were on for the mission tomorrow, August 6, "We're on for tomorrow… wanted to let you know… most of us on the same plane."

"Yes sir… I got word from the operations sergeant a few minutes ago," I said wondering what else he had for me.

"Look… the way it's going to be here is that we probably won't be on the same plane as a crew… lots of shuffling around," he said and then, "I asked for you as flight engineer… need your skills and we work well together, so I will ask for you as much as possible."

"Sir… OK… I appreciate that… yea, if you can make that happen that works for me, thanks."

"You are welcome… see you at the briefing in the morning," he said and rushed off to a pilots meeting at the squadron headquarters shack. Over two weeks after my first mission I finally got scheduled with most of our original crew, Lieutenant Cahan, Ed, John Hill, and me on a mission. Most units I found out didn't have crews stay together much; it probably wasn't true for the big bomber crews. We all had to adapt to other pilots and crew, concentrating on the job was priority and ignore who and what.

Rumor has it that the invasion of southern France may be happening shortly. We've been bombing targets in Italy, looks like a shift to France soon. Talk is that we could be home for Christmas if the Allies keep up the progress. Christmas would be great but we all have our doubts, sounds nice for morale

Walking back to my hut, Gene was waving me over and said he heard a rumor that we would be bombing targets in France, "Nick… got word on aircraft assignment, you and me will be on planes dropping chaff… maybe over France."

"Great… crap…. dropping that stuff is not easy… damn it," I said frustrated remembering training in the states and the mess it makes inside the plane and the handling of the chaff dispensers.

"France… really… guess the rumors are true," I said still steamed about dropping chaff.

Gene was pretty sure, "Real reliable source on France… don't tell anyone else… OK?"

"Nick… I know its crap but let me give you some tips on getting it done without getting on your nerves… OK?"

Gene reassured me there was an easier way to dump this crap. Stateside training didn't have much on chaff dispensers and when we did it, it did not work well, hated dealing with the whole contraption.

After Gene's instruction session I grabbed my copy of the latest Stars and Stripes newspaper and went to my bunk to read and relax before chow. Feeling a little nervous, I thought I'd get over this but the feeling is back, the same as the first mission. This is number two, more to come and need to get my mind clear. Wrote letters to Mary and home, walked over to Cahan's tent so he could censor my letters. I settled in back in my bunk with my paper.

Ken and Jeff walked into our hut and asked, "Hey… you want to get a ball game in with the 442nd?" Ken asked with bat and mitt in hand

"Yea… gotta get my mind off the next mission… are you guys on for tomorrow's mission?"

"Don't know… we've been pulling a ball game together haven't talked with anyone about missions," Ken remarked looking anxious to get another player on the 441st team

"OK… let's go."

"Ed… are you in?" I said, as he was lying on his bunk reading Yank magazine.

"Yea… I'm in… let's go."

Off we went for the rest of the afternoon… we won… then on to chow, rumor discussions, steak and potatoes. Nice meal and off to sleep for an early wake-up.

Aug 6: Early wake up, chow and mission brief—France targets!—Prep for D-Day??—Date classified—Long mission 5 hours!—No fighters—Strange sight, watched another bomb group pass in front of our formation, pilots & command pissed—Dumped chaff, pain in the ass—Some planes landed at Corsica for fuel, we came in on fumes!!—Several planes damaged from flak, including ours—Don't like the bouncing around from flak bursts—Shrapnel hitting the plane's skin feels like a big baseball bat hitting the plane

Aug 7: Another long mission to France target—Hit road bridges that connected to the landing areas—Ken, Jeff, Ed and Gene on mission yesterday and today—Same crew as yesterday—Ken's plane as spare came back early—Saw for first time, British Spitfires 12 of them for escort, no German fighters or flak—Cloud cover scattered at lower and higher altitudes, nice ride—Hope all missions are like this one, can get spoiled, "Just Wait" all the old timers say!

Aug 8: Late day mission, clear scattered clouds, no problems with target ID—Target in Italy close to France border RR bridge—No fighter escort, No Show??—Flak from a boat over the Med, no problems not even close—No fighters, weather real good

Every day melted into the next, the same for weeks melting into the next week. It seemed as if I had been in theater for longer than a few months. Gene was not scheduled for a mission the same time I was off; we spent some time off the base for something I had not experienced yet… boar hunting. I did a lot of duck hunting in Michigan, but boars were a different tactic. Armed with rifles instead of shotguns and targets on the ground versus in flight.

We were able to get a Jeep from transportation, signed out two M-1 Carbine's and headed off base to a place where Gene knew we could hunt in the open.

"OK… let's get going, you're going to love this," Gene said as he put the Jeep in gear and headed off base to a hunting area he had used when he first got to Sardinia. One thing he said when I arrived last month, and I agreed after only being here a short time, was that the locals were not very friendly. It showed many times with the locals working on the base and when we would travel to a small town or village close to base. They had seen a lot of fighting putting up with the Germans, Mussolini, and now the Americans that bombed the hell out of the area surrounding the airfield.

The landscape varied with open fields and hills, it was dry about 80 degrees and a nice breeze. We headed northeast of the base towards the center of the island to a region called Barbagia… it took us about an hour and a half by winding road. The road was open and clear of traffic except for a few farmers with carts and some old broken down cars.

"There… over the right side of the hill… that's where I was two months ago and got one boar for a roast," Gene said as he pointed over to some open field with small hills around.

"Looks like groves over there," I said as I noticed a huge open area with groves of trees.

"Yea… those are Chestnut trees."

"Are they ripe yet?" I asked.

"Don't know… its been warm here they might be."

We found a spot to park off the road at the edge of some trees and brush at the base of a small hill

"OK… grab your M-1 and we'll head out over there," Gene pointed out over the field to the north and led the way.

We must have rustled through the brush and hills for two hours, nothing to see or shoot at and then the silence was disturbed with a gunshot. It startled us at first. We stopped and looked around in the direction of the sound and noticed a Sardinian with his son pointing at a spot where it appears he shot and hit a boar. We didn't see or hear them until the shot was heard

"Well, how lucky is that?" I said looking at the boar lying in the field in the distance. We both looked at each other in disappointment.

Gene shaking his head side to side said, "Well… two hours wasted… lucky shot I guess."

"Better luck next time… let's head back," I said.

"Its been fun... something to do... reminds me of hunting in Michigan," thinking back to my trips during duck hunting season, Ken, Jeff, Rich and I would head out for days. Great memories, now today I've got more with Gene in a place I never expected to see or visit in my lifetime.

"Oh yea... where in Michigan?" Gene asked. He grew up in northern Ohio and I thought he had mentioned that he would travel to Michigan to hunt deer.

"That's right you mentioned you used to get to Michigan to hunt... we usually went off the water in the thumb area around Cass City."

"Ken's parents had access to a family cabin in the country, so we would go there... it was about two hours north of Detroit... real open and rural small town."

"Boy, do I miss hunting there."

Gene responded, "We used to travel to Grayling up north... I have a cousin that lived there so we had an open invitation to visit and hunt on their property... nice area... great time."

"Hey... why don't we look through that grove area, Chestnut trees might be ready for picking."

"OK... let's go... maybe there will be some ripe ones on the ground," I said

Chestnuts grow inside spiky green shells, they open when they are ripe. As the nuts ripen, they fall from the tree so they should be all over if they are ripe.

We made it back to the Chestnut grove and began looking around, "Oh yea... here they are... not all of them are ripe but there are a lot on the ground," I said as I put my M-1 over my shoulder and started filling my pockets.

"We'll have to use our hats after our pockets are full... wow, there is a lot of them," Gene said. He added, "We can roast these when we get back."

We filled our pockets and then used our hats to haul the ripe chestnuts back to base for roasting, a chestnut party... what a treat. Arriving back at the base and our hut we emptied our pockets and hat full of chestnuts and proceeded to find a pan and open fire to roast the chestnuts. We had a treat for our fellow crewmates and us; it was a calm evening and the chestnuts tasted great. It was a long day and one I won't forget, it didn't feel like I was in a war zone.

> *Aug 9: Went to the beach house that the 320th officers set up at a Cagliari beach area, nice sun and relaxing, got a little sunburned— Wrote home and got a letter from Mary, she sent pictures of her, my sisters and ma—She looks great*

> *Aug 10: Practice mission today, formation flying, COL wants us to tighten up on our formations, better protection—Baseball game with the 444th, they won—Still had some chestnuts in my foot locker, finished them, must go to that grove for more with Gene, Jeff, Ken, and Ed*

> *Aug 11 & 12: Briefings for water survival, gunnery, war news update—Normandy invasion becoming a real success, Germans on the run—Played cards with some guys from the 442nd, won $50!!*

Days blended together, but not being on a mission made me feel like I was missing out and needed to be flying to keep my skills sharp. I can't get my mission count up while I stay on the ground waiting. Then, checking the operations posted missions for the 13th looks like Ken, Jeff, Gene, Ed and I are scheduled.

> *Aug 13: Up at 0230, take off at 0445—Mission to Toulon France, enemy gun positions—Visibility poor, really bad haze, sun low created visibility problem—Enemy destroyer off shore put out a smoke screen, didn't help with haze—Missed target!!—Not a good mission—Saw the Spitfires again for escort, no German fighters—2 planes badly damaged from flak east of targets—Lost plane from flak, saw it hit left wing, it was blown off, two chutes spotted, rumor has it pilot and co-pilot didn't get out, two captured and the rest missing or dead—The site of their plane was surreal played ball with these guys now some are just gone!*

> *Aug 14: Another early mission—Target St. Tropez gun positions—P-47's and Spitfires showed up for escort, no*

> *German fighters—Excellent bomb run, saw a huge red explosion (secondary explosion) southwest of the south gun position—Better results than yesterday—More damage from some flak—8 planes shot down & 1/3 of our group planes damaged heavily since we started France missions earlier this month—Lost some new friends that I started to get to know, great guys, very sad*

Back from mission, tired from the long flight over the water and back. Everyone was ordered to report to the officers club at 1400 hours; just enough time to brief the intelligence officer on mission observations and get some chow. The club had mud and brick walls and a tile roof, it was built by local labor. It had two rooms, one for the bar and the other was a larger room for recreation with chairs, tables, benches along the wall and a couple of dart boards.

Gathering with the rest of aircrew personnel, conversation chatters all around. What was going on? Ken, Jeff, Gene, Ed and I are standing close to the door by the recreation room and noticing a security presence keeping any "bat boys" or other civilians working on the base away from the club, "What's going on with all the security?" I said as we continued to speculate.

"I think it is D-Day for the invasion of southern France… it's got to be… can't be anything else," Gene said with confidence.

"Well… yea… makes sense to me but could be an all out effort for Italy as well," Jeff said.

"Are you in a betting mood?" Ken said to Jeff, "Twenty bucks its France… um?"

"I'll go for twenty… anyone else?" Jeff said.

"Are you guys nuts?" I said.

"This isn't worth twenty bucks."

The silence breaks as Captain Smith approaches the crowd; we all stand up at attention, "OK… OK… at ease and just take your seats… real informal… OK."

Pausing to take a breath, Captain Smith begins, "Sergeant, will you close that outside door please?" Gazing across all of our faces and waiting for the door to close, "Tomorrow we're gonna help make history… the newspaper headlines in the States will read "Allied Troops

Invade Southern France", that is Operation Dragoon," he continued after clearing his throat, "Our job will be to clear the land mines in the beach area for the first wave of invasion forces."

"We will be dropping strings of one-hundred pound demolition bombs… thirty from each ship."

"The 441st will be putting up two nine-ship squadrons and… it will be a night takeoff."

One of the bombardier officers stuck their hand up with a question, "Sir… how are we going to carry thirty bombs when we only have twenty sets of bomb shackles on the bomb racks?"

Captain Smith responded, "The ordnance guys have already worked that out… they say there is enough room to wire five extra bombs to the other bombs and each side of the bomb bay."

"They will be on the bottom so they would be first out for the drop," then an added warning, "So… don't bring back any bombs… dump them if you can't get a target drop."

"No guarantee that a rough landing would keep those bombs in place."

You could cut the mood with a knife with the "what the hell" looks on our faces as we heard about the bomb rigging setup.

Captain Smith looking down at his operations order on his clipboard continued to brief, "The 320th… the 319th… and the 17th will be putting up eighteen planes from each of the four squadrons… over half a million pounds of bombs on the beach."

"Our combined efforts will be a significant effort to support the infantry clearing its path to gain a strong foothold on the beach and their inland push," he continued, "the first wave will hit the beach at 0800 hours… so, the reason for a night takeoff in the dark for an 0715 hours drop on our target."

"Time to target is going to be 2 hours from here, the target area is "Baie de Cavalaire"… and you all may not know but that during peacetime this was a posh resort beach… no resort beach events tomorrow." Some chuckling in the crowd, he continued, "This is a big deal, maybe not as big as Normandy, but it will be big."

"There will be carriers, cruisers, battleships, destroyers, and troop carriers… C-47's will be dropping paratroopers with lots of fighter cover from the Navy, our P-47's and P-38's based in Corsica and Italy," then something not normally heard of for missions, "Only lead crews are going to have any briefing before the mission… pay attention, this is how we will line up."

Captain Smith got up and walked over to the dart board, turning the board over to show a bare surface, he did a crude drawing of the six runways on Decimo, "After loading operations the crew chiefs will taxi each aircraft to the west side of the runways… planes will be straight in line, all seventy-two of them… and the spares, eight of those," tapping the board with his pencil pointing at a west and east side he continues, "the 319th will do the same lineup on the east side."

Captain Smith started to give some detailed instructions, "All planes will be facing the runways… engine start is 0420 hours."

"Watch the plane on your right, when you see it turn 90 degrees and it starts to taxi, get in line behind him."

"No engine run ups before taxi… crew chiefs have that covered, we can't have more dust swirling around especially when it will be dark… let's keep the confusion to a minimum."

"Question in the back."

"Sir… are we using our landing lights on takeoff?"

"No… ground crews and engineers dug up some old Eyetie searchlights, they will be positioned at each runway end beamed flat down the strips."

"The war has progressed enough for us here and in Europe and its time to move forward."

"This briefing is classified Top Secret and will not be discussed in casual conversation."

"Your professionalism in conducting missions for this squadron and bomb group has been superb and I do not expect it to change," he said with a look of pride in his voice and stance, "We will succeed and we will be full on to support landing forces on the 15th "

"There are a lot of asses on the line here, including yours."

"Group and squadron operations staff have been putting together our missions… they should be posted by now so check your assignments."

"I can't emphasize enough on how dangerous this is going to be… so be on your best game… I know you are all the time, but this is an all-out effort… be safe and accurate," then as an afterthought he said, "Oh, by the way… no pleasure trips off base, you are all confined to base."

"Wake up for the lead crews will be 0230 hours, the rest at 0300 hours… stay sober and focused… dismissed."

He finished and left the area as we all looked at each other encouraged that we will be involved in opening a second front in Western Europe… southern France. We all had a worried look not wanting any mistakes for such a mass effort up in the air on a dark and crowded airfield

"I'll take my twenty bucks," Ken said to Jeff grinning like a bar hall gambler to the loser of a big pot of cash.

"All right… give me a rain check for the cash… you'll get it… damn," Jeff said, he was sure it was Italy versus France.

After checking the posting board for assignments I am on two missions for the day… a very long and stressful day tomorrow. Gene was with me in our hut, don't know where Ken, Jeff and Ed were; we spend some time talking about home and family. Gene's a straight shooter; he has been a good mentor since arriving in Sardinia, a calm and confident person.

"How's the wife… Mary, is that her name?" Gene asked.

"Yes… Mary… miss her a lot… seems like forever since I saw her," I said as her face appeared in my mind.

"Her letters say she's doing good… misses me of course and can't wait to see me."

"She keeps busy working at a law office in Detroit… and lives at her parent's home."

"We were able to get together in Florida before we took off for Sardinia."

"That was so nice to have her with me in Florida… my first time there and it was Mary's as well."

"I never asked… are you married?" I asked Gene.

"No… just engaged…waiting to get home to have a real good celebration."

We talked more about our loved ones and got homesick real quick, but it was good to talk about it. I better write home and get my letters to Lieutenant Cahan for censoring.

Six ships taking off at the same time and in the dark is dangerous and pilots need to have their best pilot skills on, no room for error.

Ken, Ed and Jeff walk in and look concerned, "What's up?" I said, we all were nervous about the early morning takeoff.

Jeff talked first, "Ken and I were at the operations office checking our assignment and the pilot for my plane is Lieutenant Trunk... well... rumor has it from one of the other crew on board that he was sick to his stomach... throwing up."

Ken interjected, "Yea... and he hasn't gone to the flight surgeon to stay off mission."

Ed interjected, "I don't like this either... I'm not on his plane, but someone has to say something."

"Wait... how do you know that?" Gene asked Ken.

"Word gets around... his co-pilot said he doesn't look good... he needs to be on sick call."

"Isn't Trunk the group's test pilot and instructor?" I said.

"Yea... but..." Jeff started to answer when Gene interrupted, "You better say something... go over his head and say something."

Jeff returned, "He might be OK in the morning with some rest tonight... he's a good pilot... don't know."

We all looked at each other concerned wondering if we should go to the operations officer and flight surgeon, our interference might be perceived wrong and out of line.

"If he looks bad in the morning before you get on that plane, say something Jeff... OK?" Ken said as we all chimed in to try and relax Jeff.

Sleeping was difficult knowing the mission risks during takeoff... not worried about getting to the target and even those wired bombs... just the takeoff in the dark. Tossed and turned to what seemed to be forever then finally fell asleep, then the harsh reality of a wakeup with a flashlight in the face... it was 0300 hours.

Pushing aside the mosquito netting and getting up feeling surprisingly rested I got cleaned up and headed over to the chow hall. All of us are anxious being involved in such a big effort, finished breakfast and got my gear together and waited for the trucks to take us out to our plane.

It was a little chilly and you could feel a slight breeze that carried the smells of the island, our base, chow, oil and gas. Climbed in the back of the truck, the ride was bumpy and dark only feeling the presence of my fellow crew, couldn't see their faces. The driver yelled out the plane tail numbers as he stopped at each plane, stopping again the driver yelled out, "Tail number 23… out here… move out."

Getting out of the truck at our plane, number "23", I looked over the airfield with the searchlights showing the magnificent site of the silhouettes of eighty planes. Perfectly lined up wingtip to wingtip, "Lieutenant… magnificent sight, isn't it?"

Looking around he responded, "Wow… quite a sight… it'll be a great mission."

Mass B-26 Take-Off for Operation Dragoon

Gathering the crew Cahan gives a short pep talk, "OK guys stay sharp and keep your eyes open… everyone in your positions and watch out for other planes on takeoff," then looking at me, "Nick… stay up front then head back to the turret just after we take off and keep an eye out… OK?

"Yes sir... ready," I responded as we were dismissed to get in the plane for a quick pre-flight. Ground crews did it before taxiing the planes but a quick re-check should do. I talked with the crew chief and he told me everything checked out... the variation on the magnetos was less than 100. The generator function, engine run-up and taxi checked out according to the crew chief. Shoving the flak vests and parachutes into the plane we loaded the rest of our gear and got settled in for takeoff and the synchronized movement of the rest of the group.

Cahan and Merrill did the startup sequence perfectly, "Master switch on... right magneto on... prop levers forward... mixture rich," Cahan gave the direction to Merrill as he acknowledged the left engine start and then the right engine. The props look good, engines sound good. Listening over the intercom, "Oil pressure in the green... good to go... watch out for the plane on our right."

"Sir... on our right, they're moving out... right turn," Merrill said to Cahan

Cahan gave the direction, "OK... ease off the parking brake and let's move behind... pilot to crew, eyes sharp prepare to takeoff."

Thinking about our conversation with Jeff last night I didn't even think about his concerns until just now. In some small talk with Cahan before taxiing, he thought he saw Trunk at the officer's mess this morning but could not get a good look at him... must be OK... hope he's OK.

There was an eerie look of the mass takeoff, planes with no lights appearing as shadows in the searchlights set up at each end of the runways. There were only twenty five to thirty feet between the nose and the tail of each plane as they lumbered on the taxiway like elephants bobbing around the circus ring for the greatest show on earth. It was 0430 hours and looking out between the pilots I was watching the engine gauges and was noticing the silhouettes of planes as they began to taxi and takeoff. Then out of the corner of my eye a sudden appearance of a red glow and then... a booming explosion.

"We lost one... what happened?" Cahan said in a shocked tone, "That had to be the second takeoff flight... I think."

Lieutenant Merrill was speechless then, "Tower broadcasting a halt in takeoffs… Roger… holding," he said telling Cahan and responding to the tower directions

"Sir… tower wants us to hold."

Cahan looking over to Merrill and me, "OK… standby." We looked at each other wondering what happened and who may have been hurt or killed. Then the tower gives the order to continue takeoffs. Looking off into the distance it was dark and murky; the searchlight's glare hid the view of the sky and any glimmer of the other planes after takeoff.

Cahan and Merrill got us in place as the plane on our right was now in front heading for the south end of the runway to takeoff. Maneuvering in place at the end of the runway waiting for our turn, Cahan is hard on the brakes running the engine RPM's for takeoff… 2,700 on both engine tachometers… then he releases the brakes as directed and the plane lunges forward. Manifold pressure 52"… airspeed moving normally… approaching 100 mph Cahan eased the wheel back as the nose lifted up and at 130 the main gear were off the runway, we are up.

The sky was dark and we can barely make out the planes on our right side as we continue to ascend to altitude for the rendezvous with the rest of the formation.

Then not quite two minutes after takeoff, "What the hell… another one?" Cahan shouted and we saw a glow and then heard a large explosion that we could feel as we flew over a crash site.

"Who was that?" "Keep your eyes peeled… watch out for other planes," Cahan shouts as he looked out his side of the cockpit at a plane below that crashed in to a small hill.

"Get on the radio Ed… give them a position for what we just passed over," Cahan tells Ed Geronimos who was the radio-gunner.

"Roger sir," Ed said as he got on the radio with the tower and sector control

After passing the crash site he immediately looked forward to concentrate on climbing out on heading 340 to altitude and the rendezvous point, Isle de Asinara, a small isle off the north shore of Sardinia. The sky was beginning to turn lighter like a plum blue, enough light to see well and make assembling for the mission easier and less dangerous. We formed up in squadrons of nine planes at about 7,000 feet; Cahan noticed a gap in the formation like there was a missing plane... must have been the one we flew over.

"Can't think of who would be in the formation gap... what do you think? Cahan said to Merrill wondering who crashed.

"I don't know... must have been mechanical... hope they're OK."

I thought of Jeff's crew, don't recall where his plane would have been in the takeoff lineup. We turned with the rest of the squadron and headed out over the Mediterranean, you can see the island of Corsica at our right. Next land we will see is the target area about 200 miles ahead. Headed back to my turret gun, don't expect any fighters today. I should be able to see pretty good off in the distance.

Cloud cover was partly to mostly cloudy, 6/10 to 8/10 coverage. You can see the blue water below through the cloud breaks then all of a sudden I can see naval ships... everywhere, as the sky gets brighter. What a sight, it seemed endless. Escort fighter planes, P-47's and P-38's cross over the ships below, lots of them. The landing time approaches for the infantry to storm the beach. I can feel a slight concussion sensation of booms from cannon fire, must be the battleships firing below us. We're getting closer to the IP for our bomb run, 12,000 feet. Watching battleships firing from this altitude looks surreal.

Over the intercom Cahan gives us the heads up, "Gentlemen we are starting the IP, bombardier get ready."

Sergeant Jim Ross is in the nose and he will drop our bomb load when he sees the lead plane drop; leads have the Norden bombsight for target identification. "Sir... bomb bay doors opening," Jim said as he waited for the site of the lead bombers dropping their loads.

"Roger... make sure all bombs get out of the bay area... don't trust those wired bombs," Cahan told Jim.

I can see the coastline and the ships on the water, still too many to count... no flak or enemy fighters... weather is good and cloud cover over target is 4/10 coverage.

"Bombs away," Jim shouted out.

As I was turning my turret around to see forward, the bombs were beginning to drop from the lead planes and now ours: you can hear a screaming whirling sound of the bomb fins falling through the air. A funny sensation in the plane as our bombs leave the bomb bay, it lifts in the air and drops slightly. Then suddenly a WHOOM along with a huge fireball of red, yellow and black in front and below us and then the clangs of fragments from bomb casings slamming our plane, "Hey what the… what was that?" Cahan screamed. The tail gunner also startled screamed, "Damn what the hell was that?"

After a few minutes Cahan came back on the intercom, "We're OK… we're OK… it's not flak… two wired bombs bumped and exploded," he sounded nervous and shouted, "Everyone OK?" Cahan said, "Wow… it was like slow motion, I saw two bombs wired together drop out of that lead plane and then watched both turn at each other and touch at the fuses… then BOOM."

We were all startled and wondered if flak hit us, then Cahan realized that those wired bombs from one of the lead planes must have bumped together as they left the bomb bay exploding in air just below their plane.

"Sir… engineer gunner OK," we all checked in as OK.

"OK… damage report… anyone see any damage?" Cahan gathered damage assessments and contacted sector control, no one is dropping out.

"Don't see anything from my view," I said.

"Sir… a hole underneath the left stabilizer, no control surfaces," our tail gunner Sergeant Fred Cook shouts over the intercom.

"Way too close… don't see anything else."

"Roger… thanks," Cahan responds.

We'll need to get on the ground to see any real damage.

"Sir… any changes in engine or generator functions?" I asked.

"No… all looks good, must not have touched the engine," Cahan responds, "Stay in the turret for now until we get closer to Decimo."

"Roger sir."

"Jim… check the bomb bay for any hang-ups."

"Yes sir... heading back to check," Jim disconnected from the nose intercom and walked back to the bomb bay, "Sir... all bombs have dropped, no hang-ups."

"Got it... thanks."

Cahan and Merrill start our turn to return to Decimo; target hits were good and we head back for the next mission. No flak or enemy fighters. Had to look down at all the naval ships in the area as we turned back; I'm still amazed on the number assembled, hope the infantry is getting the job done.

Mission flying time was four hours and thirty minutes long. We approach the runway and Cahan makes a perfect landing. We taxi to the parking area to do a post flight check. We all got out and stretched our legs and immediately looked around the plane to check for damage. Looking over the surface and engine areas I noticed some hydraulic fluid leaking and a hole about the size of a coconut in back of the right engine nacelle. The bomb bay doors looked dented, doesn't look bad and there are more dents underneath aft of the bomb bay. Ed noticed some holes in the left wing about the size of a baseball; this plane isn't going anywhere for a few days.

Fred was looking at the hole just out of his view in the tail gunner position and pulled out a rough piece of bomb casing embedded in the hole. "Look at this... if that would have been a few inches further to the center fuselage... um... well I'm OK... keeping this one for the record."

I looked at the piece and we looked at each other and just shook our heads in wonder and went on to finish our post flight.

Merrill and Jim notice some holes on the left wing near the engine nacelle, amazingly no damage to the control surfaces of the wings and tail

"Sir... any word on who dropped out on takeoff?" I asked Cahan and Merrill as we continued to post flight our plane.

"Yea... one crew got out of their plane, no word on the other... let's get over to Intel for our briefs then we'll know more."

We finished up and waited for our ride back to the group headquarters building and the next mission brief; I'm on for the next flight in about two hours.

Our ride back to the headquarters building to get our quick mission brief and crew assignments was bumpy and dusty. I thought about Jeff and his concern for the pilot, Trunk, and his stomach problems. If he had the flu, he should have been grounded. Arriving at the headquarters area, the Red Cross had provided some coffee and donuts for us as we waited for our brief and transport back out to our planes for my second mission

"Nick… Jeff was on the second crash plane," Ken pulled me outside the building near the Red Cross hut, "No one knows what the condition of the crew is… there is a volunteer group going out with the flight surgeon and operations officer to see where they crashed."

"I don't think I can get off my plane to help… I better not try… are you going?"

"Yea… there's six of us plus the officers," Ken said, "Gotta go… I'll let you know later when you get back… be safe."

"You too… hey, was the pilot sick?" I asked thinking about our conversation and concern yesterday.

"Don't know… you bet there will be an investigation."

"See you later," I said and went off to get my gear and get on the truck out to the airfield for the next mission

Flying with the same crew as the first mission this morning, different plane tail number "03". We are carrying one thousand pounders in the bomb bay for a target near Arles, road bridges that link to the beachhead. We took off at 1358 hours, clear skies with minimal cloud cover, British Spitfires and Navy Hellcats along with our P-47's and P-38's provided air cover. Our bomb drop pattern was right on destroying the bridge and approaches, all planes returned to base. No damage, flak or fighters and landed at 1819 hours. It's been a long day, frustrated not knowing Jeff's status.

Riding back to the squadron area for post flight interrogations and then get a cup of coffee and bread at the Red Cross hut, I saw Gene heading in my direction.

"Nick… I've got news on Jeff's plane," Gene didn't look like he had good news, "They were all killed in the crash… I'm sorry… so sorry."

Shocked and not knowing what to say I stood there starting to feel the onset of a faint feeling and then emotions that I couldn't control, I started weeping. Gene grabbed me looking into my face, "Nick... steady... it hurts bad I know... got to settle down and deal with it."

"Sit down and take a breather... grieve here and get it out," Gene was sitting next to me with his hand around my shoulders.

"This is hard for you and Ken... it's harder being so close," Gene gave more advise, some welcome and some I didn't hear or want to hear. "I'm shaking... how do I stop this?" sobbing and asking Gene for help, help he couldn't give.

"Nick... look at me... look at me," he got in my face and looked straight at me, "Let's get over to the chaplain... got to talk this out... OK?"

"Yea... I don't know what to do."

After a long visit with the chaplain I headed back with Gene. In our hut I saw Ken... cried out eyes, red... a blank stare on his face," I should have stayed on a mission... the area we searched was a small hill... some locals looking around... didn't hit any buildings."

"Finally found the impact site and realized how scattered the wreckage was... it was still smoking," then Ken started choking a little on his words and then, "I found Jeff... the only... it was his head... don't know where the rest of him was."

Ken stopped and began sobbing again... extremely painful experience. Ed didn't say a word but was brokenhearted on his own. He instinctively let us grieve our way, he knew how close we were in school and how that made this death more significant for Ken and me.

Aug 17: Class A uniforms today, squadron assembling at the Allied Cemetery close by—Hard to write this, lost close hometown and high school friend Jeff, killed on takeoff for 15 Aug mission—Pilot was sick, WHY WHY??—Hard to deal with, Ken and I talking with the group chaplain GOT TO DEAL WITH IT!!

Hot August sun, we looked un-military in our wrinkled uniforms as we assembled in a formation for the funeral of Lieutenant Trunk's plane crew, Jeff's last mission. I had seen this cemetery from the air but never thought about its purpose… standing at parade rest the chaplain begins the service looking over eight flag draped caskets. You don't feel like anything will go wrong… then reality sets in when you see your friends and other crew get killed.

I remember seeing the film "A Guy Named Joe" not long ago, Spencer Tracy was a pilot in the film and was killed in a scene where his plane was hit by flak and crashed into an enemy ship. The next scene showed him walking in waist deep fog seemingly alive and then an angel comes up to him, "Yeah, you're dead, but you have to go back and help out this fledgling pilot back on Earth, give him the benefit of your experience." The next scene has Ward Bond, Spencer's flying buddy, consoling his girlfriend, the beautiful Irene Dunne, "Flyers may crack up once in a while, sure, but they never really die." I couldn't help but think about that scene as I looked over the caskets… Bull Shit. The presence of those caskets in front of all of us brings home the reality of where we are and what we are doing. Sherman from the civil war, a general and an aggressive fighter said… "War is hell", well, it is from my view, it may be worse than this I'm in the air and not on the ground. Then… an old timers words to me personally… get your mind straight and think of yourself being dead already… move on and do your job.

Aug 17 (continued): Formation of four B-26's flew over funeral formation in tribute, missing man formation on the third pass—Taps sounded and started to get teary eyed—After taps stopped, silence then called to attention by Captain Smith, right face and we marched out of the cemetery to our trucks and back to squadron area—Dusty ride back to my hut, carefully brushed off and folded my Class A's, put them in my duffle bag—On for a mission tomorrow—Wrote letter to Jeff's parents, home and Mary and Rich in England with the 332nd BG, hard to write about, sick and empty feeling—Ken is taking Jeff's death hard like me, we don't talk about it, the chaplain is going to be my best friend, he did help greatly the other day when it happened

Aug 18: More gun position targets in France—Great target hits—Could see P-47's strafing targets, huge smoke plume from docks at Toulon—flak hit us hard as we turned away after bomb drop, 9 planes hit, 2 bad—Close calls for flak, a burst hit our right side just forward of my turret, shrapnel piece entered and was about the size of a golf ball and smoking, got down from my turret seat and smothered the smoke with the fire extinguisher, not bad—More hits on my Plexiglas no damage—Those pieces are really jagged, coming at you they could kill or rip you apart—Saving this one in my footlocker—P-47's, P-38's and Navy Hellcats provided our escort cover—The Hellcats are like P-47's to me, flying tanks lots of firepower, P-38's are a very unique and effective fighter plane, real fast with two engines

Aug 19: Early wake up for mission—Bridge targets in France—P-38's and P-47's below us attacking targets, no approach to us—4 unidentified aircraft seen at our 4 o'clock at about 10,000 feet moving away from our formation—No flak—Missed target but cut off approaches to rail road bridge on two sides of the target area cutting off north and east approach by enemy forces

Aug 21: Early mission, off to Italy RR Bridge at Borgo San Lorenzo—Saw Spitfires and P-47's on escort—3 of 4 direct hits destroyed target area—Saw another B-26 group far off in the distance bombing their target, flak looks heavy, WOW it was intense, saw one get hit and burst in flames—No damage to our group, no flak or fighters—Colonel Fletcher flew with us today in "21" with the flight commander

Seems like I have been on every mission since Jeff's funeral, Ken and I have a hard time talking about it, we ignore the subject and do other things to stay busy. Got into a ball game with Ken, Gene, Ed and others in our squadron with the 444th guys, tie score until the last inning when I hit a long home run with two on base… felt real good.

Headed back to my hut with Ken, we talked about the game and then the subject of Jeff's death surfaced, "Nick… don't say anything to anybody… I got a copy of the statement for the record from Captain Smith and the exec officer." We arrived at our hut and Ken showed me the copy. "I don't want to know where or how you got this," I said in a frustrated tone

The last part of the August 15th record reads,

> *The cause of the accident cannot be accurately attributed. The aircraft may have been deflected causing him to stray from the formation. On the other hand, Lt. TRUNK was reported to have been quite sick this morning, vomiting and experiencing stomach cramps. His determination and courage may have caused him to proceed on this combat mission when his physical condition should have forbid it*
>
> *He made no attempt to contact us by radio so further attempts to ascertain the exact cause would be only conjecture. In our opinion the actual cause of the accident cannot be ascertained*
>
> Signed Captain Smith
>
> Signed Captain Berge

"OK... now what?" I asked as I finished reading, "What can you do?"

"Look, here... Trunk was sick and should not have been flying," Ken said sounding angry and frustrated wanting to blame someone for this tragedy.

"Stop, just stop... I don't like this either... but, they're all dead... dead," I said throwing the paper on the ground, "We can't change this and Trunk probably thought he was strong enough to get on with the mission... wrong as it was... he went on with the mission."

"That takeoff was dangerous... all of us knew that... we were fortunate enough to only have one plane crew killed."

"Look... we've been here a short time compared to the others... there's more to come and more death to friends we don't know about yet."

"Let's get over this... I'm sad and sick enough already... OK?" I said shouting to Ken and left to go outside and just be alone.

Ken sat down on his bunk... after an hour or so he tracked me down as I was heading over to the Red Cross hut for some bread and coffee, "Nick... I can't stop thinking about Jeff... I guess I need to blame someone... it doesn't bring him back, or the others we've seen get shot out of the sky."

"I'm sorry… I'm really sorry."

Looking at Ken's relieved face, I knew his apology was sincere, "Ok… let's get on with the day and get a game going."

"Let's go."

I know I had to get my mind off Jeff's death… no one could change what happened, got to learn to deal with it. There will be more death of close friends to deal with, but Jeff's is just too hard to take.

The 444st won again against one of the 319th Bomb Group's squadrons, beer and some sandwiches from the chow hall after the game… I don't know who arranged… nice afternoon.

Checking the operations board for missions, I'm on with most of my original crew. Gene and Ken are on today… late day mission takeoff. Lieutenant Cahan came up to me at the operations office, "Hey… heard you got your third stripe?"

"News to me sir… really?" Surprised as I found out that I got my third stripe, then the squadron personnel clerk handed me the order. He must have seen me at the operations board. No ceremony, just a needle and thread to add stripes to all my uniforms… Sergeant Bentas… has a nice sound to it

"Congratulations… Sergeant, well deserved," Cahan shook my hand and headed off to his hut and me to mine

"Ken… want to get some target practice?" I said not having a lot to do but wanting to let off some steam, and celebrate.

"Hey… you're sewing sergeant stripes… me too," I noticed Ken sewing stripes on his shirts.

Ed was on his bunk sewing on his stripes, "Hey… I got orders too."

"Yea, how about that… Sergeant."

"Let's go… want to get an M-1 or just .45's?" Ken asked, rifles were more fun especially for distance shooting.

"I'll pass on the practice… need to write home to my wife, you guys go out and have some fun," Ed said as he continued to sew on his new rank.

"Let's get M-1's."

We signed out our rifles and wandered around the squadron area over by some wrecked German planes left behind and shot lizards sunning on cactus or scurrying through grassy areas. Saw and shot at some rats as well. Nice fun for the afternoon… no misses. Nice warm day… sunset with lots of clouds and nature's colors. I slept well.

Easy wake up, I sewed some stripes on a few of my shirts after breakfast chow. Talked with Gene about home and Mary. He told me about his home in Ohio and his fiancée and plans for a big wedding when he gets home. We talked about getting together after the war and meet each other's family. He lives about three hours from Detroit in Bowling Green, Ohio.

All crews are gathering for the mission brief for today, August 24th Montpellier Rail Road Bridge in France. Takeoff at 1500 hours, it's going to be a late return, 29 B-26's, one spare. It is a long ride over the water, lots of rumors of moving closer to the coast of France and Italy maybe the airfield at Alto, Corsica or an inland French airfield somewhere. We are stretching our fuel limits with the targets now, so a move is probably coming soon. Sounded routine with no flak or fighters expected, but it turned out to be one for the books.

Keeping an eye out from my gun turret I can't see directly below our plane but I can see far ahead or behind quite a distance with a 360-degree view. I can see the bomb explosions in the distance after we turn away from the target area to head home; on occasion I would look down through the waist window gun positions to see the bomb hits. As the formation turned away from the target the plane to our right wing, tail number "16" looked like it was having engine trouble and turning off to its right at a steep dive.

"Engineer to pilot," I said over the intercom, "Sir… "16" is dropping out and losing altitude fast."

"I don't see any smoke, but the prop on the right engine looks like it is stopping and restarting."

"Roger… we noticed," Cahan responded and little did I or the rest of us know he was talking with Lieutenant Jenkins in "16" and indicated he was dropping out.

Cahan got on the radio to sector control, "Colgate", and asked permission to follow and escort, the plane on our left wing also asked permission to escort.

"Colgate... this is "06"... our right wing number "16" is having severe engine problems and losing altitude... permission to follow and escort... we are over water, he can't make it to a land base... over?"

Colgate got back quickly, "Granted... sound off position for air sea rescue... over."

"Roger... position 43 degrees, 10 minutes north and 4 degrees, 40 minutes east... turning east... over."

"Got it... watch your fuel... who is your left wing?"

"Our left wing plane is tail number "09"... "16" is heading down to a real low altitude... he may have to bail out." Cahan concentrated on maneuvering and taking lead on the escort to cover the crippled plane. "Sir... "16" doesn't look like they're going to recover," Ed reported his observation from the open waist windows as we turned to follow. "Sir... they're jumping out... one... two... three, four... five, just five chutes so far," then Ed sees a sixth crew trying to jump out, "Pull your cord... NO... NO... he didn't open his chute," he shouted out.

After the sixth crew left the plane it hit the water and broke up violently throwing large and small pieces of the plane over a wide area. The five chutes of the survivor crew landed in the water, it looks like they didn't have enough time to throw out their life raft.

"Sir... didn't see a life raft drop out at all," Ed reports, still shocked watching the sixth crewman not able to pull the ripcord for his chute.

"Ed... Nick... get our raft package out... get ready to drop," Cahan gave the order.

After contacting the other plane, "The other escort is going to get theirs out as well... we're circling around the five survivors... get ready."

"Colgate... we are dropping rafts for five crew in the water... out." After a few minutes Ed and I get the raft package ready to throw out.

"Sir... ready to drop," I said kneeling with Ed waiting for the signal to let go.

Cahan leveled our plane and headed toward the five survivors floating in the water. He lined up as if we were going to strafe the crew, slowing down a bit, "OK guys... count of three and drop... ready."

"Steady... steady... coming up."

"One… Two… Three DROP," Cahan shouted as we dropped at his command and watched the rafts fall into the water close to the crew. After our first turn and pass over the crew we could see them climbing into the rafts. Lieutenant Cahan directed us to drop some dye canisters and smoke bombs to mark the area. We circled for about thirty minutes to make sure they got in the rafts and air sea rescue was contacted. I think the pilot and co-pilot didn't make it out alive.

Pilot to crew, "We're going to head back… just heard from Colgate that air sea rescue is on their way… looks like they are all in the rafts."

Cahan led one last pass over the crew and rocked our wings to confirm to say goodbye for now. I saw them waving to acknowledge.

Bad things can happen fast and you can never know when it will happen. I thought back to our training at the ditch facility at Lake Charles… nothing like today. The five-crew members should survive, sad for the pilots and their families. Be ready all the time for the unexpected is the lesson for today. No enemy fighters around, real lucky, this could have been a really bad day for us and them. We landed at 2035 hours; getting dark I hope the crew had been rescued by now. We found out late in the evening that air sea rescue couldn't find them, never heard from them again. Don't know what happened, they were a mere twenty five miles from the beach on Corsica, all they needed was a few more miles

Aug 24: Good mission drop on target in France, Montpellier RR bridge—No flak or enemy fighters—After bomb run watched our right wingman plane go out of formation, severe engine trouble, 5 bailed out pilots killed, plane broke up on impact, circled and dropped rafts for them until air sea rescue notified, scary—Air sea rescue never picked up the 5 crew, where did they go??

Aug 27: Early wake up and mission today over France, take off 0850 hours, landed 1245 hours—Gun positions at Ile Ratenneau France—Excellent bomb pattern on target—Large explosion from one of the bomb hits with red and green flashes WOW, looked like fireworks with different colors—P-47's escorting and attacking ground targets—Target guns seen firing at our naval ships, stopped when they spotted us (I suppose), bursts gave away their positions— Flak was light and inaccurate—No clouds, clear with some haze— No enemy fighters seen, only P-47's in the target area strafing—Last mission over France, Allies moving inland fast, out of our range with full tanks of gas

Aug 31: Early and long mission over Italy, takeoff 0810 hours and landed 1640 hours at Decimo—3 Spitfires escorting B-26's from another group in the distance to their target area—10-12 P-47's seen southeast of our position by the Po River Valley area—Target area RR bridge at Legnago, we destroyed the north end of the bridge completely!—Flak was heavy, you could see the gun flashes on the ground firing at us—Flak damage to the plane, no penetration that I could see or the others—My Plexiglas seems to get hit a lot from small pieces of shrapnel—Tired and needed to stretch after landing—We had to land at Ghisonaccia Corsica for gas, one B-26 had engine trouble and stayed at Corsica base, returned crewmembers in our plane and one other plane that landed to refuel at Corsica back to Decimo

We were stretching our fuel range limits for enemy targets in France and targets in Italy. Lots of talk about moving closer to each front… the logical move for now is Corsica, Land of Napoleon.

Crews Gather after Mission at the Red Cross Hut for Coffee, Bread or Donuts

CHAPTER 4

ALLIES MOVING ON

Shakespeare's Henry V, 1598:
"From this day to the ending of the world,
But we in it shall be remembered—
We few, we happy few, we band of brothers;
For he to-day that sheds his blood with me
Shall be my brother; be he ne'er so vile,
This day shall gentle his condition;"

Missions are getting longer due to targets being further out from our base in Sardinia; Allies are making progress throughout Italy and France. So far I have fourteen missions to my credit through August. September weather on Sardinia is pleasant with daytime temperatures at the low 70's; nighttime cools off a little to around 60. The humidity can be a problem but the breezes off the water make it bearable. One peculiar thing about the water temperature is that it gets warmer into September and October, so our visits for the 320th Officer's Beach Club make for a great day on the beach for swimming. I was told that the water was actually colder in June and July. I still get picked for some KP duties and latrine cleaning on occasion.

Since Jeff's death on the 15th of August there have been more killed, some I got to know only briefly and some I wish I could have known better. I adopted the philosophy that I can't worry about what will happen each day. I will do my best keeping my focus on the mission and let the chips fall where they may. Breaking the boredom at times was hard, especially if no one wanted to play ball or head off base to the coast or hunt wild boar. Periods of days off not flying were also filled with lectures on medical issues, enemy aircraft identification, gunnery, refresher map and navigation training, and war news. The "Yank" magazine and "Stars and Stripes" newspaper have news on the war effort but the generals don't like the presentation of the news. General Patton especially didn't like these papers because of the jokes directed towards him and other brass. We had Armed Forces Radio, but no one in my hut area has a radio so the newspapers, letters from home and squadron or group war briefings were the source of information and war news. I really enjoyed the cartoons in the newspapers, Sad Sack, Bill Mauldin, Willie and Joe; on occasion those of us missing our female companions (wives and girlfriends) back home got a hold of the British newspaper "The Daily Monitor". It had the "Original G.I. Jane" cartoon that reminded of us what we are fighting for… cold shower time; Yank and Stars and Stripes had some good pinups on occasion. Zane Grey novels are plentiful for our reading entertainment.

Met a friendly guy the other day that arrived here a week or so after me by troop ship, Jerry Raschke, nice guy, decent and eager. He started flying missions later in July. A recent mission of his, that I was not on, was one he would never forget and we all heard of his heroism upon his return. It was supposed to be a milk run, we all think that it will be, and it turned out to be a story he could tell his grandchildren.

The mission started out fine then on the IP and the very beginning of the bomb run they experienced some light flak that hit their plane just as the bomb bay doors were opening. Jerry explained, "Just as the bombardier was shouting out… "Bombs away"… he said… Oh, Oh." Something you don't want to hear, the bombardier saw a hang up on his board that indicated bombs were still on board. One or more were still on board and probably armed. Jerry continued to describe what happened, "The pilot was pretty busy keeping us on track, he asked me to come forward to see what was the problem."

To his surprise as he entered the bomb bay he could see three 250 pound bombs with the arming wires out of the fuses on one and two with partially removed wires. All of them up against the bomb bay doors. He tried to get the wires in the two partial removed wires, keeping in mind the doors were still open and they were at about 10,000 feet. He walked out on the catwalk in the bomb bay, no parachute, and started to get the wires in the fuses. The bombs were wedged crossways in the racks, he could try and get the wires in but it might be better to get them out of the bomb bay and fall out. He straddled the bombs and worked at getting them loose and out of the bomb bay; with the doors opened for so long it adds a lot of drag on the plane and then he heard one of the engines sputter. They were using up a lot of fuel and now an engine was acting up. All the bombs were finally let loose and the doors closed, because of low fuel and engine trouble they were escorted to a fighter base just outside Rome. They landed on a short airstrip and overshot the runway damaging all three landing gear. They got off the plane and noticed a small fire in the crippled engine. They didn't try to put out the fire, they noticed it was spreading fast and evacuated the area as fast as they could; it exploded just as all the crew reached a safe distance. This event gave them the opportunity to see a little bit of Rome, the Vatican and Coliseum; they finally got a ride back to Sardinia on a C-45 transport two days later. Rumor has it that the pilot put him in for the Distinguished Flying Cross (DFC)… some milk run.

> *Sep 6: Special ceremony, got to get out our Class A's— We assembled on the runways, the 320th, 319th and 17th were in formation, big assembly, Parade and a Brass Band, well done, we didn't forget how to march!!—42nd Air Wing commander General Webster attending, he passed on the command to the second in command Col. Doyle (General rank coming soon you can bet on it)—All groups awarded the French Croix de Guerre for supporting the French Army in May fighting at the Gustav Line breakout—Col. Fletcher got an award, DFC, and there were others with Silver Stars and Air Medals—Weather not too bad, no rain and got warm in our uniforms—Dismissed and repacked my Class A's*

Continued to find things to do; Gene, Ken, Ed and a few others went with me to the boar hunting area with the goal of getting a boar.

No luck again… but we did get more chestnuts for a squadron party. It was a nice day with a few clouds and nice breeze, not too hot as the calendar was getting closer to mid-month.

After a break of about ten days I'm on mission with a crew I have not flown with before. Our target is in Italy, a railroad bridge at a place called Castel San Pedro. Gene and Ken are on the mission; Ed is off today.

> *Sep 10: Mid-day mission to Italy, RR bridge Castel San Pedro, almost five hours—No flak—2 Unidentified aircraft southeast of us at about 9,000 feet flying south, couldn't ID the outline of the planes, Enemy Fighters???—We never fly a straight route to target, sort of zigzag—Flew over Apennines Mountains, Adriatic coast, Po Valley—Haze but unlimited view, clouds look like a painting with blues, grays, white fluffy texture, beautiful site—Good bomb hits on target—One B-26 dropped bombs through its doors, switch malfunction—One B-26 landed on Corsica low fuel*

Just one day off then another mission to Italy with a different crew assignment than the mission on the 10th. Getting to know more guys I haven't previously met.

> *Sep 12: Early mission takeoff at 0800 hours, returned 1245 hours—We are really stretching our limits on fuel and bomb load, more planes land at Corsica because of low fuel—Saw P-47's in the target area strafing targets during our bomb run—One B-26 landed at Grosseto, Italy with engine problems—We missed our target, cloud cover (8/10 to 10/10) prevented a good view for the bombardier—Flak at the IP, the bomb run and on breakaway, Heavy—Our plane and three others hit, wings and fuselage damage from bursts below our plane—Flak shrapnel sliced a hydraulic line, fluid seeped in the heating ducts… what an ugly smelling misty odor, pilot had to shut off the heater it got so bad*

A day off to refresh, then another mission set for tomorrow with some familiar faces, Cahan as pilot, Hill, Ed and me.

Sep 14: Early takeoff at 0830 hours, target defensive position at Mt. Oggioli—P-47's and Spitfires dive bombing and strafing gun positions in the target area—Flak hit us during bomb run and breakaway, 4 planes damaged, felt minor hits on our fuselage, no penetration—Great target hits, covered the entire target area

September 15th was a mission that all of us would never forget… the luckiest and hairiest so far. Our mission was to hit a German defensive area southwest of the town of Rimini, takeoff at 0835 hours with 51 B-26's from our bomb group. The target was a long way off; we would be flying across the width of Italy to the Adriatic Sea. We took off in clear weather over Sardinia, and then about one hour into the mission we could see multiple layers of cloud cover.

This was a significant effort; our squadron had fourteen planes in this large formation. It normally wouldn't matter where our plane was in the formation, but today it would calm nerves at least temporarily. Today we were on the top squadron in the formation. The flight was going well as we reached the west coast of Italy; there were five squadrons, nine planes each that were stepped down in trail.

Looking ahead from my turret, we were passing through 7,000 feet and I could see ahead of us a base cloud, a solid base cloud. It wasn't dark, maybe it wasn't too thick, and it was impossible to know how deep the cloud was until we got into it. Captain Smith our squadron commander was the mission commander, he would have to make a decision on what to do. I heard over the intercom from the pilot, Lieutenant Rodgers, that Captain Smith's decision was to fly through it in formation

"OK boys… we're going to tuck it in and go through this cloud… keep your eyes open," Rodgers said and he took hold of the controls along with our co-pilot Lieutenant Simmons.

"Bentas… stay in the turret and keep your eyes peeled for other ships… we're on the high squadron but there might be some strays… OK?"

"Roger sir… hanging on," I said and wondered if we would get through this in one piece.

"Roger sir… I can see pretty good… the plane on our right wing tail is in the normal distance," Ed responded.

"Thanks… stay sharp," Rodgers said with a nervous tone in his voice

As we entered the cloud we couldn't see anything, not even our wing plane; none of us have ever been in this situation before.

Rodgers was concentrating on the lead plane just before we entered the cloud cover, he held the plane as close in formation as he could knowing that if he drifted out he would disappear, still close but invisible. This is a bad combination of close and not visible

"Look at the airspeed," Simmons shouted as Rodgers was holding on to the wheel and concentrating on looking forward and keeping steady.

I could feel the plane a little sluggish then over the intercom I heard, "This yoke feels mushy… can't risk stalling… push the throttle to the envelope… balls to the wall," Rodgers said to Simmons as we accelerated bringing the airspeed up avoiding a potential stall.

We started to see a lighter sky inside the plane as we approached 9,000 feet and then suddenly we popped out on top of the overcast. Rodgers throttled back, "Take it back to 2100 RPM," he said to Simmons and sounded surprised that we didn't see anyone else pop out of the overcast. Then looking over a 360-degree view in my turret I could see planes popping out and skimming the surface of the overcast. A bright sun with blue sky overlooking a fluffy white cloud blanket was the perfect picture of B-26's popping out all over.

Then Rodgers shouted out over the intercom a little giddy, "Wow… forty-five B-26's flying through this overcast and no two came out together… I think a prayer of thanks is due."

We all felt the same; there were approximately three hundred crew carrying one hundred and eighty, one thousand pound bombs on board. Lots of radio chatter after all of the planes came out of the overcast; we got back into our typical squadron formations and continued on to the target.

B-26's Emerging Out of the Clouds

Approaching the IP, nerves were still frayed and that was evident when the lead bombardier forgot to open his bomb bay doors on the bomb run

Someone on the plane behind him shouted over the radio, "Hey, Plouck (lead bombardier in the lead plane), are we on the bomb run?"

He replied, "Roger."

"Then you better get your bomb bay doors open."

The doors swung open on the lead plane and the bombs dropped out immediately.

Flying back to Sardinia after the bomb run was loose and a little sloppy, the pilots were emotionally and physically spent, not to mention the crews' nerves. This could have been a significant air disaster.

All planes landed safely and we proceeded to debrief and get back to our squadron huts to settle in and relax. Before we could head back we were told to report to the officers club. Now what was going on? Captain Fay, our executive officer for the 441st was there and was handing out absentee ballots for the upcoming presidential election. Didn't realize there were so many pilots that were only twenty years old and couldn't vote, I was twenty-two so I was on the list and got my ballot. Jokingly, there was reference to Franklin D. Roosevelt as King Franklin the First running for his fourth term.

The battle lines in France had moved well beyond our range, we were now involved in "Operation Sesame", an operation supporting Allied forces in northern Italy. Our missions, at least for now, would be in support of the U.S. Fifth Army performing missions in front line support. The British Army called their involvement "Crumpet Two". U.S. and British forces were trying to maneuver up the boot of Italy into Bologna, but highly skilled German paratroopers were blocking their efforts

> *Sep 16: Takeoff at 0914, landed at 1340—Target defensive area NW of Rimini—Dropped "frags" anti-personnel bombs, small and dangerous bomblets—2 planes landed in Italy to refuel, stretching our fuel range still—No fighters—Flak hit us on the bomb run to breakaway—Milk Run!—Hit target with good concentration of bombs*

> *Sep 18: Takeoff at 0821, landed at 1253—New crew members except Ed Geronimos—Target barracks are Casalecchio Di Preno (spelling??) Italy—P-47's seen near the target area, no enemy fighters—Flak during bomb run and breakaway, scattered not too accurate, sporadic explosions, no damage—Flying in tail number 23", sharp silver paint scheme looks like new, nice plane*

We were really stretching our range and on every mission there were planes that would need to land short of Sardinia to refuel. The west coast of Italy at any fighter base or on Corsica became regular stopping places for gas. Fighter base airstrips are shorter than bomber base strips; pilots have to be very careful in order to land safely within the length restriction. This was especially dangerous if the plane was damaged because a go-around is not an option.

> *Sep 19: Got the word to pack our stuff and go to the officer club area, bring our cots, I guess we're sleeping outside??—Movement*

> *orders for Corsica!!—All personnel getting ready to move our group equipment to Navy LST transport ships, some stuff on B-26's—Getting closer to the action, no more long flights—Heard a rumor of Italy for next movement a few weeks ago, GUESS NOT it's Corsica!—Ken got tagged for detail duty supporting the move*

A flurry of activity all around the squadron and group buildings, I'm packing all of my personal items in my duffle bags. Missions aren't stopping so when we go on one we need to have our stuff tagged for shipping. My next mission is on 23 September and I'll probably land at Corsica on return… hope I don't lose anything.

"Ken… can you keep an eye on my stuff?" I said to Ken, he was not scheduled for a mission

"Hey Ken… can you watch my stuff too?" Gene asked, "I'm on for the same mission."

"OK guys… you owe me big time… just kidding."

"Hey me too… Ken," Ed said to make sure we were all covered.

"I'm not on for a few days… at least until we get to Corsica," Ken said as he was told to be on detail duty for the move a few days ago.

Gene woke me up on the 23rd; we got cleaned up and ate an early chow. Headed over to the group operations office for the mission brief, the target for today is the Borgo Forte Rail Road Bridge our scheduled takeoff is 0930. Flying with Lieutenant Cahan and a co-pilot O'Mahony, Ed, a bombardier Lieutenant Anderson and me on tail number "06".

> *Sep 23: Mission today over Italy attacking the RR Bridge at Borgo Forte—Took off at 0938 hours, landed 1247—Good flight, weather good, scattered clouds—Flak hit us as we broke away from the target after the drop—Good pattern of hits—One B-26 hit with flak, not bad—Did not return to Decimo Sardinia, landed at Alto Corsica NEW HOME!!—Ken's keeping an eye on my stuff, Ed and Gene's during the move*

As we returned from the mission, we could see the familiar site of Alto Corsica; it was a frequent stop for our planes if you were low on gas.

It was shorter than Decimo, which had six strips. Alto was better suited for fighter planes. It was narrow; pilots know it is a challenge to land a B-26. A single north/south strip less than 5,000 feet with steel mats as a base. The steel mats were Corps of Engineers planking for airstrips known as pierced steel planking or "PSP". PSP was one of the most versatile tools the U.S. military had for constructing quick airstrips or roads. Each piece of PSP was 10 feet by 15 inches with interlocking tabs and round holes to let the dirt fill in within the planking. One bad thing about PSP is when the tabs would bend upwards they could puncture tires and if you're landing fast it could cause a horrific landing, blowing the tires out crashing. Another bad thing about PSP is that when it was raining the water and mud that seeped up through its holes would create a slippery mess. One pilot described it as slippery as owl shit.

Alto field was located eighteen miles south of Bastia. Bastia is located on a rock-cliffed coast in the northeast part of Corsica. It is a beautiful island with picturesque views of mountains and the blue waters of the Mediterranean. We understood that the native population was wild, like Napoleon… that turned out to not be the case. The strip was a "stone's" throw from the Mediterranean on the east, with 8,000- foot mountains on our west that ran north to south on the island. Those mountains provided shade on our side way before the sun would set in the west

The winds generated from the west over the mountains were a problem for landings and takeoffs; the prevailing winds from the west would hit the mountains and then roll down the eastern side over our airstrip. Pilots had to deal with the turbulence this created; unexpected jostling of the plane would give a hell of a ride. Because of the short runway and difficult winds for landing and takeoff the group commander asked our higher headquarters to reduce our bomb loads to 3,000 pounds versus 4,000. Instead they countered and directed the group to reduce other weight factors, less radio equipment, less ammunition, and one less crew. Also they wanted us to remove the waist guns, two of them, with the exception of lead or back up planes.

After our post mission briefing with the interrogators we gather at a makeshift shack for our squadron. Different setup for all of us, the tent shortage gave us less than comfortable accommodations with more personnel in each tent. That is until we put up more tents… we'll get there. I was able to catch Gene when he finished briefing in the squadron area. Ed showed up as well.

"What do you think?" Gene asked as he looked around at the possibilities for getting comfortable.

"I just want to know where I'm going to bunk down for the night… Ken's on the detail for getting our stuff here… wonder where they are with moving?" I said, thinking we should set out on our own to get a tent up and set up a comfortable place to settle.

"Gene… let's get with the engineers for some tent equipment and get started," I said as Gene was finishing his coffee.

Ed chimed in, "We need to get proactive and get with the engineers for what we need to get started."

"Yea… let's go… I need to get settled."

We got word that our equipment and the rest of our personal items should be here tomorrow; I took some shaving gear and change of clothes with me in a flight bag on the mission.

Gene and a few others that would bunk with us got a hold of a tent and plenty of stakes. We even found some unused PSP for the floor… better than wood that is scarce right now.

While we were preparing the ground to put up our tent we noticed a couple of Frenchmen approaching. They were talking up a storm and gesturing something at us and laughing.

"What the hell are they laughing at?" I said.

"Don't know… maybe we're doing something wrong… but what?" Ed said

"Anybody know French?" he asked.

"I don't… maybe they speak English… what do you think?" Gene asked and put down his tent mallet to go over to them and ask them… what's up.

Gene was carrying on, in a friendly tone, and they finally were able to say to him in broken English to find out what the hell was so funny.

He turned around and headed back to us shaking his head and with a smile on his face started to explain what the hell was going on, "Well guys… here's the scoop," Gene points towards the mountains and said, "When the rain starts… which could be soon… it tends to run down from the mountains this way down to a flat area… where our tent is right now."

"When it comes down it is fast and it creates a flood plain… right here."

"OK… now what?" Ed asked

"Well… instead of digging a narrow shallow drainage ditch, we need to make it about twelve inches deep and eighteen inches wide." Gene said with wide eyes and telling us what the Frenchmen indicated. "So… if we're going to do that, let's build up the floor before we put down the PSP… what do you think?" I said. All of us nodded 'yes' and started digging.

"Seems a little much… don't you think?" A passing officer smirked. "Yes sir… but when it rains, we'll be dry… a Corsican Ark," Ed returned the comment. The officer just shook his head and went on his business

The ditch, tent floor and finally the tent canvass came together and we made it as comfortable as possible. It was a tent with a higher stance than others in the area; a solid level floor with the dirt from the ditches and the PSP on top was perfect stabilization for the tent and all of our bunks and personal stuff.

On occasion we got tagged for KP duty during our off duty time. Jerry Raschke and I were one day. Reporting to the mess sergeant in the early morning we were supposed to unload boxes of steaks from a supply truck and stock the kitchen and supply areas. The bad food we've been experiencing, we thought, were going to get considerably better. "Nick… steaks for tonight… can't wait, finally a good meal," Jerry said with a big grin.

"You bet… seems like it's been forever since we had steak," I said also with a grin and expecting a great dinner. We finished our KP duties and got cleaned up as best we could and went over to the chow tent. Much to our surprise we got some slop that sort of looked like stew.

I looked at Jerry and then told Gene and Ed about what we saw this morning; we were definitely expecting a steak and potatoes meal for dinner

"What the hell… this looks like leftover… I don't know," Jerry exclaimed in a disappointed tone.

"I don't know either," I said as I watched the chow cook slop this whatever it was on my tray.

After choking down dinner Gene, Jerry, Ed and I set off for our tents, we took a path that took us past a shack where the mess sergeant was sitting with a few other sergeants. We stared at them and noticed they had what looked like a nicely grilled steak on their trays. We continued to move past the area and then stopped.

"What the hell was that… did you see that?" Jerry said.

Gene looked at Jerry, Ed and me and said, "That's a lot of nerve… damn that really pisses me off."

"You know what we should do… let's tunnel into the mess supply tent and get us some steaks and potatoes… are you guys up for it?" Jerry had a devious look in his eyes and he inspired us to agree.

"Let's do it… let's wait till dark," Gene said as we left the area to wait with shovels and empty duffle bags in hand waiting for the cover of darkness

About an hour later we proceeded on our mission to confiscate… that is acquire… proper nutrition. We successfully tunneled into the mess supply, got our steak and potatoes and went back to our nice high floor of our tent and secured our find

The mess sergeant found out later in the evening that there were missing food supplies, the sergeants were furious. The MP's were notified and they searched the entire area and never located the acquired food. We ate really well for a few days as we also got a hold of pans and built a fire pit by our tent for cooking.

Back on missions, it's been six days since we flew; Ken and the others who were detailed to move the squadron and group finally showed up. We were able to fit Ken in our high-centered tent. Good for all of us; the rain came on really hard and we were the only tent above water… we were envied. The 30th of September was tomorrow and the mission looked like a milk run… can't always bet on that. The target was fuel dumps west of Cremona, Italy with a late morning take off.

> *Sep 30: Took off at 1119, landed at 1407—Beautiful view of the Apennines Mountains and Po River Valley with scattered cumulus clouds at about 4,000 and 6,000 feet—No flak or fighters—Milk Run!!—Good hits on target—Ken and others finally made it a few days ago, we fit him into our tent, he was impressed with our high floor especially when the rain started and flooding from the mountain runoff came—Food missing from mess supply… um!—Wonder what happened??—Dinners will be real good treat for the next three or four days!*

Generally speaking Corsica was a beautiful place and the Special Services Squadron set up more facilities and provided sports equipment for baseball, volleyball and football. The island has scenic woods and rivers throughout with cool water that was just right for skinny-dipping. Jeff would have given us more on the island's history… Napoleon was born here in 1769 in a small village named Ajaccio. It was located over the mountains from us on the west side of the island; he was exiled to the island of Elba just offshore to the east.

Missions scheduled for tomorrow include three different flights and target areas all in Italy, Pastrengo Dump Area, Peschiera RR Bridge, and Messanino RR Bridge. Gene and I are on the first flight, Ken is on the second and Ed on the third

> *Oct 1: Took off at 1109, landed at 1332—Great weather, Ceiling And Visibility Unlimited (CAVU)!—No flak experienced on our flight, noticed other flight at nearby target fired on with some big guns, not accurate, lots of big bursts, must be 105's versus 88's—Saw P-47's west of Piacenza, no escorts for us—The view was spectacular with the blue sky, mountains and outlines of the Med shore line*

When the rain came, we had a lot of water leaks from holes in the tent ceiling that we would patch up as we found them. All of us wondered why there were so many holes with patches; what we found was out was that the previous occupants on Sardinia started a hobby inside this tent and others

"Gene… hey… what the hell is it with all of these holes and patches," I said pondering why such a thick canvas would get so many. Gene was a long time resident of Sardinia and would know the history of the holes. "Well… let me tell you a story," Gene was grinning as he continued to explain, "Once upon a time in wartime Sardinia, some energetic air crew were sharpening their skills."

Wondering where this was going he says, "Those energetic souls decided to get some expert practice without leaving their bunks… so… they took aim at irritating flies… and they were big… really big," he was building for a climax in the explanation.

"They took their .45's and commenced to eliminate those pesky flies," Gene finished and we all looked at each other and shook our heads. Nothing more was said… we all would have done that to stay busy… as long as we didn't hit anyone. Did they get any flies?

> *Oct 3: Mid-day takeoff at 1245, landed 1630—P-47's escorting, A-20 spotted and heading east as we flew over Moneglia, lone mission I guess—Bad flak, very intense with over 100 bursts as we started the IP for the bomb run, scary lots of bangs on the skin of the plane, Pilot and co-pilot windows cracked bad—Flak only lasted 30 seconds seemed like more time than 30 seconds—Cahan is a great pilot, landed looking through the cracks—CAVU for weather, beautiful views of the mountains and Med on return—Cleaned up in the mountain stream, really cold but refreshing—Lower ranks getting latrine duty, Don't Forget Matches!!*

From the 3rd of October to my next mission on 12 October we were scheduled for practice missions in the southwest area of Corsica. Routine practice runs reminded me of stateside missions over Louisiana and Florida. Flight engineers, like me, were tasked to ride along with the pilot, co-pilot, and bombardiers to monitor all the planes systems. We made run after run at 12,000 feet on the tiny Isle de Cavallo using a Norden bombsight dropping little blue bomblets on a pretend target. Each run gave the pilot and bombardier practice to synchronize the airspeed and altitude, the Pilot's Directional Indicator, and the bombardiers' lateral corrections for the bomb run. The goal was to spend the minimum time straight and level on the bomb run and get the bombs on the target. When we fly longer on the bomb run, German flak gunners have a much better chance of knocking us out of the sky. Once in a while we would wander off the base to see the island; it was scenic with plenty of wooded areas, green covered mountains and the view of blue water from the Mediterranean. It was nice off base but on base we lacked some basic facilities such as showers; more makeshift buildings were being built providing better cover for chow and offices. We washed ourselves and our clothes in a stream that came down from the mountain… it was clear, fresh and cold. Washed up with brown bar soap, really strong smell, standing knee deep in the stream in khaki boxers… by the time I finished washing my legs and feet were blue and my fingers looked like white raisins.

Mail caught up with us, received several letters from Mary and home. Received a letter from Rich in England with the 322nd Bomb Group; he got my letter about Jeff and took it hard. Ken and I think about him often and miss him more and more… get that empty sick feeling in my stomach every time I think of him.

My daily afternoon routine was to check the operations posting for missions… I'm on for the October 12th mission that is going to Italy, a late day mission. The weather is changing to fall temperatures with more rain and getting much colder at altitude, especially at 12,000 feet. Cahan, Ed, and I are on again… a few of us originals back together… we were assigned to tail number "14", great plane.

Oct 12: Late afternoon mission takeoff at 1418, landed at 1737— Target German troop concentration area SW of

Bologna—Saw other bomb group on east end of Bologna and they received intense flak—We got flak after the bomb run as our bomb bay doors closed, jostled around with the close burst concussions—Lots of clouds at various levels with turbulence, got bounced around good, hit the bulkhead with my head several times finally put my flak helmet on… Ouch, have a bump on my head—Wish we could pick our plane for missions, "14" is a great ship with good performance, no write ups, a real tough veteran, weathered and scarred but a sexy B-26—On again tomorrow Gene, Ken, Ed, and me

Oct 13: On mission again, Cahan, Ed and me—Took off at 1016, landed at 1340—Hit Padua RR bridge Italy—Good hits, lots of scattered clouds—No flak or fighters—Rumors and Intel saying German Me 109's in waiting, look out for fighters!!!—We better get our waist guns back in, so screw the weight, get rid of something else!!—Wrote letter to Mary—Red Cross hut had some hot chocolate, nice change

Oct 14 &15: Weather getting colder, finally got some washing basins for cleaning up—Some cold rain, glad for our ditches and high floor, got my sewing needle out to fix more patches in the tent roof—Wrote letters home to Mary, Pa & Ma—Talked a lot with Ken, Gene, Ed about home, sports—Ed was tracking down a radio for our tent, listen to good music from our favorite enemy "Axis Sally", she sure has a sexy voice seems to know everything about us

Having some time off from flying, Gene, Ken, Ed and I signed out a Jeep to head into the nearest village to get a taste of French hospitality in Bastia. These natives are a lot friendlier than the Sardinians; they seem more appreciative of our efforts to liberate them from the Nazi oppression. We put the canvas cover on the Jeep since it was still raining and headed out, nice to get out of the routine and get some sight seeing. Bastia was a short ride north of the base about 18 miles with shops and cafes. We found one that looked clean and sat down to enjoy the taste of some civilization. Wine country is just over the mountains. As we sat down for some wine and bread, we saw several U.S. Navy sailors wandering around; there was a PT Boat base here. We overheard some of them talking and they were looking for girls and fun. A sailor's reputation intact… be careful out there boys.

US Navy PT Boats Docked in Bastia, Corsica

Corsica was the first French territory to be liberated from Nazi and Italian occupation; it was eight months before the Normandy landing. The resistance, Free French, played a significant role in liberating the island, which was one of the most densely occupied areas in Europe. There is a sense of free spirit in the air and you can see it on their faces, warm smiles and service… plenty of wine and bread.

> *Oct 17: Went into Bastia, nice French town off the water to the north, very scenic with the green mountains and blue Med—Saw U.S. sailors wandering around, we didn't talk with them they were out for girls and drinking—Saw the Navy base where we noticed the PT boats docked, they are impressive boats—Returned in the late afternoon and listened to Axis Sally, read the Stars and Stripes and wrote home—Heard the officers*

having a wild party, they got a lamb from town, butchered it and roasted it in an open fire pit, lots of noise and bad singing of popular songs—Maybe we should sneak over and get a bite

It may not seem like much but having a Red Cross presence with us really was a morale booster. After each mission there would be hot fresh coffee with donuts, sometimes it was bread. I would go over and have a taste for something to do if I was not on a mission, usually when those on mission that day would return. I always wanted to talk about how it went and just chat. It is a time when you feel a part of the crowd and can get to know other crew. There is no thought about if the guy you talked to yesterday might be dead tomorrow.

We need to change our uniforms to winter wear, our khaki's are too light for the cold that is coming so we got some issue for our winter wools. Nice to have some new clothes to wear, my khakis were getting kind of thin and worn. New clothes for the colder weather came just in time, it has been windy the last few days and when you mix in the rain, it gets miserable.

Another mission scheduled for tomorrow, Rail Road Bridges at Mantua

Oct 19: Saw 8 Me-109 enemy fighters swoop towards us then off away from us, we had NO ESCORT!—They did not attack WHY?—Target was a causeway and bridge at Mantua—Noticed the 319th BG formation getting attacked by the 8 fighters in the distance 3 B-26's shot down they were off our tail in a smaller formation than ours—We tightened up for better firepower—Learned after we landed that 3 crew from the 319th were wounded real bad—I did not get a chance to shoot

After we landed and did our post briefing in interrogations, I went over to the Red Cross hut for coffee and donuts. I met Gene there, we talked about how lucky we were today especially with our waist guns removed for lighter weight.

"It's a damn good thing that the Luftwaffe and the German backed Italian Fascists Republican Air Force didn't know we had missing guns and less firepower," Gene said shaking his head.

"I know… it could have been real bad… I could see them making some pretty aggressive runs on the 319th "

"We had better be putting those guns back in the waist mounts," I said as I sipped the hot coffee.

"I was nervous about getting attacked… I spun my turret around watching and waiting."

Gene looking over to the other crew coming back from the flight line, "There's more from the third attack flight… wonder if they lost anyone."

"Know anyone from the last flight mission?" Gene asked me, "Yea… Ed Geronimos was on the third mission… hey, there he is."

"Ed… over there," I waved at Ed and he saw Gene and me and headed over.

"Wow… that was scary… no fighters, just saw them attacking what was left of the 319th bomb runs," Ed exclaimed with a shaky hand holding his coffee cup.

"We hit the bridge hard and looks like we blocked the rail road bridge by Brenner Pass… the pilot said that we blocked the only viable route for German forces to resupply in northern Italy."

"I know I was nervous… when I saw those 109's coming towards us, I only thought about how I needed to aim my turret gun," I said. I was remembering the experienced trainers at gunnery school in Texas and how they described a real fighter attack.

"We overheard chatter from the 319th on all the call outs… it was confusing."

We spent a lot of time talking about what we would need to do when an attack started, trying to remember gunnery school and the gunnery lessons we learned here when we arrived. There are going to be some gunnery briefings tomorrow that will get our focus for the next encounter… whenever that may be.

Got the word that there is going to be a parade tomorrow on the strip, the Twelfth Air Force commander Major General Cannon, is presenting the 320th with the Distinguished Unit Citation for outstanding performance of duty in enemy action at Fondi on May 12, 1944… I was still in the States… wish I could have been there. This parade had a lot of brass attending from the U.S., British, and French forces; there were also nurses in formation from the nearby hospital unit. Since I was assigned to the 320th I was able to wear the unit citation on my uniform, if I would transfer out then I could not wear it. The citation is a gold framed blue ribbon that was worn over the right pocket, it is presented in the name of the President of the United States.

The 320th successfully bombed the Pisani Bridge in the Po Valley, the Brenner Pass rail lines, and the Ossenigo railroad bridges… the 9th of October missions turned out to be a good day for the Allies. The Germans really got a beating and suffered some severe losses. Recon photos taken after the attacks indicated that the bombings caused a huge tie-up of German southbound traffic to supply its forces in Italy. The rain has been relentless, and it has prevented some missions from getting off the ground. The rainfall flowing down from the mountain developed into a river that ran through our tent area and most of our stuff got soaked… what a mess. We worked hard at getting gravel in places to help make paths through the small lakes and ponds that seemed to be everywhere. Most of the tents had to be moved to higher ground… our tent survived and is the envy of those who doubted our efforts

Planes that could take off through the clouds and rain looked real shaky from my view. I liked to watch the planes takeoff when I was not flying… always like to watch them fly and maneuver. I went over to the clinic and got my updated shots in the arm and ass… I was sore for a few days.

Finally a break in the rain and we started to put up missions again, I'm on for the 31st. We are heading to Bologna to support the Allied advance; target is the Railroad Bridge at Bozzolo. Cahan, Ed, and I on the same crew again this time on tail number "02".

Oct 31:Took off at 1238, landed 1432—We could not drop bombs due to 10/10 cloud cover—No flak and no fighters,

> *we started putting the waist guns back in the deal with fighter attack—Getting back to the tent and must help with moving stuff around, weather is not cooperating—Hot coffee and donuts from the Red Cross after missions is a real treat*

All of the facilities on Alto and our living area are getting better, when I wasn't flying I was getting our tent and helping others get their leaks fixed or personal stuff moved. We did find time for some relaxation in the enlisted man's club, which doubled as the mess hall. Finally got a working laundry system, our uniforms getting a little rough, what a godsend. There was movie viewing in an open-air theater affectionately named "Dan's Ri-Alto" which had a concrete floor with a few hundred seats and a circus tent overhead

Listening to the radio was a good pastime; we could listen to baseball games and music from Armed Forces Radio and occasionally from Axis Sally. Sally had some good information that didn't match the reality of our mission success... all propaganda with some good music. Radio Monaco at Monte Carlo had the best music unquestionably in the Mediterranean Theater of Operations.

The Red Cross opened a club in Bastia that served coffee, sandwiches, and yes... ice cream... this was a great getaway when we could leave the base. The Post Exchange store finally got their stocks to Alto Corsica from Sardinia... soap, towels, paper, envelopes, magazines, and newspapers were available again.

The bomb group command was given permission to grant leaves in the area to rest camps in Rome and Capri, some of the officers got to Cannes France on three-day passes at a resort on the French Rivera. Rank does have its privileges... this didn't last long, the weather was unpredictable and the command was worried it couldn't get their pilots back immediately after the three-day expiration. I did not request any leave, seemed not right. I could keep myself busy here with some of the activities and places available; I'll wait till I get home.

We continued to conduct our favorite off duty trips here on Corsica... boar hunting. Signed out a Jeep, some M-1's and headed towards the mountain areas to get a boar for roasting. Gene and Ed got one each on one of our trips… nice treat; we shared with the rest of the squadron.

If we were not on details for concrete or building projects, we played baseball and volleyball. Letter writing was a favorite pass time and especially re-reading letters from home. Mess hall food got a little tastier; I still yearned for my SOS. Many of us found some long lost friends from the 17th and 319th Bomb Group's that go back to gunnery school in Texas, airplane mechanics school, and basic training. We made plans to meet in Bastia at the Red Cross club whenever we got some time off. Just when we thought it was going to be a permanent station, rumors started to fly that we would move again and very soon.

CHAPTER 5

MOVING AGAIN

General George S. Patton, Jr.:
"Don't tell people how to do things, tell them what to do and let them surprise you with the results."

I slept in this morning, there is no mission scheduled today... its November already. The chill of the night is starting to take its toll; I sleep with socks and long johns to stay warm under a G.I. wool blanket. Took my mosquito net off my bunk yesterday. Got up and dressed and headed over to the chow hall with Gene, Ken, and Ed. On the way over we stopped by the squadron operations bulletin board to see what was going on for the day and any briefings or training scheduled. Our missions and our living conditions have been plagued with recent rainy weather. Rumors of the group moving to France are getting strong and we all think it will happen soon. Speculation is that France's airfields have some decent living accommodations and they are near nice villages and towns'... real brick and mortar buildings with porcelain thrones. Real toilets will be a nice change from the latrine shacks and daily cleansing rituals.

"Gentlemen... what are you up to?" Captain Smith walking by the group board stopped by to talk with us, "Got some news... Colonel Fletcher is being rotated back to the States and Lieutenant Colonel Woolridge is assuming command of the group tomorrow, November 2nd."

"He was in the 319th as the operations officer and a former commander of one of its squadrons... so he will be by tomorrow to give us a pep talk."

"Sir, do you know him well?" Gene asked.

"Yea… sort of… he's a straight shooter and a lead from the front type… so I feel good about it."

"Oh… also more news on the 42nd Bomb Wing… the 17th and our group will be moving to France, Dijon airfield… so you can stop listening to rumors," he said with a grin, lots of talk around the squadron about moving maybe to Italy or somewhere in France.

"Yes… France is good… any word on timing that you can tell us sir?" I asked

"Well… the higher ups are thinking somewhere around the end of this month, may be sooner… and there will be more planning for the move… so any volunteers for detail is appreciated," Captain Smith said with a grin and a wink, "Or we may select volunteers."

We looked at each other with grins and shrugged our shoulders, then Ed said, "We'll wait to be volunteered, sir," Captain Smith understood the humor of the moment and went on to different topics of home and what we may need in Corsica to make our living conditions a little better. He is a descent and direct person, you can definitely feel his sincere desire to lead and also be concerned about our personal welfare. After chatting with the Captain it was time to get some chow; maybe… just maybe the mess sergeant got a hold of some real eggs or maybe made some of my favorite breakfast… SOS. Finishing chow we ran into the squadron operations officer at the chow hall and he told us that Captain Smith would soon be Major Smith. He also told us that Ken, Ed and me are being put in for our rocker stripe… Staff Sergeant… three up and one down. Gene already has his Staff Sergeant rank… and could be expecting a promotion to Technical Sergeant… three up and two down. More pay and rank… we might even be exempt from KP or other details… maybe.

After chow and some coffee I got at the Red Cross hut I went back to my tent and wrote letters home to Mary, Pa and Ma. I took my small box out from my footlocker and thumbed through all the letters I received from Mary so far. I spent the rest of the afternoon re-reading her letters; I was missing her more than ever.

Nov 1, 2 & 3: Got the word on moving to France!!—And more good news I got my fourth stripe Staff Sergeant, should be sewing it on in a few weeks—New group commander Col Doyle, Captain Smith to be Major Smith—Wrote letters home and re-read Mary's letters, Miss Her A lot!—Living conditions improving, like getting off base to Bastia and boar hunt with Gene, Ed, Ken—Officers had a real drinking blow out party for the outgoing group commander on the 3rd, Loud Music, Smell of roasted lamb in a pit, Really bad singing of popular tunes, Needed Ear Plugs!—The enlisted got together and had our own party with some steaks and some local wine that somehow got on base, don't know where the steaks came from, All Was Good!!

The Allied efforts seem to be making real progress; there are still rumors of the war ending by Christmas… I'm on board with that when it happens. There aren't any missions scheduled so far but the rumor is that the 4th will be an all out effort

Gene came into the tent and came over to me while I was reading, "Nick… we need to get to the group's briefing room, there are more missions coming for a big push."

"OK… let me put these in the box," I said, there were rumors flying around that the Germans are trying to recover their supply lines through northern Italy. Last month we had bombed and destroyed some vital supply lines, they may have rebuilt some or all of the targets we hit. Gene and I walked over to the briefing room and the group headquarters building; Ken and Ed are already there along with the rest of our squadron and the other squadron's gathering as well. Lots of chatter about moving and what's coming, German fighters, the other groups in recent missions have spotted Me 109's and Fw 190's over northern Italy and southern France. Recent attacks on the 319th aggressive, Intel says they were part of Herman Goering's "Abbeville Boys" or sometimes called the Abbeville Kids", his top fighter squadron. Their planes have distinctive markings, yellow painted noses for one and the letter "S" behind the cockpit overlaid on a shield and the typical German emblems. The unit had the designation Jagdgeschwader (JG)

26 and the official Luftwaffe name as *Jagdgeschwader Schlageter* Any yellow nosed Me 109 or Fw 190 seen was reported as being flown by JG26. British and U.S. bomber crews were respectful of them due to their ability to penetrate our fighter escort screens and shoot them down. An undisputable opinion was that JG26 had some of the best pilots in the Luftwaffe.

There was a lot of chatter and some laughing and joking around, and then the shout of "Ten Hut" as everyone rises to attention. The group operations officer along with the intelligence officer enters the room. The squadron commanders and the deputy group commander are standing off to the side.

"At ease gentlemen… get comfortable," Major Stevens, the operations officer said as he looked down at this notes and then he looked up and continues, "We are going to be putting up several missions over the next few days… sometimes there will be more than one mission per day for crews… we are still working on the crew configurations and plane assignments."

"Let me give you a preview of what's going on… or rather what we will be going after," he paused and turned the page of his notes, "OK… here goes, we'll hit the road fills at Dolce and Ossenigo in the Po Valley."

"We'll also go after the railroad bridge at Casseano Di Adda between Trento and Verona on the line that runs through the Brenner Pass… this will block enemy supply lines east of Lake Garda."

"Brenner Pass is a key target… the more we can destroy to prevent a resupply of northern Italy the better off U.S. and British ground forces will have in beating back the enemy."

"Targets may change overnight but any and all rail lines throughout the Brenner Pass area are targets of opportunity to cut off the enemy."

"So far we are looking at seven missions to hit various pieces and parts of the target areas," pausing he hands the briefing to the Intel officer, "Captain Lee… your turn."

"I don't have to tell you that the Germans will be building up their flak guns around this area… it is vital for them to have their supplies get through to continue fighting in Italy," then he added a caveat,

"However... we don't think the Germans have had enough time to put flak guns in place, especially with all the damage we've done to roads and causeways in recent missions."

"Also... this is almost 100 percent... German fighters... the Abbeville Boys."

"Any questions?" Captain Lee looked over the gathering and was met with no questions just looks of concern for what was to come. Flak is one thing, but aggressive fighters'... tough missions... hope our little friends cover our ass

With that final request for questions we were dismissed. Detailed briefs will be given just before takeoff tomorrow. I am not on for tomorrow, Gene is and Ed, Ken and I are on for the November 5th mission

November 4th... mid-day takeoffs for the first mission today... when I can and when I am not on mission, I like to be near the flight line as our planes take off. Each plane made their way down the runway and off smoothly with each one creating a mist cloud from the standing water on the PSP. Everything looks good so far; weather is partly cloudy but its not raining. Each plane turned east after takeoff and over the water to form up at altitude. The next to the last ship moved in place at the end of the runway and started to run up its engines, the pilot released its brakes accelerating to takeoff speed. It got about nine hundred feet down the runway when I saw the left main tire blow with a big bang that got everyone's attention. It was going too fast to just stop. It veered off to its left and I watched it hit a ditch and finally skid off into the woods on the west side of the runway.

The fire trucks started to roll out to the scene and anyone watching started to run towards the crippled plane. Just as we started to run a fire started in the left engine and was spreading fast; I could see three crew scramble away from the plane with help that was nearby and run like hell clearing a good distance. Our squadron flight surgeon, Captain Randolph and his medic Sergeant Carter were on the line and close by the scene, they were able to help the pilot, co-pilot and flight engineer get out and away. Then the unthinkable... an explosion as the fuel caught fire engulfing the plane. The explosion caused me to react and

I hit the ground… just as I got off the ground to continue running, I was thrown several feet landing on my back from the concussion of the bombs exploding. The four other crew did not get out, they were trapped inside and were killed instantly… I still wanted to run towards the plane. What could I do at this point? Nothing.

I was shocked by the intensity of the fuel explosion and then the bombs going off. Smoke and fire soared into the air over three thousand feet when the explosions occurred. The plane was from the 442nd squadron, "39" the tail number. I may have played ball with those guys or cards, or laughed with them in the club or sat with them to chat in the chow hall… I don't know. The plane's wreckage was not too far from the tent area so it was visible to everyone. The explosions rattled the entire base area; it was probably felt in Bastia eighteen miles north. If we can find bodies, the 442nd will have a funeral to deal with… the reality of Jeff's death hit me again.

Nov 4: Today is my little sister's birthday, Matina, I hope she got my letter—Watched mission takeoffs today and it was a day that reminded me of Jeff's death, plane lost on takeoff after tire blew out, I saw it happen right before my eyes, four crew killed from the 442nd—I got a hold of the group chaplain to talk later in the evening—Long day with the incident picking up the pieces, I can still smell the smoke from the fuel and bomb explosions—Colonel Fletcher gave a good bye and farewell speech to the entire group gathered, he thanked us all for our efforts and to keep up the great work, he was well-liked and fair, he was on more missions than I was aware

Gene and Ed talked about the mission for today, they were on the first mission hitting RR bridges, flak damaged 3 planes (2 light damage, 1 badly damaged but made it back OK)—They had to circle around and hit the target from another direction—P-47's in the target area strafing but no fighters—Weather clear

Getting up for the mission today, November 5, was hard... I couldn't sleep well at all, seemed like I didn't sleep at all. I headed over to the group's briefing room with Ken for the mission briefing. Ken and I checked our plane and crew assignment on the bulletin board and went into the briefing room to find a seat. I am on my favorite plane, tail number "14".

"I was talking with some guys that were on yesterday and they said that there was some flak during the bomb runs... they saw P-47's and Spitfires," Ken said looking around the room pointing out some of the guys he talked with.

"I talked with Jim and Chet... over there."

"Flak wasn't bad, one guy was wounded from the 444th turret gunner."

"What happened to the Intel report on the fighters?" I said thinking about the Intel officer's comments yesterday.

Ken looked at me, "I don't know but we better be ready... maybe today is the day."

Shaking my head up and down, "Yea... maybe," the chatter was broken with the shout of "Ten Hut" and we stood at attention

"At ease... take your seats," the new group commander Lieutenant Colonel Woolridge, soon to be full colonel, said as he walked to the front of the room next to the maps and boards covered up.

"Gentlemen... we had some excellent success yesterday, and we will be continuing our efforts today."

"There are four target missions today that will concentrate on two railroad lines connecting Northern Italy with Yugoslavia and Austria, all in the Brenner Pass."

"Major Blevins will continue with the brief... good luck," Colonel Woolridge handed off the brief to the group's operations officer. The operations sergeant for the group, Staff Sergeant Morris removes the covers from the boards revealing maps, photos, and time schedules for takeoff

"Good morning... today there will be four targets in the Brenner Pass."

"Marco Railroad Bridge…" Pointing to the map location, "Roverto Railroad Bridge…" Moving pointer to the next target, "Cismon del Grappa Rail Road Bridge, and…"

"The Voghera Railroad Bridge," tapping the pointer at the last listed target

"As the colonel said these are vital enemy supply links to their forces in Northern Italy… we need to keep at this and destroy their capability to resupply."

Major Blevins continued to brief the times for takeoff, call signs for the group, sector control and mission commander for each target. Captain Smith is going to be the mission commander for the second target, my mission on "14" tail number.

Then the Intel officer has a few words, "Gentlemen… flak may not be a problem, but be aware… and, yes, there is a 100 percent probability of enemy fighters… stay alert," he sounded quite sure of his estimate.

He added plane identifications reported by the 319th and 17th recent missions, "There are reports of Me 109's, Fw 190's and Italian Mc 202's." Italian Mc 202's were similar in appearance to the 109's but with different paint schemes.

Colonel Woolridge dismisses us and we head out to get our gear and wait for the trucks to take us out to our planes. Something I don't often think about but am continually warned about is the prospect of capture after parachuting out of a crippled plane. We've had some shoot downs where a few have been captured, one actually got away with help from partisans. These missions today are no different than others; I just have to think of my training and protecting myself and get back to base. I don't know why I just started thinking about this now.

The planned take off for our mission is 0955 hours, our plane tail number "14", is located at the end of the formation. It is exceptionally clear today; the standing water on the PSP runway is not as bad as yesterday. The tire blown on the plane yesterday had to have been caused by a PSP tab sticking up that no one noticed. Ground crews spent yesterday afternoon and early this morning walking the runway looking for bent tabs that could cause a tire to blow on takeoff or landing.

Lieutenant Evans, a pilot I have not flown with, lifts us off gently at 140 mph and we head east over the water to form up. My observation position between the pilots gives me a bird's eye view of the clear sky and the planes forming up ahead. Our squadron, the 441st, has fifteen planes and the 444th is providing four planes for this second mission. After we form up with the rest of the planes, I head back to my gun turret and watch for fighters and observe the bomb run. The clear weather provides the perfect site of blue water below… it is something to see. We eventually make landfall over a town called La Spezia. From my turret venue I can see over 100 miles, turning my turret 360 degrees I can see Cannes and Nice on the French Riviera to the west and the Swiss Alps in the northwest. Pisa is visible off to the east… what a site… breathtaking.

Magnificent 360-Degree View

"Sir… engineer to pilot," I said as I noticed one of our squadron planes dropping out of formation.

"Yea… go ahead," Evans replies.

"I can see one of our planes… tail number "20"… dropping out on a slow turn northeast, over."

"Roger… got it… thanks," Evans confirms.

"The spare is moving up to take its place… looks like "84" tail number.

"Tail "20" has engine problems and heading for the barn."

"Yea… I see him… scanning for flak and fighters, out."

"Roger… stay sharp everyone," Evans exclaimed to the rest of the gunners

We are well over the northern part of Italy and we did not have escort fighters, our little friends, for cover. I'm getting nervous based on what the Intel officers said in the brief this morning… I've got a bad feeling. The formation was tightening up close on leads and wing ships for better protection and concentration of our defensive guns firepower.

Turning my turret around forward then to our right side I saw in the distance shadows of planes in a formation at twelve o'clock. They couldn't be our little friends; we would have been contacted if they were in the area. Looks like they are separating and turning towards us.

Then just as I noticed the color and shape of the planes I shouted over the intercom, "Four fighters at twelve o'clock high!"

Another shout out, don't know who, "Three at ten o'clock level… two more at one o'clock… four at nine o'clock high." The whole German Luftwaffe was out there it seemed

Evans shouted out, "Gunners… shout out positions… we're tightening up… lead them… make your bursts count," Evans was making sure we could get in close to our wing and lead planes to concentrate fire on the fighters.

The smell of cordite from the firing of our guns started to fill the air in the plane, those fighters were circling us like jackals. Each crew shouted out relative positions from their position perspective which made the shout outs confusing. I could see each enemy plane approach and then perform a split "S" exposing their belly, which was heavily armored, as it passed underneath. My heart was pounding as I swing my gun turret around to lead the approaching fighter on our right side… I fired several short bursts. With all of us firing you could feel the plane shudder. I think I missed, my tracers went behind the fighter as it passed; running through my mind are the instructions from veteran gunners at gunnery school. I'm nervous... need to settle down and concentrate... get scared later after we take out these fighters. Then I realized that the noses of the planes were yellow... Abbeville Boys, Luftwaffe's best are on the attack

I heard shout outs over shout outs and tried to concentrate on where and look out from my view at the same time and call out positions. I could see dozens of parallel ribbon thin vapor trails streaking by... machine gun rounds from the fighters. Then I heard hits between my turret and the tail gunner... loud and hard... no explosions... small holes from their .50 caliber rounds, they went straight through.

"Fighter at 3 o'clock level passing under to our right side," I shouted and turned around towards the left side where I say another, "One o'clock... coming fast." I stopped my turning... aimed and fired. I could see my tracers hitting the plane rear of the pilot and into the tail... I got a piece of him.

The first pass was fast... you could see them in the distance reforming and coming in... in pairs. This time from all directions... it looked like they were going to hit each other. I saw a pair coming in at twelve o'clock high and took aim and fired a long burst.

"Two at nine o'clock low," I heard from someone on the intercom.

I looked around and couldn't see at the low position.

"Twelve o'clock high," I shouted and took aim again at the pair on the one fighter to my right. I could see their tracer rounds coming right at us. I fired again... three bursts... then a long burst at the attacking plane... I could see my hits across the left wing and then the tail, the 109 turned over and passed by; I could see smoke trailing from the wing. It sped off away from our formation; probably damaged... another piece of a fighter... can't confirm a kill.

More shout outs heard over my head set, trying to figure out which ones are for me, "A pair coming in straight and level at 4 o'clock," I shouted

Then I heard our tail gunner Sergeant Hal Noel shout out, "I've got him," then like slow motion I watched his rounds hit across the engine and into the cockpit. I could see the pilots head bounce back and blood splatter over his shattered Plexiglas canopy. The plane turned over and headed straight down… one kill.

In between attacks runs by the fighters I noticed that one of our planes was hit and heading down, smoke trailing from both engines… I see three chutes, then an explosion and a plane in pieces falling into the rocky Italian landscape.

No time to think about who or what… another run in pairs again, "Two at three o'clock high," I shouted back, "I'm on it," I fired a long burst at the plane on my right side view and swivel my gun turret to my left over to the other plane attacking. I can see my rounds hitting the first plane then smoke from its engine. The other plane passes beneath us and performs a split "S" down and away.

I could hear our tail gunner Hal shouting out and then, "Damn it… my gun's jammed… trying to fix… damn it… damn it."

I wanted to help but I saw another pair coming at us from eleven o'clock high, I fired a long burst and missed… then my gun jammed, "Damn… damn…" I worked to clear the jam and charged it twice and then tried to fire again and nothing. Working the jam… tried again… then a jolt as my guns fired. I wasn't aiming at anything… but my guns work again.

More shout outs and then a calm… the remaining fighters pull way off in the distance… to the northeast towards Austria… don't see as many as the original number. Our other planes must have hit quite a few. I can see one… two… three… four… one trailing light gray smoke. In all the confusion I have no idea how many came at us… I think fifteen; maybe twenty… seemed like the entire Luftwaffe. I checked my ammo feed and was surprised that I almost fired my entire load… sure did not seem like it… I tried to fire short bursts and keep my aim true. All the confusion and adrenaline makes you lose track of reality… I was focused on getting those fighters.

Then over the intercom, "Did anyone see chutes from that second plane?" Evans shouted, "I couldn't see from my view."

I did not know another plane of ours got hit with all the confusion. Two planes down and some killed, "I saw three more chutes," I heard someone say... their fate unknown, of course... hope they can avoid capture and make it to friendly lines. The landscape is pretty rough below.

After the attack we settled down, no one talked... silence. We continued on with the mission, the only sound I could hear was the steady hum of our engines; we had not reached the IP to make the bomb run yet. The Intel officer this morning said there would be no flak... hope he is right. As we approached the IP we turned right and rolled into the target heading.

"As smooth as it gets," Evans said as we made a perfect bomb run. I could see the hits after we passed overhead looking aft. I could make out the valley and the bridge as our bomb hits seemed to destroy the entire outline of the bridge and surrounding area. We broke south towards the coast, as we headed out over water I could see another one of our planes drop out, you could see smoke starting to trail from one engine and it was turning black. It must have sustained damage from the fighter attack and then just quit. I heard over the intercom that they were bailing out and then Lieutenant Evans shouted out, "Keep an eye out for chutes... "84" is bailing out."

Hal, our tail gunner had a good view looking below, "Sir... I see one... two, three... four, I see four chutes so far."

"Got it... there has to be more," Evans shouted.

Those that could see below noticed the plane dipped a wing then rolled over and the nose began to go straight down, just then, "Sir," Hal shouted, "I see another... wow, he just made it out."

The plane plunged from about 6,000 feet into the water... when it hit the water it blasted up an immense column of white spray.

I can see the airstrip on Corsica... a sight for sore eyes. No one talked after we saw "84" go down, I heard over the intercom that air sea rescue was notified... they should be OK... no one lost on that one. Evans made a perfect approach and landing... number "14" made it through in good shape... a few holes but OK. I couldn't tell if we sustained any significant damage, we'll have to wait till we get on out for the post flight checks. Getting out of the plane my legs felt like rubber bands and my hands were shaky... I noticed Hal and he looked white as a ghost.

Walking around the plane I noticed a hole under the right wing right by the fuel tank, it wasn't a big hole but close enough to the fuel tank to be a problem. With all the firing and confusion during the attack I did notice the sound of some rounds hitting our plane. There were holes just aft of my gun turret; they looked like they went straight through. The ground crew said they would look over the plane; we need to get to the interrogations officer to sort out what happened today. Later that afternoon a ground crew mechanic said that they found an unexploded 20-millimeter German round in the right wing, if the round would have exploded when it hit… missed a bad day.

I spent at least an hour talking to the interrogations officer with Hal and Lieutenant Evans about the mission. No doubt there was a lot of chatter and shout outs to call out fighters, everyone was busy and the attacks seemed to last more than just a few minutes. After everyone let out their thoughts there was a consensus that at least 15 planes, 109's and 190's attacked us. We shot down 9 and damaged the rest, I saw several pull away from us with smoke trails but not going down and out. They came to within 100 yards and came in fast and in pairs on the second and subsequent passes. The third plane's crew, "84", were all rescued by air sea rescue, no word on the crew that parachuted from the two planes shot down during the attack.

After we finished we headed over to the Red Cross hut, the bomb group command allowed us to have a two-ounce shot of whiskey or coffee and doughnuts. I took the whiskey shot, we all needed one… headed back to my tent… laid down in my bunk and stared at the ceiling contemplating what we experienced today. Ken walked in all hopped up, he got credit for one kill, "Hey… got one today… hit a few others… exhilarating," Ken exclaimed and then he said, "I think I need to relax… I can't seem to settle down."

I looked up at him, "Go over to the Red Cross hut and ask for that two-ounce shot of whiskey… it'll settle you down… it works."

He turned around and headed out without saying a word, I continued looking up at the ceiling and fell asleep.

Nov 5: Milk run mission turned into a scary one, German fighters seemed to be everywhere—We lost two B-26's during the attack and one on the way back to base over the water—I got a piece of three or four planes, our tail gunner got one kill—Our flight got 9 fighters shot down (the final Intel assessment), there were 15 fighters seemed like the entire Luftwaffe—Abbeville Boys hit us hard and fast

Nov 6: Another mission, no fighters but heavy flak over target, Dolce RR Bridge—Still nervous, learned to focus, scared to death after I had time to think about it—I reported seeing at least 6 Me 109's being intercepted over Desenzano and another flight chasing a formation of B-26's in the distance near Cremona—Good target hits, successful mission

Nov 7: No mission today, time to relax a little—Talked with Gene, Ed, and Ken about home and wives and sweethearts, no one wanted to get off base to hunt boar or play ball—Wrote letters home sent over to officer tent for censoring, don't know who is reading my letters, hurry up so I can get them in the mail run—Wandered over to the Red Cross hut for coffee and bread, saw a movie tonight Casablanca" with my favorite actor, Humphrey Bogart, I flew over Casablanca on the way here in July—Chow is getting better, mess sergeant must have learned a lesson from the missing food last month!!!—Checked the operations bulletin board and I am on for tomorrow's mission

Nov 8: Mission to Casale Norferrato RR Bridge—Flew with Cahan and Ed—Lots of flak, lost one plane to flak No Chutes Seen!—I knew two of the crew on the plane, empty feeling comes back, I think about Jeff everyday, starting to accumulate the faces of those killed in my mind—My turret Plexiglas got hit twice from flak burst shrapnel, startled me each time, one of these days that shrapnel is going to go right through

After interrogations today, Lieutenant O'Mahony approached me, "Sergeant Bentas... need to talk with you," he said.

"Yes sir… what's on your mind?"

"Well… your name came up for detail… and you, me and several others are being assigned to get the move to France organized and completed," he said with a look like he wanted my approval.

"OK… when do we start, sir?"

"It looks like sometime around the 15th… some of what I need you for will not be needed until closer to the 20th… so you could be on a few missions until I need you full time," he looked at his clipboard and up at me, "How's that?"

"Sounds OK… who else and how many of us are on this detail?"

"Including you and me… there are eight plus the group and squadron staff."

"The other enlisted helping me are from the 442nd, 443rd and 444th you might know some of them."

"We'll be flying missions to transport cargo on our B-26's and coordinate with Navy to fill LST's with all our heavy stuff, trucks and heavy equipment for transport to the port at Marseilles France."

"After we get the LST's off loaded we'll convoy up to our new base, Dijon."

"Questions?"

"No sir… what do you need me to do now?"

"Nothing now… let's meet after your next mission, I'm on the same one… we can meet at the officer's club with the rest of our small team… OK?"

"Yea… see you then sir."

See how easy it is to be a volunteer? Really doesn't sound too bad… nice change.

The lieutenant, soon to be captain, and I got together with the rest of our small team and got our assignments and tasks that needed to get completed in order to leave Corsica and move to Dijon. Since I was a flight engineer I could tag along with the B-26's used for carrying cargo to France, just like the practice missions and pilot training flights I've been on. The group and squadron logistics and transportation officers were in attendance and then we were assigned to an officer for any detail work required. We got familiar with everything we would need to do coordinating movement... nice to have a desk job for a while. From the 9th to the 12th we worked with each other to get ready to move... got scheduled for a mission tomorrow

> *Nov 13: Flying today with Cahan and Ed on tail number 23" one of my two favorite B-26's—Target Ala Station and Stores (supply) target—Flak guns seemed to follow us to target and after we broke away on the way back, guns locations throughout the route to and from—Flak damaged 4 (2 slight, 2 heavy) all made it back—P-47's seen attacking targets in the area—Saw a huge storm system north and west of Padua, lots of lightning*

There is no time to do anything else but plan and meet. Our days are filled with meetings and paperwork with group and squadron staff to coordinate our move. I might be on two missions, I've been flying with newly promoted Captain Cahan on recent missions, and he told me he requested me for at least a few more missions.

> *Nov 17: Target today Avisio RR Viaduct—Took off at 0808, landed 1142—Flew with Cahan and Geronimos on my favorite B-26 23"—P-47's escorted us today from Elba to and from the target, glad to see them around, a few gave chase to enemy planes seen off in the distance—Target was missed, lots of haze over Po Valley—Flak damage on 6 planes, we had some hits that penetrated with small holes*

> *Nov 18: Flew with Cahan and Ed again, on "23"—Took off at 0911, landed 1324—Going after the same target as yesterday where we missed, we hit an alternate target with success, enemy had a good smoke screen over target area—Weather was hazy with 3-4/10 cloud cover—Alternate target was the Pizzighettone RR Bridge—Flak damage to 2 planes, we didn't get hit with shrapnel—8 P-47's met us over Rimini, good cover, did not see any German fighters—**This is my last mission from Alto Corsica**, time to get the paperwork done and move to Dijon, France—Wrote letters to Mary, Pa & Ma*

can't say anything about moving yet until we get there—Axis Sally probably knows more than all of us, What's Her Opinion? Just play the music!

Got the order and it's official… Staff Sergeant Bentas… another good sounding name and rank… sewing my stripes on. Gene found out he made Technical Sergeant… Ken and Ed also got orders to put on their fourth stripe. Captain Smith is now Major Smith and O'Mahony was promoted to Captain. Cahan was promoted to Captain and moved over to the group as an assistant operations officer, he will move into that position when we get to France. We got our stripes sewed on and were headed for much better living conditions in France. Cahan has been a good mentor and pilot, I'll miss flying with him. Morale is getting higher and a motivator for a cooperative environment due to the official move to France

You don't realize just how much equipment, trucks, Jeeps, and personal bags there are until you get into a detail supporting the move. Where did all this stuff come from? All of us that were assigned to the movement detail were told to meet in the group's briefing room. Gathering in place we were chatting and then the group's operations officer, Major Blevins entered, then a shout of "Ten Hut."

We all stood at attention as he began, "At ease… grab a seat and get comfortable… I've got a few announcements and then we can get back to work."

"First things first… we've been doing some pre-planning in anticipation of moving, so now we have the order."

"Yesterday's mission on the 20th was the last mission from Alto, Corsica."

"To make it official the 320th Bomb Group is relieved from operational status with the Twelfth Air Force effective November 21, 1944… and reassigned to the European Theater of Operations (ETO) as part of the First Tactical Air Force—Provisional effective November 27th 1944."

"Also, the Thirteenth Tactical Air Command and the 42nd Wing are intervening units… and will be located with the 320th and the 17th at Dijon."

"What that means as far as chain of command… we are a part of the Ninth Air Force in the ETO under the 42nd Wing as the First Tactical Air Force—Provisional… we will be supporting several numbered U.S. Armies and the French First Army."

"They will be pushing the Germans back to The Fatherland… so let's get this done… you should have been pre-planning… now we get down to the real movement."

"OK… done… get with your already assigned teams and let's get going… dismissed."

With that we broke up and Captain O'Mahony called us together to get going on tasks for the next week.

He started with a scheduling briefing, "OK… I will be supervising the scheduling and loading of B-26's with whatever will fit in the bomb bay and inserted in side," he looked at me and said, "Sergeant Bentas… since you're a flight engineer I need you to work with the operations staff and schedule other engineers for these transport flights… OK?

"Got it…no problem," I acknowledged and then asked a question, "I assume we will only have the pilot, co-pilot and engineer… correct sir?"

"Spot on… also make sure when you watch everyone loading the plane, keep an eye out for any obstructions to controls located throughout the plane from the cargo."

"We don't need any snapped cables or broken hydraulic lines… OK?"

"Roger, sir."

The all-out effort to move and pack was in full swing; the transport missions to Dijon on B-26's were calm with no enemy air activity. I flew on six transport missions and got to see the airfield and then a quick turn around to get back to Alto Corsica to reload. The landscape was a brilliant green with rolling hills, forests, farmhouses and small villages scattered along our air route. Dijon's airfield was pock marked with bomb craters that the Army engineers were in the process of repairing.

The remaining hangers were in real bad shape with only their steel frameworks in place. There were scattered wrecks of German planes of various types. Flying over Dijon and the surrounding area gave me a view of some of the villages that we were going to be occupying… real buildings and indoor plumbing… morale is going up. There was an incident that we didn't expect; a B-26 from the 444th was lost in bad weather one day. It was never found; we lost a crew of three.

> *Nov 22: WOW, we moved a lot of equipment and small items using B-26's as transport planes, we stuffed them—LST's will be moving our trucks loaded with heavier equipment and about 400 personnel for convoy from Marseilles port to Dijon—B-26 lost due to bad weather two days ago, crew and plane lost, no one knows where or how*
>
> *Don't know if I'm on a B-26 or convoying from the coast of France to Dijon, I will volunteer to ride versus fly—Looking forward to living in a real building (maybe) and real wash up sinks and toilets—Got to see Dijon on several flights in and out, needs a little work, Army Engineers working hard to make ready for our group and First Tactical Air Force (Provisional) units, heard a squadron of French Air Force to be located with us, Fighters I think—P-47 fighter squadron will be on Dijon*
>
> *Nov 23: Got my wish for convoy, can't wait to see the French countryside—Route is safe according to the MP's, weapons will be at the ready for any enemy stragglers (German and Vichy French soldiers)—Packing up, next entry in France when I get there!!*

We drove to Bastia where the Naval base and docks were located and boarded our trucks and Jeeps for the ride to the French coast. I've never been on a ship this size… the appearance from the outside is impressive. The ride to Bastia was my last since our LST will be leaving as soon as it was loaded. A part of my duty was to be one of six commanders for the convoy from the coast of France to Dijon after we disembarked

The weather was getting cooler; the water was calm in the harbor and the word was that the weather would hold for a few days... smooth sailing was the forecast. We watched our equipment being loaded and personnel found their places on board and got settled with their bags. The LST finally finished loading and prepared to cast off; our sea crossing will be two to three days. One thing we didn't realize or ask about was what kind of services and accommodations were on board. To our disappointment the entire ship had only three toilets, one chow hall in a cramped space, one washroom, and one water station for drinking. There were long lines for everything... if you were not in line you probably would need to be soon in order to get any relief. All of us, over four hundred, couldn't wait to get to back on land.

Our trip across the water was uneventful, we dropped anchor in the port of Marseilles, France... from the top deck you could see the entire harbor. For as far as you could see, there was row after row of Liberty ships, LST's, Minesweepers, and Destroyers. Smaller PT Boats were patrolling the harbor area as docked LST's were unloading. Our ship will have to wait its turn. Something we would all need for our trip and new home in France was French currency and a G.I. issue French guidebook; there was also a lecture we would have to attend on the things we should not be doing in France.

After hours of waiting, we were told to get ready to disembark. Moving towards the pontoon bridge to the beach didn't take too long. We couldn't wait to get off this ship, for now we would all settle in at a bivouac area just off the beach to spend the night. Our trucks, Jeeps, and equipment were offloaded into a staging area. From the staging area we would organize our convoy and then head to Dijon.

We must have looked like unorganized gypsies as we formed up to move out. The trucks and trailers looked like we just threw our stuff on them; we put everything we thought we could use including non-military building materials. Most of us had figured out, from experience, how to make life comfortable so we brought it all... we were going to be happy. We didn't care what we looked like; we just wanted to get to Dijon and set up our housekeeping. There was an Army unit arriving on the same day that had their equipment in the staging area next to ours, what a contrast of fresh and new to the old and tried. Their equipment was neatly stacked and packaged, ours was just thrown in; we got some odd looks and comments directed towards us "those raunchy Air Corps types"… get over it, we're content.

LST's unloading at the Port of Marseilles France during and after Operation Dragoon

Lieutenant Vosler was the officer in charge of the convoy, he called all of the commanders assigned together before we left for Dijon at 0500 hours, "OK… gather around… let's get our order set," he said to me and the others

"I'll be in the lead vehicle… Bentas, you're with me… Anderson, you're about ten vehicles in with a Jeep… Jolson, the next Jeep about ten down and Petersen with Jones in the last Jeep."

"Keep in touch by radio… we'll do two hour checks… weapons on safe, but be aware of any problems… contact me if you need anything."

"I got an Intel brief last night and we should be clear of German or Vichy stragglers on our route… if you're fired at, return fire if you have a target identified, contact me immediately after… I should be able to hear your fire so I'll know there is a problem."

"MP's have the route marked and like I said, we should be clear of any trouble… check your weapons and radio function and let's get going," looking around at the area and then to us, "Any questions?"

"Sir… what is our departure time and what time do you expect us to make Dijon?" Sergeant Jones asked.

"We leave at 0700 hours… my reports have the roads clear of traffic, the MP's know we are coming through."

"I'm optimistic that we could make Dijon by 1800 or 1900 hours… be prepared to sleep in makeshift spots or tents."

"There should be tents or places to bed down when we get there… most of our planes are already on the ground or leaving this morning and throughout the day for Dijon."

"Anything else?" Hearing nothing, he continued, "Set your watches to 0525… mark… OK, let's get going… 0700 hours I'll start pulling out… get the word out." He dismissed us to our assigned convoy vehicles, and we got the word out for a 0700 hours departure time.

Chow line is not too bad so we got a hot breakfast; each person got a box lunch with an apple for the road. We stocked up on C and K ration boxes, extra water and gas cans.

The time… 0655… almost time to go… 0700 here we go. I started the Jeep and put it in gear, let out the clutch, and headed out of the staging area up to the gate where an MP directed us out to the main road… here we go. So far the MP reports are correct, the road was open for traffic; we've not been deterred or needed to stop because of traffic problems. The traffic we did pass by was military, some tanks, trucks and Jeeps with trailers and troops on board. No sign of enemy stragglers, we've been by several checkpoints with MPs on guard with no problems so far. Looking around the countryside we saw farmland over green plains and rolling hills… scenic and peaceful looking. The farmhouses were painted a light brown and some had a dull pink color. We also saw crucifixes along the road at various spots… French citizens stopped to watch our huge convoy pass staring in amazement at such a large column of friendly vehicles. The weather was cold with no wind and occasionally a warm sun through an unthreatening overcast. We passed at one point, about three hours in, a stretch of highway with a site that I was amazed to see. There must have been over a thousand German trucks, tanks, small Jeep-like vehicles, trailers and wagons littering both sides of the road… it seemed endless. Just as we passed that scene we would come upon quiet villages and towns that looked like they were not touched by war; there were cafes, restaurants, and even movie theaters open for business. Fortunately for us we were not detained at checkpoints for more than five or ten minutes… MP's pushed us through. Finally after nine hours on the road we made it to the outskirts of Dijon… we turn on the marked road southeast to the airfield. We will park our trucks and equipment at a staging area on the airfield next to buildings that the engineers had repaired. Personnel will be transported to Longecourt where the group headquarters was being set up later this afternoon or in the morning. There are tents set up here that we can bunk in for the night… our B-26's are still landing in one's and two's. There were still some missions being flown out of Alto, they would land at Dijon after bomb runs on targets. Gene, Ken and Ed are still flying missions. I should be able to catch up with them in a day or two… I'll get a tent or room set up for us in the squadron area.

The 320th Bomb Group set up headquarters in the oldest Chateau in Longecourt, the 441st and 442nd are also in Longecourt near the group in smaller chateaus, the 443rd and 444th are in the nearby village, Bessey les Citeaux. The Services Support Squadrons are set up in Dijon and a village close by in Neuilly. Army engineers have been hard at work getting the runway in shape for the rest of our group's B-26's, the 17th Bomb Group's, the French Air Force planes and our P-47 fighter squadron. The engineer units are located at the airfield. The 42nd Wing Headquarters set up in Longvic just outside of Dijon. The airfield is going to be crowded with aircraft from U.S. and French air forces. The 441st officers will have rooms in the homes of villagers and the chateau in Longecourt; the enlisted will be in tents... tents again. The best thing is that we will have running water, wash up sinks and showers with porcelain thrones for comfort.

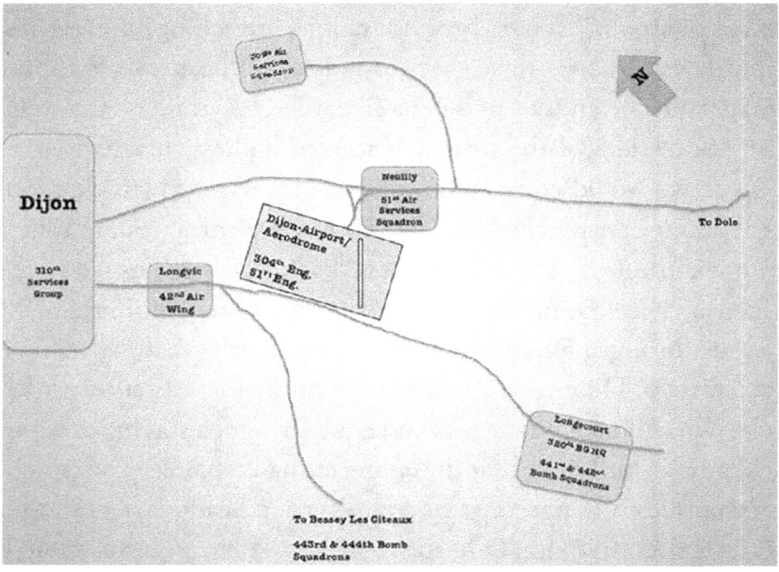

Dijon and Vicinity of the 320th Bomb Group and Co-Located Units

CHAPTER 6

GETTING SETTLED

> *Prime Minister Sir Winston Churchill:*
> *"This is the lesson: never give in, never give in, never, never, never, never—in nothing, great or small, large or petty—never give in except to convictions of honour and good sense. Never yield to force; never yield to the apparently overwhelming might of the enemy."*

Tents… tents… what a FUBAR. We thought all of us enlisted would have a chance to fit into local homes and chateaus… instead, we are putting up tents. It is a good thing we brought all our rag tag building materials from Corsica to make solid floors in tents and other makeshift structures or other creative conveniences. However, we did get a break for at least a few days to be housed in Mrs. Monnier's Chateau next to a bar in the Chateau de Longecourt. The French are grateful for their liberation; we get enough admiration and thanks from them that will last a lifetime. Now it's time to get our tents in place… lots of work to do. I have not been on a mission since last month and I'm still a part of the movement detail.

The weather is getting colder… the locals think it will be a colder winter this year… that remains to be seen. We set up our squadron enlisted tents just outside the Chateau… I've got my spot picked out, and I'll have my hands on good flooring material and a new issued stove. My plan was to make the tent sit high so that any flooding that might occur from melting snow and unexpected heavy rain would keep us high and dry. We did get to stay in the Chateau until our tents went up… it was cramped but nice to be inside. Jeff would be ecstatic talking about the history of this place, it was built in the 12th century… it has a moat and the family has had this place in their lineage since the 1600's. It's a beautiful place with an elegant interior. While staying in the Chateau we made French Fries in the fireplace… you could not miss the scattered appearance of bloodstains around the mantle and walls. No one asked what or how. For the first time since arriving overseas, I am not living in close proximity to the airfield. It is a nice change to live among the civilian population in homes and to interact with locals. The French are friendly and warm, especially the children

Chateau in Longecourt—441 Bomb Squadron

Enlisted Tent Area—Longecourt

Ken, Gene and Ed will be pleased; they were supposed to be here yesterday... one more mission out of Corsica for them. There isn't much there and they are living out of a ditty bag and the clothes on their backs. I was able to get their personal bags here in one piece, and I have the tent in place with all of their stuff. I found some discarded ammo boxes that I cleaned up to use for shelves and set them up in the tent.

I heard a couple of trucks pull into our area and the sound of the rear door flap opening and hitting the truck's tail making a loud clanging noise along with the chatter of conversations. Must be returning crews... I saw several B-26's circling with our group markings about an hour ago. I headed over to the trucks to see if Ken, Gene and Ed were on board.

There they were with their bags and gear.

"Hey... Nick... where's my room," Ken said sarcastically and looking at the big Chateau expecting to have a luxury room indoors.

"Well... let me get the valet to take your luggage over to our luxurious tent with immaculate floors, comfortable beds and warm stove," I said with tongue in cheek.

Ken was a little disappointed, he thought that what he heard about tents was a rumor to be squashed, "What... is this a big FUBAR or what?" he exclaimed. Gene and Ed looked at each other, definitely disappointed.

"This way guys," I said. I grabbed a few bags and walked over to the tent I had set up for us.

"Welcome to the chateau de Gene, Ed, Ken and Nick," I said trying to soften the mood

"Funnyman... this is really it, huh?" Ed said in a disappointing one

"Yea... this is it," I said.

"I was able to get together some good wood planks for the floor, discarded ammo boxes for shelving and a new issue stove for the heat... I did my best."

"I also want you guys to notice that it is higher than the rest of the tents... flood water protection... not bad, hey?" I said still trying to soften the mood. They looked around disappointed with no response. "I was able to scrounge up some newer footlockers that weren't so beat up," I said encouraging them it was as good as it could get for now.

They threw their bags and gear towards their choice of bunk and sat down rubbing their faces and settling in with the disappointment.

Gene chimed in having lived in some rough places before any of us arrived in Sardinia and said with a sigh, "Well... this is way better than what I started with in Sardinia when I got there... and, it will be OK... just settle in."

"We are in France... the war may end soon... we're OK," Gene continued turning disappointment to a tone of dealing with our living conditions... it really wasn't that bad.

"Let me tell you about the locals... they are warm and friendly... I've been in Dijon a few times and it is friendly," I said bringing up some positive aspects of our location and living conditions.

"The Red Cross has a canteen and there are cafes, restaurants, a movie theater and cabaret entertainment."

"Get unpacked and settled and I'll show you around... I have some detail duties to finish," I said and I headed out the door.

Ken called out, "Nick... thanks for getting us a good spot and taking care of our stuff."

"You're welcome… I got the best for us, some of the privileges of being in charge of logistics for the movement," I said with a grin and wink and turned around to head out of our tent for my duties. I stopped and poked my head back in the tent, "Hey… there is wine in the Chateau and I've got connections."

"We'll head over later… I'll show you guys around just in time for chow."

Besides having to deal with the cold and some snow there were some extra amenities being set up in Dijon to boost morale when not flying. The Red Cross in cooperation with the French are opening up several locations. Movie theaters, cafes, restaurants, clubs and the Red Cross canteen were opening. The "Scrub House" was the name of the canteen. Regular schedule truck rides to Dijon and back was set up to give us all a chance to see the city and get to know real French hospitality… a definite morale booster. Military Police regularly patrol the streets and roads throughout.

After settling in and showing Gene, Ed, and Ken around the area we got word that the squadron commander, Major Smith, is mustering us for a briefing. We headed over to the 441st briefing room and found a seat to wait

Seeing Major Smith approach the room, Sergeant Buijak calls the room to attention, "Ten Hut."

The major enters and calls us to our seats, "At ease… as you were, I've got some information I need to pass on to you as we get started conducting missions out of this airfield."

Looking down at his notes on his clipboard he continued, "We will be going after German targets in German territory… we haven't done that before, so this is a first for the 320th and this squadron."

"So… let me emphasize, we are located about 100 miles from the German border… they are ready and willing to do whatever they need to protect their homeland."

"According to the group Intel officer I need to pass on the following information for all combat personnel… it is 100 percent certain you will see more flak guns and they will be accurate."

"Also... the German civilian population, as you may suspect, has been subjected to a great deal of bombing from our bombers and fighter planes attacking targets where they live," he stood back a bit and cleared his throat, "Let me be clear... they have been known to use clubs and pitchforks on airmen who land in their location," again he cleared his throat and added, "Whether you land in a crippled plane or parachute down you may encounter a highly agitated civilian with an effective weapon."

"From this point forward, you will always carry your .45 pistol and you can add extra magazines if you like... protect yourself if you are menaced by civilians and you definitely feel threatened."

"Find German military personnel to get arrested properly... a better way to carry your pistol is on a chest harness, it won't fall out when you pop your chute."

"One last thing... the targets we will be going after are in southern Germany, which is predominately Catholic," he added, "You might want to use the phrase "Ich bin Katholik," it means, "I am Catholic," if you encounter hostile civilians."

"I'm not telling you to convert but this phrase may save your life." This brought a few chuckles and comments from real Catholics to the rest of us to become Catholic

"OK... OK, settle down... any questions?"

"Oh... can't forget this, there is a mission scheduled for tomorrow so check the operations board for assignments later this evening... now, any questions?"

No questions or comments heard from the squadron assembled, Major Smith dismissed us.

> *Nov 30: Finally time to write in this journal—Lots completed during the Group movement, got to ride in an LST for 3 days, NEVER AGAIN, cramped with long lines for everything, miserable and glad I didn't join the Navy—Very scenic ride from port to Dijon in convoy, beautiful country, saw a stretch of road with many destroyed German tanks and trucks—Arrived in Dijon at the airfield to assemble, got billeted in the Chateau de Longecourt for a few days*

Set up our tent with good wood planks and made it high for flood/water protection, learned our lesson on Corsica— Gene, Ed, and Ken arrived a few days ago and they looked disappointed, getting better attitude; it isn't really that bad, I set up a good tent with newer bunks, stove and footlockers—Clubs in Dijon being set up, Germans were not good to the French, they are very thankful for their liberation Tasted French wine from the Burgundy region, Very Good!—

The chateau is an elegant building, too bad we aren't billeted inside, the officers have that privilege—Finally settling in to write home, Mary must be worried about the absence of letters, our mail hasn't caught up with us yet

Major Smith gave us a briefing on German civilians and what they might do to us if we parachute into enemy territory, Don't Get Shot Down!! OR Make sure you have your pistol in place when you exit the plane, protect yourself OR find a German Military person to properly arrest you OR How about trying to evade and return to base??

The weather has been nasty and is preventing missions, there were several planned and then cancelled for bad weather. Missions for December 1st and 5th were scheduled and able to take off, I was not on the rotation for either assignment. I am done with my detail duties for the movement and anxious to get back into flying… that is, when the weather allows. Snow is accumulating around the tent areas and is making travel on the Route de Dijon into the city slippery with ice and patches of packed snow on the road. The skies are cloudy every day… occasionally you can spot a small exposed patch of blue sky, but it disappears just as soon as you see it… the rolling clouds overtake the view. Sleeping in uniforms with heavy socks is the norm to keep the chill off… the supply sergeant said that new sleeping bags are here and we will get our issue.

Dec 1: Getting cold out, temps in the low teens and colder at night, thank God for our stove and our newly issued sleeping bags, I still sleep in my uniform with heavy socks—Gene, Ken and I head into Dijon to the Red Cross canteen, Ed got tagged for a special duty in the squadron area, no KP, we'll talk later—Met up with some Aussie friends we met last week, they sure have some stories, I may have to visit Australia after the war and see what the Outback is all about—Also met a Canadian that lived in Ontario across the Detroit River, nice swapping stories of Detroit and Windsor

Administrative actions caught up with all of us… several of us were awarded Air Medals, including me, and others getting promoted. I cannot remember which missions I got Air Medals for, but I've got the paper work and certificates. I have two so far. Mail finally caught up with us and I received four letters from Mary and three from Pa.

Gene, Ken, Ed and I went into Dijon on several occasions to visit the Red Cross canteen. We saw a French "Who Done It" movie that had sub titles; it was not Hollywood quality but interesting, the name was in French so I don't know the title. These theaters also featured Hollywood films; we saw Casablanca again, my personal favorite. Some of the theaters also presented cabaret entertainment featuring music, song, and drama vignettes in a restaurant setting. At the Red Cross canteen we saw a register, there were names of G.I.'s in the area in other units. Gene noticed a guy he grew up with in Ohio and the rest of us saw a few names we recognized from basic training. Across the street from the canteen was a place called "G.I. Joe's Rendezvous" that featured American food when it was available. Food was scarce at first for the French, a result of the harsh German occupation.

An interesting rumor heard from several G.I.'s was that General Patton had personally asked for the 320th to come to France to support his troops. We were not surprised if it were true, we had an accuracy record recognized by the 12th Air Force as one of the best. Patton was moving fast towards the north of us in the Alsace Lorraine region pushing the enemy back into Germany. We typically didn't associate with ground troops or other units, we were a close knit group and stuck together.

> *Dec 4: Read and re-read letters from Mary, Cannot wait to see her again, I'm glad she sent pictures of her and family, getting homesick—Gene, Ken, Ed, and I scrounged wood for our tent stove in Longecourt, I think we pissed off some locals, we may need to get into the woods to cut down some big trees—We can also burn the heavy pressed paper binding wraps that the bombs are packed in, that is when we can get them before anyone else—We also scrounge for old ammo boxes and crates discarded at the airfield*
>
> *The Red Cross hut in the group area has some good coffee and hot chocolate occasionally with donuts, yum yum, nice treat— Not much to do, sometimes its feels too cold to sit down and read or try and get a card game going—The Stars and Stripes finally got delivered and copies of Yank, nice break from the worn out Zane Grey novels and old magazines—I was able to scrounge another radio so we could listen to music from Axis Sally, the one we had on Corsica got lost in the move... Somehow she knew who we were and where we were, I guess our move wasn't so secret??—Axis Sally has the best music and we laugh at the propaganda and make fun of it*

All of us in our tent were scheduled for missions and then cancelled because of weather. Gene, Ken and Ed mentioned how cold it was at altitude. It was a part of flying and the natural occurrence when flying up to 10,000 feet or more. Our bombing missions were mostly between 8,000 and 12,000 feet. Our current temperatures on the ground hovers around the mid-teens, as a plane climbs the outside air temperature drops at a rate of approximately three degrees for every 1,000 feet ascended. So if you climb to 14,000 feet the temperature drops to about minus thirty degrees... frostbite is a real concern. There are heaters in the plane but... they don't work real well, my only real complaint about the B-26. On a mission over Italy we caught a chunk of flak that severed a hydraulic line and a heating duct. The hydraulic fluid seeped into the heat lines; when the pilot turned the heat on, a choking mist filled the cockpit and made its way throughout the plane... not good, makes you sick. Dealing with the cold is a challenge, and we rely on our heated suits, gloves, and boots. Also important is to avoid breathing on or near the window and Plexiglas surfaces, they get fogged and iced up real bad and you can't see.

Mission scheduled for December 10th, my first out of Dijon and the weather has cleared enough to proceed. The target is Rastatt Railroad Bridge near Karlsruhe east of the Rhine River, Germany. This was the target on December 1st and 5th, sounds like it's still intact. The mission reports from the 1st and 5th indicated 8/10 cloud cover around the target; there was some breaking, but evidently not enough to get a good bead on the target for the lead bombardier. We took off at 1119 hours and returned at 1442 hours with our bombs... could not see the target. The clouds were thick and they only broke as we returned to Dijon.

> *Dec 10: Mission today, really bad cloud cover, real cold—No bombs dropped, returned with all of them—I hate landing heavy with a full bomb load—Returned to Red Cross hut after post mission brief for some hot coffee and donuts, burnt my lips on the cup it was so hot but it tasted Great!!—Played cards with some guys from operations at the Red Cross Scrub House canteen this evening, nice break to get into Dijon—Getting colder, more snow today*
>
> *Dec 12 & 13: Cancelled missions, weather, of course—Played cards at the canteen again—We have Italian POW's doing chores and KP, I guess they can be trusted, Making sure I have my pistol with me, don't trust these guys—More reading from Stars and Stripes, talk of an end to the war by Christmas, everything is too frozen to continue to fight!—Wrote letters to Mary, Ma & Pa, got two letters from Mary*

Another mission scheduled, December 14th target is the enemy defensive area near Otterbach, Germany. After our mission brief and arriving at our plane on the flight line, we did our preflight checks, and I entered through the waist openings squeezing my way in with my cumbersome winter flying suit. I did more checks inside and headed forward to sit between the pilots for engine start and takeoff. The same warnings of heavy flak and possible fighters seem to not have come true for the last two weeks. The 17th Bomb Group has had trouble with fighters intercepting them just before they hit their target… they lost three ships yesterday. We are rendezvousing with P-47's… ten of them for protection. Our plane is tail number "11"… never flew on this one. Engine starts and performance all look good as we prepare to taxi for takeoff

After takeoff we ascend through the clouds to form up, the view is limited and we have a 6/10-cloud cover… we can still see our wing and our lead plane, so far so good. This could be another fly through the clouds scare I had over northern Italy last month… that was scary… way too scary. Looking around from my perch in the turret, it is nothing but cloud cover, still 6/10 cloud cover. Our altitude is about 12,000 feet and we are on the IP. I heard over the intercom from the pilot, "Well boys… looks like we are not dropping our bombs, lead bombardier can't see anything and neither can anyone else."

"Strap in… we may run into some clouds with some turbulence."

"Roger, sir… can I head up front, I don't think I'll see any fighters with this cloud cover?"

"Yea… come on up," Lieutenant Domke said.

I squeezed out of my turret seat and made my way forward gently passing by the bomb bay and the radio compartment. I stopped between the pilots and plugged into the intercom connection by the co-pilot's eat

"Sir… generator function looks fine… I looked through the ship on the way up and everything looks good… except for the cold," I said with a bit of humor

Domke responded with a grin, "Thanks… gauges look good up here, have a seat and relax… grab some coffee from my thermos."

"Thanks, sir… sounds great," I said as I found a spare cup to fill with some hot coffee, "I see the cloud cover is the same, I'd say a 6/10."

"I agree," Domke responded, "I wish we could dump the bombs… landing with a full load is not fun."

"I know sir, it scares me too."

Flying along on our way back to Dijon we pass through clouds, we experience some slight turbulence of no concern, then over the intercom Lieutenant Domke hears "21" put out a distress call.

"Sounds like engine trouble, left engine out or running rough… can't hear through some static."

"How far are we from Dijon?" Domke asks Lieutenant Bobbitt.

"Sir… about twenty miles."

OK… can you see him?" Domke asks.

"No sir, I can't."

"OK… pilot to crew… watch out for a distressed B-26 tail number "21"… keep on eye out," Domke exclaimed to the rest of us.

Our radio operator, Sergeant Canzonetta moved to the nose of our plane to watch out. He noticed a plane descending with a smoking engine. Then he reported, "Sir… I see three chutes, they look like they opened OK… another one."

"Roger… anymore?" Domke asked as he and Bobbitt looked for the plane descending out of their view. Canzonetta had a great view of "21" and did not see anymore chutes, "Just four… nothing else."

"They're taking it in for a landing, just the pilot and co-pilot… they're heavy… hope they make it down OK," Domke exclaimed with concern in his voice, he knows from experience how dangerous a landing it is with one engine out and a heavy load in the bomb bay.

We landed safely and didn't see a wreckage as we taxied to our parking area… "21" must have landed OK. Turns out the pilot made a perfect landing and one for the books. Three of the crew landed in open fields, one landed on a farmhouse roof crashing through with both feet. Word is he got stuck halfway through the roof with his legs dangling through the ceiling. Lucky guy… good thing he landed in France and not Germany.

After our short interrogation brief I went over to the Red Cross hut for hot coffee and donuts. Everyone was gathering around for coffee and conversation and I met up with Gene and Ken who were on the mission today. We made plans for going into Dijon to see a movie this evening. The PX is getting setup and we are able to get personal items and candy bars for ourselves but also for the children we see in Dijon and Longecourt. I am storing some for our upcoming Christmas party that the orderly room personnel are planning in Longecourt.

"Anyone know what film is being shown at that movie theater?" Ken asked

Then someone listening in on our conversation blurted out, "The Fighting Seabees… John Wayne is going to war again."

We looked at each other and thought, "Well… its probably good, Susan Hayward is in it," Gene said with wide eyes.

Ken reacted with, "Yea, lets go… I'm in love with Susan Hayward."

"I'm heading back to the tent to get ready," I said and put my cup down on the counter and headed off, Gene and Ken followed. We got into town and had a good time watching the movie… the Pacific war scenes looked really warm… makes you want to ask for a transfer to the Pacific Theater

Dec 14: Mission a total bust had to return without dropping on target—Lots of clouds—Watched a B-26 in trouble, we thought it would crash land with bad engine and full load, crew jumped out and pilot & co-pilot land perfectly—Went into Dijon and watched a movie "Fighting Seabees" with John Wayne and Susan Hayward, good action but the warm scenes versus our cold weather motivates us to ask for a transfer to the Pacific

Dec 15: No mission today—MP's put Dijon Off Limits, trouble with civilian disturbances, rumor is that the mayor of the town (a Nazi collaborator during the occupation) was attacked and hanged and his body dragged through town by a group of angry civilians, Don't know when we can get back to Dijon, stay away from the mess—Townspeople are also seeking women who collaborated (slept with) with the Germans, they shave their heads in public humiliation Snow starting again, light and cold—Ed and I went out to get wood and other items to burn for our stove, we may have to cut down some trees, details being formed to take six-by-six trucks into the woods to cut down trees, French authorities have granted U.S. troops permission to cut down trees for firewood—Didn't know I would become a lumberjack in the Air Corps!

The days went by slowly and the cold was a constant feeling whether dressed warmly or not. Constant cloud cover with cold and light snow, not a lot of accumulation but it kept coming and was not melting. If you take the war out of the picture, the scene was looking like Christmas… a peaceful time but with the homesickness feeling of not being with loved ones during the holidays. Decorations in Dijon and those in different areas of Longecourt are popping up; the squadron and group offices have some makeshift decorations with trees and figurines of familiar Christmas symbols. I found a tree with a perfect top around the east side of the Chateau that would look good in our tent as a Christmas tree. Don't know why no one else noticed it… I got a saw from the orderly room tool box and cut off a small portion and also found a piece of wood to make a stand. It will look good in the open corner of our tent.

Gene, Ken and Ed were in their bunks sleeping or reading, too cold to do anything else and Dijon was still off limits as far as we knew. I opened the tent door flap and brought in our tree.

Ken looked up and said, "Hey… what do you know our own Christmas tree… thanks… now we need some decorations."

"Don't have decorations yet, maybe we can buy some at a shop in Dijon," I said, "I'm going over to the orderly room to see if Dijon is still off limits… I'll be right back."

"Gene… got anything for the tree?" Ken asked.

"No… let's get into town if we can, don't have anything here," he said, "I wasn't in Sardinia last Christmas."

"My fiancée said she would send some tree decorations… hope she mailed them in time."

As I headed over to the orderly room I saw the mail being unloaded in the orderly room… looks like a lot of boxes. Mary said in a previous letter that she and Ma would put together a Christmas package with

Greek Christmas cookies and other treats… hope they made it. I was getting excited to see if my package made it… it did and I found one for Gene and Ed and a few letters for Ken. I found out that Dijon is open for business, the off limits restrictions were just lifted by the MP's.

I made it back to our tent with my arms full of mail and yelled for someone to open the door flap, "Hey… open up… got packages… open up."

Ken opened the flap to let me in, "Hey… Christmas has arrived… what's here?"

"Package for Gene, Ed and me… a few letters for you."

"Is Ed still sleeping?"

"Yea… he's been sawing logs for hours," Gene said, "Hey… looks like I got the Christmas decorations and… looks like wrapped Christmas bulbs… hope they're not broken."

"Me too… my Mother made some of her Greek cookies, they're packed pretty good… hope the taste is still intact," I said ripping through the paper wrapping to get my first taste of Ma's cookies… they are really good with coffee… dunk and eat… dunk and eat.

Finally unwrapping to get at my cookies… looks like several dozen, "Oh yea… let's have a taste," I grabbed a cookie and eagerly put it to my mouth to take a bit, "Umm… still fresh… wow, this tastes so good I can't stand it."

"Hey, how about sharing… its Christmas time… huh?" Ken said, he had tasted my Mothers cooking before and had these cookies.

"OK… OK… grab one… I'm going to ration you so they last a long time."

Gene had a few presents and some decorations but no cookies… I was the cookie man and would have to ration my find. They were tasty and I had to take another… I'm going to find some hot coffee for dunking.

"Ed is still sleeping, we need to wake his ass up," Ken said contemplating waking him.

"Just let him sleep… I'll give him a treat when he gets up."

Mail call is the best part of any day when it happens… today was special… it felt real good.

December 16th, a day that crushed the hope of the war ending soon… initial word was that the Germans attacked in force through the Ardennes Forest in Belgium. That location is about two hundred and fifty miles from us… it's nerving to know that the enemy has regrouped and may overwhelm our forces. Who is to say that they could cross the Rhine less than a hundred miles from here? I could be an infantryman by the end of the week.

The German advance and the continuing weather problems that prevent us from getting off the ground is nerving. Not having the ability to get off the ground as well as find our targets in heavy cloud cover frustrates the group operations staff. It is frustrating to us not being able to support our ground troops in fighting back the Germans. There are plenty of rumors of bugging out and fighting as infantry. The Allied air force units north in France and those still in England will concentrate on the Ardennes, if they can get up with this horrible weather. We need to concentrate on the region of Alsace Lorraine and eastward into Germany. There are plenty of marshalling yards and defensive areas we could go after.

Dec 17: Mission scheduled, defensive area at Otterbach, Germany, took off at 1130 hours, landed 1505 hours, long mission and COLD!—Flak at the target and as we broke to the west, no damage—Big clouds at high altitude but CAVU at the target—P-47's escorted us, no German fighters but Intel says they'll be back, Intel says they are running out of gas and the Germans tow their planes to the end of a runway to save fuel, Desperate!!—Axis Sally plays some good Christmas songs, makes us homesick—She said our end is near, referring to the Battle in the Ardennes and the wonderful and powerful German forces

My cookies from home are under lock and key, I do share and they are just great, Thanks Ma & Mary, Dolly and Matina probably helped—Our Christmas tree looks great, we all have been stocking up on PX stuff for a planned Christmas party for the French kids from the surrounding villages

Dec 18: Cancelled mission for me—Weather has us socked in, the battle rages up north and we are hearing that German tanks are heading towards the Rhine River northeast not too far from us— Squadron briefing today, **Be Ready to Move "You Might Be An Infantryman Very Soon"**—*Pray for weather break to help!!*

Gene and I went over to the squadron operations office to check the bulletin board for missions. All of us are on for tomorrow, the 19th looks like a big push with all four squadrons on the mission. Someone is optimistic on getting through the bad weather or the weatherman is wishing the weather to clear. As we were going over to the Red Cross hut for coffee, the personnel clerk stopped us.

"Sergeant Fulk… hold up," he shouted, he had a piece of paper in his hand

"Sergeant… I've got orders for you."

"What?" Gene was surprised wondering if he had more medals or… maybe a rotation order?

Looking at the paper the personnel corporal handed to him he looked up at me with wide eyes of surprise, "I'm going home… tomorrow is my last mission… number 66… I'm going home." The look on his face could brighten the room, he had the biggest grin and he was ecstatic

"Congratulations," I said happy for him, "When do you get out of here?"

Gene looking at the order says, "It looks like the first of January… I've got to process out and try and get to a repo center for shipment back to the U.S., with what's going on up north I'm worried that these might get cancelled."

The personnel corporal said, "Sergeant, for now these stand… that's not to say they could not change, but plan on getting home in a few weeks."

Gene said, "No argument here… thanks."

We headed back to the tent to pass on the news… Gene felt really good, sort of unbelievable. I would miss him… he has been a good friend and mentor, happy for him but sad to say goodbye soon.

We were notified that there would be an early briefing at 0900 hours for the mission tomorrow, which is going to be the time from now on for all the missions unless notified otherwise. In order to give a good window of preparation we may be getting up at 0400 or 0300 hours to get our gear, chow and any preflight checks done in this cold. We take off at 1300 hours; I suspect there is more news on the battle going on north of us. Rumors are plenty on moving out because of German tanks spotted across the Rhine near Hagenau, France not far from the river and the German border

Early wake up… Gene is not happy, but it is his last mission before going home. Getting dressed and cleaned up, we are all quiet in the tent and the general tone around the squadron is that of worry and what's next. Chow is good, not much talking, definitely concern over the German advances. After chow we all head over to the group briefing room.

There is little chatter and an eerie quiet and then the shout of "Ten Hut" as the group commander Col Woolridge enters the room as we stand at attention, "At ease… take your seats."

"Gentlemen… lots going on, rumors are everywhere some are true some are false… we are going to give you the latest and then give the mission brief."

"Major Evans will give you the Intel and mission brief… any questions for me this morning?"

No one raises a hand, no questions.

Looking over to the major, "Major… its all yours… good luck today men, you are the best."

Major Evans comes to the front of the room and looking down at his clipboard he begins with the Intel brief and what's going on, "As you all know the Germans crossed through the Ardennes Forest in Belgium pushing our forces back, U.S. forces were giving ground and retreating."

"To give our guys some slack, the German advance was quick and overwhelming with lots of armor pushing through our positions… it's obvious we were surprised."

"The U.S. 7th Armored Division was able to halt the 6th Panzer Army near Saint Vith, but they may not be able to hold… the U.S. 2nd and 99th Infantry Divisions are holding near the Elsborn Ridge near the north side of the bulge."

"We are trying to confirm rumors of German Panzers that may be heading towards Hagenau and Strasbourg; they will need to cross the Rhine first."

"That advance is of great concern for us… we may need to evacuate," he continues noticing a tone of shock among us, "We will get our planes out of here with a pilot and co-pilot, destroy the ones that can't fly… and yes, the rest of us will fight as infantry until relieved."

You could hear a pin drop after that news; we looked at each other with the "Oh Shit" look on our faces. The major continued.

"Look… if you haven't figured this out, this is serious… some good news," he said with a sigh, "The powers that be are moving the 82nd Airborne and the 10th Airborne into the main bulge area… Patton is probably going to turn his Third Army 90 degrees to the north and counter the German advance."

"The Seventh and Third Armies are regrouping and preparing to defend the Alsace Lorraine region close to us… be ready to move out if the evacuation order comes down."

"The French First Army is also on the move to fight along side the Seventh and Third Armies."

I think we have had enough bad news, Major Evans switches to the mission brief, "Time to move on to what we can do… our mission today is to bomb the shit out of the Neustadt Marshalling Yards… you know what that is, supplies, troops, tanks, rail cars, trucks, and the like."

"Weather is of concern, but the weather man says it will break enough for us to hit the target."

Sergeant Evans uncovers the mission maps and timetables for the major, pointing to the map, "The mission path to target is base to Nancy… to Mannerheim… to Hagenau… to Annweiler… to target."

"After the drop turn left to Saverne… to base."

"Depending on flak… take evasive action for altitude… flight leads pay attention and coordinate, let's discuss the details after crew dismissal."

"Take off for lead ship is 1300 hours… 30 second intervals thereafter… stay on time."

"Follow standard procedures for take off and execute right turn at 1,000 feet and then ascend to 4,000 feet to form up in attack formations." Major Evans continues with detail navigation for the flight lead, flight commander and pilots. The rest of us are dismissed to get ready for the mission

I am flying with Lieutenant Wetzel today; Jerry Raschke is our waist gunner. He was the guy that had the bomb bay episode where he was able to push out hung bombs. I haven't heard whether he ever got that DFC approved.

"Jerry… we're on today on tail number "22"," I said to Jerry as we approached the six-by-six truck, throwing our gear in waiting for the rest of the crews and driver

"Hey… good to see you… I think this is the first time we are on the same plane."

"I think you're right… hear anything on that DFC?" I asked. "No… I think it got lost in the paper pile… not worried about it, it would be a nice award," he sighed, "Time to get on with it… heard any more about the weather today?"

"Cloudy as usual… I guess, just as long as the fighters can't see us and we can see the target."

We stepped up on the footstep loop on the backside of the six-by-six truck bumper and sat down on the cold bench waiting for the truck to fill up. The road to the airfield is a little icy and we can feel the slipping and fishtailing… the driver must have been a professional racecar driver. It's freezing out and it will be minus 40 degrees or so at altitude. Someone stole my original set of gloves last month and I used a lesser-insulated pair on a few missions; I borrowed Gene's or Ken's when I could. I was able to get a newer pair of gloves yesterday from supply. My fingers sometimes hurt; the flight surgeon said it was frostnip, nothing to be too concerned about… keep those gloves on.

Cloudy skies as usual, the driver stops and yells out, "Tail number "22" get out," he shouted.

The whole crew was heading out the back of the truck, sometimes the driver gets impatient and starts to roll away without us all getting out. Lieutenant's Wetzel and O'Brien are already at the plane, Sergeants Stone, Witten, Raschke, Reavis, and I get out of the truck as fast as we could. Reavis is our photographer today. Jerry has taken some photos on previous missions but not me.

The ground crew has been prompt on getting snow accumulation off the plane and clearing a path for the landing gear to get out of the parking spot for taxi. We start our preflight and start engine checks. The heaters are doing OK; I feel a little warmth from the vents. Engines fired up, all gauges and generators are functioning within parameters, "22" sounds real good so far. We took off at 1314 hours ascending up to the formation, the clouds are 6/10 to 8/10 coverage and we head to our first navigation point to the target… Nancy.

Wetzel, the pilot, hears a message from the flight lead and then tells us, "Pilot to crew… we are going to alter our flight path… we need to go around some storms," he continues, "As you look forward… there are some real nasty looking clouds and we will not be going to our first point, Nancy."

"I'll be responding to the flight lead for course changes… keep a sharp eye."

"Sir, I'm heading to my turret," I said and turned around heading back to my gun turret, I have a good view of the clouds and I can look out for our wingman and any planes in formation fore and aft.

"Roger… stay sharp."

We are flying around some distinctive cloud formations that are beautiful and perfect pictures of huge cumulus formations. After a little over an hour I lost track of the number of turns we made but we finally started the IP for our bomb run. The cloud cover is 7/10, there is ground haze and over the intercom I hear Lieutenant Wetzel talking about the identification of the target in this cloud cover. The lead bombardier is having some problems, we're on the IP and it sounds like we can see the target. All I can see are huge cloud formations.

Heard over the intercom the shout out of "bomb bay doors open" and then a few moments later the "bombs away" shout from Stone. The lead bombardier must have spotted a hole in the clouds and ID'd the target, Reavis our photographer is shooting his camera out the waist gun openings to get a good view of the bombs hitting the target. He was swearing at each click frustrated with not getting the shot in time as we passed over a cloud cover opening to see the target hits. I think he might have taken a few good ones... the ones he wasn't cussing over. No flak as we broke away from the target and headed back to base.

The clouds seemed to be getting closer and thicker as we moved away from the target area. It looked like, to me, that the weather was closing in behind us... not good. Then within a few minutes Wetzel came over the intercom, "Pilot to crew... flight lead says we are going straight through the clouds... buckle up it might get bumpy... keep an eye out for our wing and other planes in our formation."

"Acknowledge?"

"Get your flak helmets on... hang on."

We all responded, "Roger."

The instant we all acknowledged we hit our first bump; we must have dropped 500 feet and back up again within a few seconds; it happened fast and we all bumped hard inside. I saw Jerry floating below me and then slamming on the floor just forward of the waist windows. We were separated according to our standard operating procedures in the formation and could see our wingmen; we had to stay intact as a formation to fly through the cloud. This was as scary as the cloud flying during a mission over Italy, no bumps but we were blind to the other planes in the formation. At least we could see a little better to avoid collision; we had 36 B-26's in this formation. The bumps seemed endless and were hard, Jerry looked like he had been beaten up hanging on to his helmet and trying to stow his parachute pack that was floating around him. I got knocked around in the turret, I thought I would punch through the top of the Plexiglas the bumps were so hard and fast. "Pilot to crew... I know its bumpy... hang on we should be out of this soon."

Just as he told us to hang on, another hard bump, "Damn… that was the worst," Jerry shouted as he slammed to the roof and then the floor barely missing the guns that were mounted at the waist window. Reavis hung on to his camera as he bounced around near the bomb bay… I could hear all of us cussing over the intercom. Then it seemed to smooth out and the bumps were not as bad then, "Starting descent and landing at Dijon… keep your helmets on for landing," Wetzel exclaimed, he sounded nervous, and it must have been hard handling the bumps and changes in altitude up and down. Then I heard him tell Lieutenant O'Brien to adjust flaps and then landing gear down… can't wait to get on the ground.

After we landed and taxied to our parking spot I pulled my helmet off and slipped out of the waist windows with my gear. I brushed away the snow from the hard ground and kissed the earth thankful to have made it back in one-piece… turbulence was the worst I have ever experienced.

> *Dec 19: Cold today for the mission took off at 1314, landed 1629 hours—We hit the target despite the cloud cover, small break in the clouds opened over the target area—ABSOLUTELY THE WORST URBULENCE COMING BACK FROM THE TARGET!!—Our gunner Jerry Raschke got bounced around real bad, we all had our flak helmets on to protect us, and we could have gotten some bad knocks on our heads—Need that whiskey shot to settle down—What a send-off for Gene on his last mission!*

Then the usual gathering of crews around the Red Cross counter after this crazy ride, lots of hot coffee and donuts… no whiskey. Jerry and I head straight to the smell of the Red Cross coffee, Gene is already there and he looked happy but white as a ghost.

"Wow… what a send off… I have never been bounced around like that on any of my 65 previous missions," he said as he started to calm down, "I hope I don't get a ride home like that one… that was scary."

"Well… we all made it, so count your blessings," Jerry said as we tipped our cups of hot coffee on nervous lips… our donuts tasted like high-priced pastries from a French bakery.

Dec 20 & 21: Cold-Cold-Cold, can't seem to keep the tent warm even with the stove burning constantly—Gene is getting ready to rotate back to the states, no more missions for him, to date I have 40—Word is, no more rotations, we are here for the duration—Battle of the "Bulge" still raging, we got word that a German Panzer unit broke through Allied defenses near Hagenau, NOT GOOD, we may have to evacuate—Wrote home to Mary—I still have some cookies left, I ration them and dunk them in my coffee at the Red Cross—I may be fighting in the infantry by Christmas—Everything around has the Christmas atmosphere, it is dulled by the "Bulge" news, don't know how you can fight on the ground with this cold, French say this is the worst winter in recent memory, maybe the last 100 years

CHAPTER 7

BATTLE OF THE BULGE

Gen. William Tecumseh Sherman:
"War is hell."

Prime Minister Sir Winston Churchill:
"If you are going through hell, keep going."

Intel message to the 320th Bomb Group for December 23, U.S. and Allied forces situation known at this time:

> German forces captured 9,000 U.S. troops in the Schnee Eifel region on the Belgian-German border.
>
> The U.S. 101st Airborne and the 10th Armored Division of the Third U.S. Army have been directed into the vital road junction in Bastogne, Belgium to prevent enemy forces from gaining a major road system to continue their attack.
>
> Armor elements of the German 6th SS Panzers have captured the U.S. fuel depot at Stavelot, Belgium.
>
> German Panzerbreakthrough at Hagenau, France, heavy fighting reported.
>
> Allied Headquarters recommends evacuation of key airfields in the path of potential German unimpeded advances.

Colonel Woolridge, the 320th Bomb Group commander is dismayed by higher headquarters directive and orders the operations staff to issue movement orders for evacuation to an airfield west of Dijon, a field location not yet determined. His order includes the destruction of B-26's that are beyond repair and cannot fly, the issue of rifles, ammunition and infantry gear in anticipation of fighting with other Allied ground forces. A pilot and co-pilot only will relocate flyable B-26's; all other personnel will assume combat infantry and support roles to deter German forces. Just as soon as this was ordered, higher headquarters rescinded, there is grave concern that the French will be shocked and overwhelmed. The war effort cannot afford such an emotional setback after having gained so much; German forces will be defeated and pushed back. Fight in place; plan missions as the weather permits and as directed by the 42nd Wing.

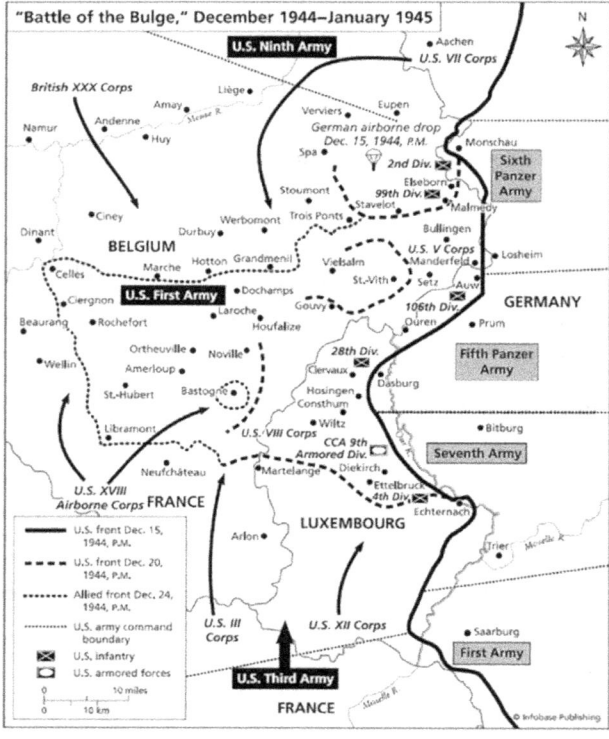

Battle of the Bulge Situation Map

"I can't believe I'm hearing this… evacuate, now stay in place," Gene said as he was scratching his head as we heard about the evacuation order and the almost immediate rescinding of that order.

"Am I going to get home or what?"

"I'm just glad that I don't have to fight as an infantry dogface in this cold weather," I said as I put more wood into our tent stove.

"There has to be some good news… some sort of break as we regroup."

"The 10ᵗ with the 101ˢᵗ Armored will be busy trying to push back and stop the advance," I said with some hopefulness, "We have got to get up in the air to hit targets… that's the key to get this moving."

"I can't imagine what the dogfaces on the ground have been going through."

"Do the infantry guys call themselves 'dogfaces'?" Gene asked to interject some humor.

"Who knows… they probably do," I responded with a grin.

"They spend so much time in foxholes and crawling around their faces start looking like dogs."

"Did you all check the board?" Ken asked us as he stepped in the tent interrupting our moment of dogface humor, "Not you Gene, of course."

"No," I said.

Ed shook his head no

"What's up?" Ed asked.

"Mission tomorrow… big push on a bridge over the Rhine," Ken explained.

"The French hit that target last week with their B-26's… it was heavily defended with accurate and heavy flak… they lost four planes." We looked at each other and wondered what was going to happen… Gene must have been relieved, but he looked like he wanted to be a part of the effort

"We do what we need to do," Ed said with some confidence, at least we won't be fighting on the ground as infantry, affectionately referred to as dogfaces.

Dec 22: Cold, snow and clouds, not a lot of flying—Germans getting aggressive, we got the order to evacuate and then no, stay

> *in place—Mission on for tomorrow, vital bridge in Germany, the French B-26's hit it last week and lost four planes, Lots of Flak!—Gene is processing out and he will sleep in tomorrow, Lucky guy I'm going to miss him—Christmas party for the Longecourt kids after mission tomorrow, I saved up my candy bars for presents*

There was a worried mood but also a mood of wanting to get up and hit German targets to stop their efforts. The tent is nice and warm, better get some rest; we are going to get a wake up call at 0300 hours.

Sleeping snuggly and warm 0300 hours came too soon, then the door opens and Sergeant Buijak enters giving us the wake up call, "Geronimos, Dixon, and Bentas… get up, mission brief at 0900."

Ken grabbed his boot and flung it at Buijak, "Get out, we're up… close the door you're letting in the cold."

Buijak dodges the boot; he gets one thrown at him from time to time. Ken must be in a bad mood, "Damn… I was so comfortable… Susan Hayward wanted to marry me and then Buijak wakes me up," he said as he got up to get dressed.

"Was I going to be the best man?" I said to humor him.

"Yea… why not, we were on a Pacific Island and John Wayne got turned down," Ken joked.

"I told her I was not in the Seabees, and she could come back home with me."

"OK… get dressed… get out and get married," Gene said as he rolled over and went back to sleep.

Standing in line at the chow hall, Ken, Ed and I run into some other crew we will be flying with today. All of us are getting used to mingling with other crew on assignments, flying together with the same guys is rare. This has given me the opportunity to meet others in the squadron… some of them are dead or missing. Jerry is on our crew with me today in tail number "07", he is the waist gunner and radio operator today.

"Hey… look at the serving line… SOS," I was excited.

"Haven't seen SOS in a long time… my favorite."

My comments drew some odd looks, I must be the only guy in the ETO that likes it… it better be good.

More conversation at the table about the bulge; we are hearing the name reference "Battle of the Bulge" more often. The conversation also steers to the weather and the 8/10-cloud cover and snow. Talk is that Patton wants the 320th to cover his ass... OK, if we can get off the ground. After chow we head over to the group briefing room, the 441st and 444th Squadrons are on for today, 36 aircraft plus two spares in the air. The SOS was very good.

Major Evans enters the room and we hear the call, "Ten Hut."

"Take your seats... at ease," Evans says and then looks down at his clipboard and then up, "Target today is the Railroad Bridge at Briesach... you may or may not have heard this but French B-26's hit this target a week ago and lost four ships."

"Flak is expected to be heavy... sergeant pull the cover off the maps and timetable charts, please... thanks." Sergeant Buijak takes the covers off the two charts and Major Evans continues, "We need to improve our odds and not let the German flak gunners shoot us full of holes... there will be a six-ship decoy flight ahead of the main force on the mission for today."

"The decoy flight will pull away from the formation just as the IP is reached... as it pulls away, it will drop chaff to confuse enemy gun radar."

"After dropping the chaff... the decoy flight will attack the flak gun positions... it will be a short bomb run with air-burst fragmentation bombs," he points to the positions the decoy flight will take and the known and suspected flak gun positions.

Major Evans continues on with briefing the pilots and navigators. The rest of us are dismissed to get our gear and move out to the flight line to perform our preflight checks. I hope the ground crews have the snow cleared and are finished with their maintenance and loading.

Engine start up is tough this morning; real cold and I don't think the ground crew did any run-up for our engines. This is going to take time and it's a good thing we headed out early, scheduled takeoff is 1230 hours. Lieutenant Lazo, the pilot is pissed, "Damn it... let's get this done... the last thing I want is a late takeoff because of one plane... ours."

We get moving and work together to get our checks done; Jerry was a flight engineer on a few previous missions so he was helpful with the functional checks. Finally, we get to the point of taxiing out for takeoff. We took off at 1239 hours... lifted off at 140 mph into the cloud cover ascending to 1,000 feet before we turn right ninety degrees heading toward our formation rally point.

After getting up to our formation, I head back to my gun turret; we are still expecting fighters... who knows if the Germans can coordinate an attack in this weather. Intel has the Abbeville Boys looking for a fight... they have to be planning an all-out effort in conjunction with the Battle of the Bulge. We have the "pucker factor" as we approached the target; this was going to be a tough one... couldn't get the French loss of four ships out of our heads. I will be able to see the decoy flight turn off the IP, the clouds are scattered at 5,000 feet and the ground has an eerie haze with limited visibility.

We have an officer for our bombardier today, Lieutenant Emmons, haven't flown with him before; I think he's new to the squadron since last month. As we approach the IP, Lazo announces over the intercom, "Approaching the IP, Emmons stay sharp... the rest of you watch out for fighters."

I could see the decoy flight ahead from my turret, and then I heard over the intercom from Emmons just as I noticed, "Decoys just peeled off to the right," he said, "We're getting close to the target."

"Roger... we see them, they're dropping chaff... look," Lazo exclaimed

Just as I turned to our 3 o'clock, I started to see small black puffs of smoke... flak, "Flak... its getting heavy for the decoy flight," I shouted over the intercom

Then flak was being directed at us as Emmons shouted, "Bomb bay doors opening... waiting for lead."

Lazo was evading flak by going up and down... not far, maybe 200 feet up then down. We had to stay straight for the bomb run. These gunners are on our path and they're good, you can see rounds of four blasts all around us and real close to our planes... they've got us zeroed in

I was turning toward the decoy flight location to see if they were still getting flak and wanted to see if they were dropping their frags on the gun positions. As soon as I turned toward the decoy flight I noticed a blast

"One of the decoy ships just got hit… its breaking up… they took the rear end off and a wing flew off," I was shocked as I watched what was happening in slow motion a large explosion with a red color in the center with thick black smoke. I don't know which tail number it was, "One chute… that's it… one chute… damn," I shouted, "Jerry, can you see any more?"

"I see one… just one," Jerry said and then he noticed, "His chute won't open all the way… he's too close to the ground." I looked down at Jerry, he had a blank stare on his face, and we didn't know whose plane was hit. I couldn't stop looking towards the area where they were hit… who got it?

The formation continued on the IP approaching the drop point. "Bombs away," Emmons shouted, you could feel the plane shudder from the weight of the bombs releasing and exiting the bay.

Lazo follows the lead and takes us into an evasive sharp left diving turn; you could feel the plane accelerating… it must be reaching 300 mph. Then, WHOOM, a fiery red burst explosion right in front of us; we flew through it in a flash, must have been an 88-millimeter shell. You could hear shrapnel clang over the surface of our plane; one piece cracked the Plexiglas on my gun turret and another one hit the pilot's window. I saw a piece hit the tail and rip the skin.

"Whoa… that was close," Lazo and Emmons shouted in unison. You know it is close when you can see the red color in the middle of the explosion. Emmons saw this while he was in the nose of the plane, he must have crapped his pants.

"Wow… that was a close son of a bitch… did you guys see that?" Emmons was almost laughing at the excitement of the moment… we almost bought the farm. It happened so fast we didn't have time to be scared… that was too close for comfort.

We made it back to Dijon safely and landed at 1517 hours, after post flight checks we went to our debriefing and found out which plane was lost. Out of 36 planes, 19 had damage and one lost. The one that caught the direct flak hit was tail number "08", "My Gal" the plane was on its 14th mission. I saw a direct hit amidships blowing the plane in half; I also saw the left wing break off after the hit. I reported seeing one chute, Jerry verified and said it didn't have time to open or it couldn't open. Jerry lost two close friends on that ship, we all lost friends… it brings back Jeff's death again.

Returning to Dijon over Heavy Cloud Cover

I was walking back to my tent; I stopped and looked around the area. The snow on the ground, cloudy skies, the fog of my exhaled breath in the air, it's dreary and cold… who's next? Can I change my mood to enjoy the kids at this Christmas party? They must feel so blessed to have been liberated and have the chance to celebrate… they have so much to be thankful for. The ship that was blasted out of the sky today… I could sit down and cry. Then I remember something one of the old-timers told me when I arrived in Sardinia… you have to accept that you are already dead. Well… that doesn't get rid of the pain when my friends get killed. It hasn't removed the fear, well, maybe some.

Opening the door to my tent I noticed the Christmas tree and got homesick not being able to see my family and my wife… how do I get over the empty feeling? Seize the day, enjoy the kids and the joy we will bring them today… they have had it much worse than we would ever know. Gene was sitting on the edge of his bunk packing some personal items in a duffle bag, too bad he won't be home for Christmas but he'll be home early next month.

"Hey Nick… how was the mission?"

I walked slowly to my bunk with a blank stare, looking down at the floor, "Well… "08" got hit by flak and went down… no survivors." I said sadly.

Looking shocked Gene wondered who was on the ship, "Who got it?"

"Dickey, Kuentz, Standicki, Dickens, Tipton, Lofton, Conant," I said

Gene stopped and put his hands over his face, he knew them all, "Damn," I could see him starting to cry and then he continued packing.

"Jerry lost two of his tent mates."

I sat down on my bunk and continued staring at the floor, then I put my mind in another direction, "I've got to get ready for the Christmas party… are you coming?"

"Yea… got to see some happy-faced kids today… it'll help," Gene's eyes were red… we all know how hard it is to hear about lost friends.

"Thanks… I'll walk over with you."

"Where are Ken and Ed?"

"I think they are still at their debrief, they said they would be coming to the party," I said, then they both walked in, "Guys… we're heading over so we'll see you there."

"OK," they both said, they were just as sad as Gene and me.

Arriving at the group headquarters building that was decorated with Christmas trees, wreaths and some candy canes and tinsel someone was able to get from home. The kids from the village of Longecourt were all over the place; small children and babies with their parents up to the teenagers attended. They had ragged clothes, but that didn't matter. Smiles everywhere… it cheered us up beyond our expectations. We had candy bars, simple toy gifts, fruit that the mess hall provided and a Santa… didn't recognize who the Santa was, and he was good. These kids would raid our garbage cans for scraps or they would ask for left over's; we did what we could to help them. They were haggard when we arrived, the Germans did not treat them well.

> *Dec 23: Lost some close shipmates, a veteran ship "08" took a direct hit over target with all lost, very sad, hard to stomach—Had to change my mindset to go to the kids Christmas party, wow they were so elated it really cheered me up as well as the rest of us—Jerry even looked happy, he lost two tent mates and good friends, he and I watched as it got hit and broke apart, one chute that didn't fully open*

> *Dec 24: Christmas Eve arrived, no mission for me, weather getting bad again, some may get off the ground—No present under our tent tree, I still have some of Ma's cookies—Mission for the 24th was a tough one with heavy flak, lots of damage, some crew wounded slightly, could have been worse—I always go to the Red Cross for coffee and donuts even when I'm not flying to chat with the returning crews—I gave away all my candy to the kids, they have not had a good Christmas since 1940, four years—I could use a good Hershey bar right now, heading over to chow and then the PX*

I finished writing in my journal; I grabbed Ken, Ed and Gene to get dinner chow. The road by the chow hall is a slushy wet glob of mud; it's like a slimy greasy layer over the road, hard to walk on without slipping and falling on your ass. Jerry was walking with us as we tried hard to stop from slipping on the road across from the chow hall. We noticed a six-by-six truck coming our way, Jerry's friend from basic training, Jim Thompson, was walking turning the corner across the street from us.

"Hey… Jim… save us a place in line," Jerry shouted and waved. Thompson stopped and turned his head, waved and nodded, "OK."

Just then an approaching six-by-six truck was trying to slow down and turn in front of us. You could see that the driver was not getting traction trying to stop; he was sliding right towards the corner of the building. The truck hit the building with a dull clunk; it looked like it slid sideways right into Thompson.

We were motionless… what the hell just happened right in front of us? Then we started to run across the muddy and slippery street, we made it across without falling on our ass. I could see a pair of legs sticking out from the rear tires, they were not moving. The driver, an MP, came around and looked down… he couldn't contain himself and began to cry.

We all stood there in shock and couldn't move or think of what to do then, "What in the hell is going on… what happened?" Captain O'Mahony shouted as he arrived on the scene. Someone ran over to the squadron office nearby and alerted him.

Then someone in the crowd said, "Sir, the truck skidded on the slush coming around the corner… Sergeant Thompson is under the truck."

Captain O'Mahony knelt down in the mud to take a look and noticed Sergeant Thompson's legs under the tires and his body firmly pressed against the building wall. It was obvious that any movement of the truck forward or backward would run over Thompson… the truck had to be moved sideways away from the building. Everyone was in shock… it was unbelievable and didn't seem real. How could this have happened?

Captain O'Mahony noticed no one was taking charge, then he took charge, "OK… everyone… get a hold of the truck and let's push it away from the building," he said as he motioned everyone to grab a section of the truck, "OK… push… push… push."

After strenuous grunting and pushing, the truck slowly slid sideways away from the building moving out about four feet away exposing the lifeless body of Sergeant Thompson. He was lying on his side; O'Mahony lifted him up a little and put him on his back. His skin was a grey color; there was a small hole right about in the center of his forehead… no pulse. His eyes were wide open with a shocked but lifeless look. O'Mahony looked back at the truck side, he noticed a protruding bolt that must have hit Thompson straight into the center of his forehead.

Don't remember who put him on the stretcher that arrived from the clinic… an ambulance was on its way. The MP that was driving couldn't stop crying, he just went back to the driver's cab of the truck and put his head down over the wheel. Thompson was on the mission yesterday, his plane was shot up bad from flak and now this... killed while heading for chow. Jerry couldn't contain himself and left to go back to his tent. Gene, Ken, Ed and I are still in shock. Chow will have to wait; I don't have the stomach to eat. I don't drink much but was able to get a hold of some good ole Johnny Walker... Gene, Ken and Ed joined in. We heard Christmas carols being sung at the officer's mess... everyone had the same idea. I just drank and stared at the tent ceiling thinking about home.

> *Dec 24: A senseless death this evening, Sgt Thompson waiting to go to the enlisted mess hall building was hit by a truck, he was killed instantly—Shocked, couldn't eat, Jerry R. was a close friend of Thompson—Great guy, ironically he had been on a rough mission and then this?—I still can't believe this, it didn't seem real as it happened right in front of us—I'm writing this before I get drunk and enjoy the company of my friends*

The latest Battle of the Bulge news received at 320th Bomb Group Headquarters on December 25:

U.S. forces capture Stavelot, Belgium.

German forces surround Bastogne and captured Saint Vith.

German forces send a surrender demand to General McAuliffe at Bastogne; the general responded "Nuts".

U.S. Third Army shifted axis of attack and heading toward Bastogne to relieve besieged U.S. forces.

Reading the battle news was about half good and half bad, we can't get up in this weather to support Patton's advance. Knowing the general he will push forward regardless... tough Son of a Bitch.

Dec 25: Merry Christmas, wish I were home… definitely homesick this day, I re-read letters from home and looked at pictures from home—Got a really bad headache, WOW head is throbbing— Gene is getting anxious not being able to leave for home till after Christmas, weather bad and the "Battle of the Bulge" could swing bad or good, Patton on the move, Go Get Um George!!—I still have some cookies left and they still taste GREAT!—Mess hall had turkey and all the trimmings, really nice!—Dijon had some good Christmas atmosphere; we spent the afternoon in town, the cold air must have been good for my headache—Dijon is a nice city

Heard from the guys on mission today that a flight of 9 B-26's made a huge mistake and bombed a place called Gettmadingen, Switzerland… an accidental drop by 444th *planes/crews—Big No-No, No word on bomb damage yet or if anyone was killed on the ground—Gen. Ike and the Big Brass will get involved for sure!*

Dec 26; Heard a rumor about Gen. Patton… his forces have relieved Bastogne, I hope so—Cold and getting colder, more snow, missions getting up and returning with no drop on target—Weather breaks show up and disappear quickly—Wood getting scarce and the locals are getting pissed at us for depleting wood supplies—Ken and Ed were on mission today, good hits came back with some flak damage—Mess sergeant got some eggs for breakfast, he must have watered them down, taste was OK I guess, trying to remember what they tasted like—SOS hasn't been on the menu lately, miss that meal

Dec 27; Too much overcast for missions, Gene, Ken, Ed and I went into Dijon to a movie, "Lifeboat" a Alfred Hitchcock film, it was OK, another good reason to not have joined the Navy—Went to GI Joe's Rendezvous for some entertainment and food, nice to get away—Wrote letters home to Mary, miss her so much!!—MP's said to be careful in town, Germans dressed as G.I.'s may try to get information from you or take you out, steal your uniforms and infiltrate the bomb group and squadron, they speak English like Americans, **Ask Them To Name Baseball and Sports facts**

More cold and snow continue to plague the operations planners to get missions scheduled. We are on alert to get out to our planes and take off in hopes of seeing a target through the overcast. There is a mix of good and bad news for the Battle of the Bulge… the bomb group posts updates on the bulletin as we receive them. The overall good news is that U.S. forces are gaining ground in the counteroffensive… the bad news is that the Germans are still trying to gain an upper hand. If the weather breaks we will have a field day… word is that the German Luftwaffe is not as strong as we would believe. They are running out of fuel and the Intel on them towing their planes to the end of the runway to save gas is true… according to the Intel guys.

Even though we were in a combat theater, life seemed to go on and the Christmas season was a mix of cheer, loneliness and fear. I lost close friends, made new ones… Gene was getting ready to leave for home soon. What's next? Better weather, I hope, and an end to the war. I am sitting on my bunk looking at an elaborate card made by the bomb group administrative staff, a nice Christmas card with pictures of the Chateau's in Longecourt and in the nearby villages where the rest of the squadrons are located. I'll send this one home for the scrapbook.

Dec 28 & 29: So cold, we go into Dijon to the "Scrub House" and "G.I. Joe's" for warmth and entertainment both days—I'm not on alert for a moment's notice mission—Dec 30 mission scheduled and I'm on with Jerry R. again

Gene getting anxious waiting to leave, looks like he'll be on a truck ride to Paris to work his way back to the U.S. on the 3rd or 4th of January—Wow, 1945 in a few days, I am just over two years in the service, seems like forever

Wrote letters home and to Mary, got two letters and a Christmas card with family pictures—Got the stove nice and cozy, right time to slip into my sleeping bag for a good nights sleep, early wake up for the mission tomorrow—I promised Buijak I wouldn't throw any boots at him for the early wake ups

Intel message to the 320th Bomb Group for December 29, U.S. and Allied forces situation

U.S. forces are gaining ground in the Ardennes region of Belgium.

Hitler reportedly ordered renewed offensive action in the Alsace and Ardennes regions against his general's advice.

General Patton's Third Army relieves besieged U.S. forces in Bastogne, Belgium.

December 30th's mission is a late morning take off; we were woken up at 0300 hours to get ready. The weather is a never-ending pain in the ass to the aircrew and ground maintenance crews. Our target for this morning is the Kaiserslautern Barracks and Supply Area; Jerry is on my plane today as the tail gunner. We are on tail number "10" with Captain Asher as the pilot, McCurdy as co-pilot, Rahl in the radio operator and waist gunner, Biddle the bombardier. Cold as hell but the sky is clearer than it has been for the past month, a break means we can get up to support getting the Germans pushed back. Our take off time is 1144 hours; we follow the standard operating procedures and head up to 1,000 feet before we turn right to form up at about 5,000 feet. There are 40 B-26's on this mission, Goering's Abbeyville Boys are still a force to be reckoned with and flak gets heavier as we head over German territory for all our missions.

I have a great view as we gain altitude; there are broken thin clouds at about 10,000 feet. Getting over Epinal the clouds break to a 7/10-cloud cover factor, visibility near the target is 10 miles with 6/10-cloud coverage.

"Engineer to pilot… I think I see enemy aircraft… three."

"They are pretty far out… now I see them turning towards us at one o'clock."

"They're coming in… fast… just above level."

"Roger… pilot to crew watch out for other enemy planes… call out when you see them," Asher shouted.

The planes are coming in one at a time; I turned my gun turret around and adjusted my aim and… fire. I pressed the trigger and held it down… I should have used short bursts. I had what looked like an Fw 190 in my sights. I could see my tracer rounds dance around the plane… I think a few hit the rear fuselage. Jerry took a shot as the first one did a split "S" right under us… I could hear him cussing as he shouted, he had missed. The other two enemy planes ran at other planes in the formation out of my view. The radio chatter wasn't too confusing… it was fast and then they were gone and off in the distance. We had just rendezvoused with our escort P-47's; they turned over and at them as they passed. I'll bet they didn't notice our P-47's. They're gone just that fast… they looked like 190's… didn't notice any yellow noses of the JG 26.

P-47 escorting B-26's

As we approached the IP we started receiving flak… it was scattered and not accurate. The further we got into the IP and the target the flak got more accurate. Asher evades up and down, the bombardier has the target and then "Bombs Away." We turn left and dive to evade flak and get away to return to base. Jerry and Rahl were watching the bomb hits… it looked like we just missed it and destroyed buildings just past the target but we hit some rail lines and trucks south of the target. The weather heading back is the same as going to Kaiserslautern. Asher makes a perfect landing at 1529 hours… we park, do our checks and then our interrogations. Headed to the Red Cross for hot coffee and donuts. Everyone made it back ok, no damage from flak and no reported hits from that one pass from enemy fighters. The P-47 escorts reported they downed two planes near us, they noticed one parachute.

> *Dec 30: Mission today, we were attacked by 3 German fighters, one pass… fired long burst at one o'clock, I saw my rounds hit aft of the cockpit, no kill—Flak not bad until we got to the target, results could have been better, there will probably be another mission to finish the job—New Years Eve tomorrow, What To Do? It's too cold to do too much, Ken and Ed talked about a show in Dijon, sounds like a good idea, I don't feel like getting drunk—I am sure going to miss Gene, he's anxious but patient to get home, he has orders for the ride to Paris on Jan 4th, he's packed and ready to go—Wrote a letter to Mary, got a letter from her at mail call when I got back from mission*

New Year's Eve in Dijon is cold and snowy but the city is alive with G.I.'s enjoying cafes, restaurants, the Scrub House as well as G.I. Joe's. There are MP's all around watching out for drunk and rowdy G.I.'s. Took the truck ride back to tent early and read a Zane Grey novel, *he Code of the West* I found the other day that looked fairly new.

New Year's Day was nothing special, it was always a let down knowing Christmas was a week ago and the season was on the way out. Another mission was scheduled for today; I am not on but will be tomorrow. Jerry will be on with me tomorrow; he is on today's mission.

January 2nd, flying in tail number "07", McCurdy pilot, Barrett co-pilot, an officer for the bombardier Elman, Kirkland radio and gunner, Jerry and me. The targets for today are gun positions and supply areas around Nunschwiller near Freiberg, Germany. It was an exceptionally clear day, bright sunshine scattered low clouds around Dijon, the weatherman says it was clear over the target... we'll see, he's been wrong before. We took off at 1048 hours; should be about a three and a half hour mission. Enemy fighters would love this weather, but I have not heard about any sightings... keep an eye out. Approaching the IP, a perfect example of the aviation weather term CAVU, Ceiling and Visibility Unlimited. Hard to believe it was so clear after all the bad weather we've had since the end of November... it probably won't last long.

Steady on the IP path, I can see gun flashes below on my right side... flak... the burst explosions weren't far behind, "Engineer to pilot and crew... flak guns on our right, get ready," I reported and just as I finished, WHOOM, WHOOM, very close to our plane and just below. We should be over the target in a few minutes and then we'll evade.

The flak is persistent; it's getting damn close. I can feel the explosion shocks from the burst around our plane. Flying on the IP to the bomb run can take maybe three to four minutes, but when flak is bouncing you, around you get nervous and minutes seem to last hours.

Our decoy flight just turned off, dropped chaff and dropped their frags. The flak guns must be all around the area scattered in pockets, we're still getting peppered, but it's not accurate.

"Bombs away... wow, it looks good," Elman, said, "Doors closing... let's get out of here."

McCurdy makes a left turn and then a steep dive, a little too steep for me but the rest of the flight is making the same dive to evade. The flak seemed to follow us for a few minutes and then stopped... the weather was still CAVU, perfect for flying and flak gunners.

I could see clouds off in the distance and a cleared view of the ground; it was white mostly with some green and brown patches of land and trees with roads clearly marked. The Rhine River below is the border... we're almost in friendlier territory. Our landing was smooth at 1422 hours... completed mission number 43.

No one said a word on the way back... it almost seemed too peaceful, it's still too damn cold. After interrogations we all gathered at the Red Cross for hot coffee and donuts... it was so refreshing.

Jan 2: My mission #43 today was good except for the flak but no real damage, odd the gunners weren't able to really zero in to knock us down, it was CAVU the entire way and back— Gene getting excited to leave on the 4th—Ken and Ed and I are jealous but don't let on, happy for him, just one mission over the 65 and go home—Chow hall had some good food tonight, steak, potatoes, fresh baked French bread, and vegetables (beans), Dijon mustard was on the table as well

Jan 3: Briefing for all combat personnel conducted by group commander, Col Woolridge… The limit of 65 missions no longer applies, sounds like we're here for the duration of the war how ever long that will be… CRAP… you could see the morale drop like a rock the moment he said it—I guess I'll be gone a while longer, Gene made it out in time—Gene wasn't at the brief but heard about it

"Hey guys… just heard the mission limit for rotation was lifted," Gene said, not in a sarcastic tone but one of sympathy.

"Yea… crap, what a let down," Ken responded, "Well we need to get off on missions and get out of this damned weather pattern to get the war over with… damn… damn it." Ken threw his hat on his bunk

I just looked around and shrugged my shoulders at Ed and we plopped into our bunks to settle in for whatever may come.

"Since we're here a little longer lets get into Dijon and do some sort of shopping or mingling, maybe our Aussie friends are in town?" I said wanting to get out of a bad mood from the news just handed us. Off to the city we went and spent the rest of the day wandering around Dijon.

No mission today, its snowing heavy, fog and colder than yesterday. It's January 4th, Gene is waiting for the truck to transport him and a few others rotating back to the States from the other squadrons. They are going to have a snowy ride to Paris.

Walking Gene out of the tent, Ken, Ed, and I slowly walked out the door after Gene, "Well guys… can't say enough but it's hard leaving you guys but I can't wait to get home either," Gene started to well up tears in his eyes, "Hey wait… I need to get your home addresses."

"I'll contact your families and let them know how things are... OK?"

"Yea... let me write my parent's home address and the phone, they'll contact Mary," I said writing as quick as I could so Ken and Ed could write theirs down

It was a slow and lonely walk to the truck, small talk mostly and then, "This is it... be safe and remember to rely on your experience and training," Gene said with a firm handshake and a strong hug for each of us. With that he turned and jumped up in the back of the truck for the long snowy ride to Paris... then home across the Atlantic. Ken, Ed, and I waited for the truck to move out and then lost sight of it as it turned out of the squadron area onto the road to Dijon and then Paris. We just looked at each other as if we lost our best friend... we did, but he'll be headed home, we were happy for him.

Jan 4: Gene left today, happy for him but miss his friendship and companionship, Glad he went home in one piece—Weather is getting really bad, we can't fly in this—Heavy snow, fog, ice and snow, we are working hard to keep the cold out of our tent—Dijon trips are a nice break

Jan 6: Battle of the Bulge leaning to our favor—Wrote letters home, think about Mary constantly, not being on mission with not too much to do makes the time go slow—We need to get our mission count up!—Hot coffee and donuts at the Red Cross, Ken and Ed head over with me, enough for today's entry

"I cannot stand to sit in a cold, freezing plane waiting to take off," Ken scowled as he returned to the tent after an alert, "Cancelled mission... again."

"What's that... three so far?" I said, "I'm on two."

Ed was frustrated as well, he had three cancelled, "Let's see... January 6, cancelled... January 7, cancelled... then," he was counting on his hand and commenting on the next one, "January 9... oh yea... we flew around for an hour in foggy soup and landed on an icy runway with all our bombs... crap."

Intel message to the 320th Bomb Group for January 9, U.S. and Allied forces situation

ᵗ U.S. Army launches attack on northern flank of the bulge around Ardennes, Belgium.

1,100 Allied bombers and 11 fighter groups attack railroad and communications centers in western Germany.

German attacks on Bastogne, Belgium are called off.

There were two more missions cancelled for me. I hate flying around with almost no visibility with a full load of bombs and returning on an icy runway. Ken, Ed and our other crewmates were frustrated. No credit for missions like these one hour joy rides… just frayed nerves for take off and landings on icy runways.

> *Jan 10: Cancelled again!—Why can't the Weather Officer get his stuff together?—Tired of getting briefed, head to the flight line to preflight and then cancel in the plane, we even taxied out ready to go—Same for taking off and turning around*
>
> *Jan 11, 12, 13: Cancel… Cancel… Cancel…—There goes the morale, getting tired of the snow and icy landscape—No time to get into town for a break, just back and forth to and from briefings and the flight line*

Intel message to the 320th Bomb Group for January 13, U.S. and Allied forces situation

ʳᵈ U.S. Army launches attack toward Houffalize, Belgium, the southern flank of the Ardennes bulge.

British forces capture La Rouche-en-Ardenne, Belgium northwest of Bastogne.

U.S. and British forces link up near La Rouche-en-Ardenne, Belgium.

At least the bulge is shrinking; reports from higher headquarters are good overall… sounds like the Germans are getting beaten back. They are still fighting and will be mad as hell when we can get up and bomb within their borders

The base weather station reported a low of 5 degrees Fahrenheit on January 14th… damn it's cold… wait till you get up to altitude on a mission. Flight suit heaters can go bad… some unruly jerk could steal your gloves. Staying warm on the ground was just as much a challenge, and I worked hard at keeping our stock of firewood for the stove. Social activities in the squadron area were limited… if you had to get some entertainment and beat the boredom and cold, you put up with the 30 minute ride to Dijon. The Scrub House and G.I. Joe's were warm places, but you can't live there.

Then a slight break in the weather, January 16th a mission was scheduled to attack the rail bridge at Rastatt, Germany. I'm not on this mission but Jerry was, Ed got on as well. Ken and I are on the ground till another can get scheduled. Ken and I stayed in our tents by the warm stove… Ken wrote letters home and I continued to read my Zane Grey novel. We decided to meet the crews when they returned for coffee and donuts. They were scheduled back soon; we'll head over when we hear the commotion of crews unloading.

Later in the afternoon, after chow, we heard some trucks pulling into the area and then the sound of crews unloading their gear and talking. It's time to head over to the Red Cross for coffee and donuts to find out how the mission turned out

Ken and I stand and wait for the crews to finish interrogations… we saw Jerry coming over. "Hey… how'd it go?" I asked Jerry, he seemed pleased.

"It was right on… and exciting," he said as he grabbed a cup for coffee and a donut or two

"What happened?" Ken asked.

"We had some cloud cover but not as bad as earlier this month and last."

"The target was hit hard… some misses but a good drop," he took a sip of hot coffee and continued, "Then we got attacked by about twenty Me 109's… you should have seen the P-47's and Spitfires going after them… wow."

Jerry was excited, "Did you hit any?"

"No… they came at us fast and then turned off when they saw our escorts… I think I got a piece of the one that passed by."

It's odd that a scary, but successful mission can raise morale. He and the others gathered around the Red Cross were just as excited. Wish I could have been on this one

Intel message to the 320th Bomb Group for January 16, U.S. and Allied forces situation

U.S. ᵗ and 3rd Armies link up outside of Houffalize, Belgium.

British 2nd Army attacked near Maas River.

German forces pushed back to the line prior to the December 16th attack in the Ardennes

> *Jan 16: Mission finally got up and did a great job… lots of Me 109's but our escort P-47's and French Spitfires did their job and beat them off, no word on how many they downed—All returned no damage*

> *Jan 18: It started snowing the afternoon of the 16th right after a mission returned, it was the first in 13 days of being grounded and cancelling missions—Snow and cold, light snow but it's falling down like a shaken snow globe—Got to get over to the operations office to see if I'm on tomorrow, its getting late—Base Weather says this snow will stop tomorrow morning*

Slugging through the snow heading over to the office… I enter the door to a warm office with a coffee pot and some confiscated donuts on a plate in the middle of Sergeant Buijak's desk.

Buijak enters the room and looks up at me, "Hey… what's up?"

"Yea… checking to see if I am on for tomorrow?"

"I do have you on… but I don't know what plane or crew yet… I'm still working that."

"OK… get me on a good plane and crew… see you at 0300 hours," I said and turned around to get my tent stove warmed up and then on to sleep.

"OK… sleep well, I'll be up late but I'll be on time," Buijak responded. He held a field order in his hand that was received two hours earlier, it reads in part,

FR: NEPHEW NR 94 1/18/1730

TO: ALL GROUPS

FIELD ORDER NR 19—OPERATIONS FOR 19 JANUARY 1945

MAPS: GSGS 4072 EUROPE (AIR) 1:500,000, STRASBOURG, GSGS 4416, 1:100,000, FRANCE-GERMANY.

TARGET NR 3—ACHERN MARSHALLING YARD

3. A. (2) (A) 27 OF 320TH GROUP WILL ATTACK TARGET NR 3…

SIGNED
DOYLE

CHAPPELL A-3 END

Sergeant Buijak sits down at his typewriter continuing to read and looks over to the detail sheets that the squadron operations officer, Captain O'Mahony, put together on crew and plane assignments for the 441st Squadron. It's getting late and he won't get too much sleep… he has to be up way before 0300 hours to wake up the crews.

CHAPTER 8

"RAINBOW LEADER, ZERO EIGHT"

> *Prime Minister Sir Winston Churchill:*
> *"Courage is the first of human qualities because it is*
> *the quality that guarantees all the others."*

Forty minutes from base. We can get back. Checking fuel transfer switches and weight balance; McCurdy has his hands full and sounds nervous calling Rainbow Leader. Generator function doesn't look good; everything checked out on the engine checklist before we took off. "Rainbow Leader, Zero Eight... my Number Two is runnin' rough and I think I'm gonna lose it," Lt. McCurdy sounding frustrated waits for Rainbow Leader to react.

Just when McCurdy was about to try again, Rainbow Leader responded on Channel "B", he had heard the conversation with Major Hayward on Channel "C" and wondered what was going on. "Zero Eight... Rainbow Leader, what's the problem, over?"

McCurdy responded, "My Number Two is running rough and I think it's an oil shutter problem, gauge says it's overheating."

Rainbow Leader responds after a pause, "Zero Eight, did you try closing your oil cooler shutter, over?"

McCurdy replied, "No, we are working that now, but I'm dropping out of formation and heading back to the barn, over."

Lt. McCurdy looked at me then Cudworth, "We got to get this fixed."

Captain O'Mahony, Rainbow Leader, acknowledged, "Got it, you may need to shut down Number Two and feather."

He continued, "Contact Boxcar for steer back to Dijon, good luck... out."

In a nervous voice Lt. McCurdy acknowledged, "Roger, out."

McCurdy and Cudworth cautiously execute a slow right turn to a south-southwest direction towards Dijon. Need to get our bearings; we can use the Rhine River east of our position as a reference point and follow south-southwest over Colmar and into Dijon. Working my way aft back in my turret gun. My view from my turret position is three hundred sixty degrees. Looking aft at our 6 o'clock position I can see our formation and escort fighters getting smaller as they appear and disappear in the cloud cover as we move away; we are east of our Schirmech rendezvous point, east-southeast of Luneville. The weather and varied cloud cover hinders our visual navigation getting back to Dijon or spotting an open level field if we need to belly in. Enemy fighters don't seem to be around so I head back to the pilot's compartment to monitor engine gauges and generator function.

Lone B-26—08

McCurdy continued directing Cudworth, "Get on the checklist for engine failure... the oil temperature is edging up, slow but it's going up."

He continued, "We may have to bailout or take it in for a belly landing, don't want to dump our bomb load over French territory."

With more anger and frustration building in his voice, "This damn cloud cover… can't see ahead… damn it!"

Lt. McCurdy looked at me and directed, "Put the safety wires back in the bomb load."

Then in a loud shout as if I were not moving fast enough, "Now!"

Startled by the shout, I was contacting John on the intercom to meet me in the bomb bay.

"Got it sir… heading back now," I said quickly and disconnected my intercom, turned around and headed aft.

John heard the loud shout over the intercom before I disconnected and grabbed the pouch with the safety wires and moved forward to meet me in the bomb bay. John and I worked around the bombs in their racks and inserted the safety wires into the fuses, this will render the bombs safe in case we dump our load over an open area. We both said nothing to each other as we put the safety wires back in the fuses. John will not be coming forward to toggle the bombs at the bombardier seat in the nose of the plane for the bomb run. It is better if he stays at the gunner position in case we have a fighter problem.

Then John looked at me and asked, "What's going on… FUBAR?"

"We will have a bad situation if we can't get the oil temperature down on the Number Two, I think it is gonna freeze up," I said.

"I sure hope the prop feathers, its bad enough with one engine out but a windmilling propeller… not good."

John with a nervous look on his face and looking around replied, "OK… I'll be ready for whatever, thanks."

"I'd rather jump out… over French territory."

I continued, "John… we'll make it, we are still at an altitude to bail out if we need to."

"We don't want to dump this plane or a bomb load on a French farmer, we can't see too well ahead because of the cloud cover."

John nodded in agreement, "I wouldn't want a B-26 dropping out of the sky without warning on me either."

I headed forward out of the bomb bay and reported back to Lt. McCurdy, "Sir, all safety wires in fuses, bombs are safe."

McCurdy looked at me and nodded in acknowledgement, he looked stressed and was sweating even in this cold at altitude. His facial expression was intense and his eyes were straining scanning forward through the windshield at the cloud cover and occasionally glancing at the engine oil temperature gauge. McCurdy's hands as well as Cudworth's were busy and their body language was tense. He is slowly moving the oil shutter control to the "closed" position on the pilot's pedestal.

Lloyd as radio operator and using navigation charts at the navigator seat aft of the pilot's compartment provided Lt. McCurdy with navigation information. "Sir, we left formation at approximate grid reference WV 0285, and we need to steer back to Dijon… heading two-niner-zero."

After a pause, he continued, "Sir… I have 1420 as the time we left formation."

Lloyd nervously continued not intentionally interrupting Lt. McCurdy's response, "We should be able to see the Rhine River just below and our left… we can use the river for dead reckoning just past Colmar, then little by little we lose sight of the river."

He paused briefly and said, "If we can see some landmarks through the cloud cover… the Rhine moves away from us on our left."

"We should be passing over Lure and then Vesoul… then on to Dijon and maybe the Dole airfield south east of Dijon."

McCurdy responded, "Roger, try to get Baggage Control."

"Report that grid reference and time… confirm heading back to Dijon."

"Try Boxcar Control."

Lloyd replied, "Yes sir."

He adds, "Sir, Besancon east southeast of Dijon would be visible just before we would get to Dole's airstrip… if we divert from Dijon steer, over."

"Thanks Lloyd," Lt. McCurdy acknowledged.

McCurdy looked at Cudworth and me and said, "I hope we can get some clearer skies ahead… we are going to be busy handling this plane on one engine."

Just as he finished and as he slowly moved the oil shutter control lever, Number Two froze suddenly, violently jolting the plane and the controls. McCurdy and Cudworth both held on with eyes wide in shock and both looking at a frozen propeller in a windmilling position. The entire plane rattled and shook; we all had a stunned wide eyed what the hell look on our faces. The plane seemed to drop in altitude quickly; I hit my head on the airframe beam above me during the drop, I know the rest of the crew got bounced around.

McCurdy shouted, "Cut fuel to Number Two… prop feather switch… do it!"

No response from the propeller to feather from the switch function on and off, it stopped with the blade flat against our forward direction.

"Hit the propeller feather switch."

He shouted again, "Try it again… damn it again… again…" Lt. Cudworth is trying to feather with no response.

McCurdy continued to shout, "Keep trying… help me make the power and level adjustment… got it?"

Cudworth responded shouting, "I got it… I got it, damn it!" "Prop feather switch won't respond… it's stuck… it won't feather…we got a windmill prop."

Shouting out again, "We can't feather… I'm trying damn it."

I interjected with some advice on the propeller function, "Sir… put the propeller toggle switches to "OFF"… battery switches to "OFF"… wait a few minutes and then back on."

"This should reset so the feather switch works."

McCurdy looking frustrated and stressed shouts back, "OK… OK… hold on, help me get control."

"I hope this works… we'll try again in a few minutes to reset the pitch to feather."

The aircraft shifted slight to a right yaw as if the aircraft was about to fly sideways. Delicately, McCurdy instinctively adjusted rudder and trim; he started to bring more power to the left engine, Number One, to straighten out the aircraft. He adjusted level to 5 degrees below level on Number One

Both pilots are trying hard to control the plane with our right engine out and a windmilling prop; Number Two is acting like a brake on our right side. They finally got a handle on control, but it is much more difficult than a feathered prop situation. The winds at this altitude are also causing a little bit more trouble with rudder corrections. Finally they gain better control and a straighter path, but struggle with the wheel and rudder controls. Number One is straining and the noise is definitely getting louder. They have their hands full; we need to get on the ground as quickly as possible. The Number One engine is straining, and it is going to get worse. The propeller feather switch malfunction doesn't make sense

Meanwhile Lloyd is having trouble getting a radio response from Baggage and Boxcar Control, nothing but static; we are not hearing anything from the formation. Radio silence from the formation for the initial bomb run is normal, so no radio traffic heard.

Lloyd didn't hear anything regarding enemy fighters in the area from the last transmission listening to Baggage Control and Boxcar Sector Control. He lets Lt. McCurdy know, "Sir, I am getting static on the radio and no response… I'll keep trying."

"No enemy fighters spotted or known in our area from last transmission."

He continued, "Sir… I think the Germans may be jamming our transmissions."

"We may not get clear until we are closer to Dijon."

"Baggage Control Channel "C" has more static, Boxcar's Channel "B" not so much."

McCurdy responded in a loud and nervous voice, "Roger, let me know when I can get on that radio."

"We have our hands full up here… not sure about the heading… recheck."

Lloyd doesn't respond immediately… finally, "Sir, we are OK on heading two-niner-zero."

In spite of McCurdy's stressed situation he lets loose with a quip about a problem similar to this that General Doolittle's demonstration pilot performed in the early production of the B-26. That pilot had a dead engine on a B-26, his Number Two, and turned and maneuvered like both engines were operating; he even turned into that dead engine with no problem. Turning into a dead engine flying a twin-engine plane is a big no-no. One major difference… he didn't have a windmillin' prop… it was feathered; his prop feather switch worked.

He said, "Remember that guy that worked with Doolittle… I'll bet he didn't get this kind of distress."

"Where is he when you need him most?"

Cudworth looked at him in a nervous grin and nodded in agreement, "Yea… what the hell… shit."

That demonstration was famous for getting the B-26 another life instead of being cancelled by Congress because of numerous early airplane handling problems and unacceptable training losses in men and aircraft.

Cudworth continued, "I guess we are about to prove how good this plane really is."

He held on to the wheel and was sweating more; simple small turns and adjustments are done cautiously. McCurdy and Cudworth are straining to maintain control; their faces are showing the stress.

After what seemed to be hours instead of minutes we are heading straighter in our flight path, McCurdy and Cudworth are getting used to the strained controls of the aircraft. They are settling down, somewhat. They look tired.

McCurdy suggests to Cudworth, "If we are going to bail out we need to be closer to Dijon… open flat fields, no farmhouses… what do you think?" He looks at Cudworth waiting for a response.

Cudworth looking concerned, "If we bail out, we have a full load of bombs on board… I know they are safe, we still could do a lot of damage if this plane hits a farmhouse… it'll do a lot of damage without bombs on board."

He continues shouting over the noise, "We can belly in… assuming we have a good flat field and keep everything intact as we ride out the forward motion… we can't just dump our load or this aircraft anywhere especially if we can't see the ground through this cloud cover."

Cudworth looks into McCurdy's eyes with a stern look and voice tone of disagreement, "I don't like the idea of dumping or bailing out."

"I think we should belly in wherever we can, closer to base… or just land on a good long runway."

McCurdy waits a few moments as he ponders what to say next then, "I think we should bail out as we get close to Dijon."

"That's it… unless we have a better option and we can see a good open flat field." He looks at Cudworth for his acknowledgement or disagreement.

Cudworth looks around thinking through what he needed to say, and then, "OK… but I think we can get this aircraft on a heading to an open field that won't hurt anyone on the ground… just in case."

And in a reluctant tone Cudworth responds, "Your call… you're the aircraft commander."

McCurdy directs Cudworth again, hoping to resolve the propeller situation, "Battery switch "ON"… propeller toggle switch to "AUTOMATIC"… do it."

"Try the prop feather switch again."

"No good… its out," Cudworth followed the "ON" directions then moved the propeller feather switch on and off several times with no result

Both have a frustrated and then worried look on their faces; the tone is definitely getting tense between them.

Frustrated with the feather switch, the control situation is delicately stable, but strained; the pilots have their hands full and need to maintain their concentration on the controls. Making my way aft to check if John, Lloyd and Bud are OK. Stopped to talk with Lloyd at the radio position, he looks frustrated; he continues trying to make contact with Baggage and Boxcar Control

"What do you think?" He said to me.

I responded, "I don't know, like I said to John before I don't like the situation… they have their hands full."

"This is a tough one, we can't get the propeller to feather, the book says we can get it under control, the windmilling is not helping… get ready to bail out for now."

"I'm going back to talk with John and Bud… hope you can get through."

Lloyd responds with a slight tone of humor, "No FUBAR… hey!" I winked an eye with a grin continuing the humor of the moment,

"No FUBAR!" I said and then went on my way.

Moving past the bomb bay towards the gunner positions where John and Bud are located, "Guys, we may need to bail out… we may have to belly in."

Both looked concerned, I continued, "I don't think we are going to have a fighter problem… keep your eyes open and stay plugged in your intercom."

"We might not have a lot of time to get ready to jump or take crash positions… roger?"

Both nodded responding in unison, "Roger."

Then Bud opined, "Do these guys know how to handle this plane?"

In a determined voice he says, "I think we should bail out and let the pilots take the plane in for a belly landing!"

John agreed, "Yea, let's get out of here, we are over French territory… we should be picked up by our guys on the ground!"

I responded, "They both have their hands full."

"Lt. McCurdy is the aircraft commander and he makes the call." In disagreement John continued, "We need to talk with him!"

I shot back, "They have their hands full, don't bother them… I'll talk with them and tell them your concerns… OK?"

With reluctant looks on their faces they nod in the affirmative.

I looked at both of them and firmly said, "Stay close to your parachute packs… be ready for bail out or belly in… got it?"

"McCurdy is probably gonna change his mind… we can't see too far forward for a clear field to dump the bombs or plane… it will be a last minute decision."

"Be ready… OK?"

"OK." Both said and returned to their gunner positions with frustrated looks on their faces

McCurdy shouted to Cudworth, "We must be getting close to Besancon… or Dole field."

"Look for an open field… I think we can belly in safely." Cudworth added shouting over the noise, "We need to get a hold of Boxcar for a steer to Dijon or Dole."

"Emergency landing at either place is better… I'll keep looking out for a good open field."

On the intercom Lt. McCurdy asked, "Lloyd, have you got Boxcar yet?"

"We are getting close to base… need to talk with Boxcar Sector Control."

In a terse tone, "Get on it!"

Almost twenty-five minutes after leaving formation, Lloyd finally has contact with Boxcar Control on Channel "B" for Lt. McCurdy. The transmission has intermittent static but is understandable, "Sir… I got Boxcar Control… I reported our last position and grid… they confirmed."

"Go ahead."

"Boxcar… this is Yellow Zero Eight I need a steer for Dijon… over!" McCurdy shouted over the noise in a nervous voice.

Boxcar Control responds, "Check your transmission… you need to steer two niner zero degrees for 40 miles, over."

McCurdy hears a broken transmission and asks, "Boxcar, please repeat, over."

Boxcar Control repeats, "Check again your transmission… you need to steer two niner zero degrees for 40 miles… you are near Besancon, over."

McCurdy responds quickly, struggling with handling the aircraft, "Roger, two niner zero, out."

Boxcar Control calls again, "Yellow Zero Eight did you receive your steer?"

McCurdy looks at Cudworth, "Can they hear us?"

Cudworth responds shouting over the noise also hearing a broken transmission wondering if Boxcar is hearing everything, "Barely… seems to be broken up a little, try again… ask for emergency landing instructions."

"Boxcar… roger out."

McCurdy responds again in a nervous voice and then asks for further instructions, "Boxcar… I believe I'll have to make an emergency landing."

Adding after a nervous pause, "Can you fix me up?"

Boxcar Control answered, "Yellow Zero Eight if you are on two niner zero you are just east of Besancon."

McCurdy hesitating then responds, "Roger… out."

McCurdy and Cudworth are getting nervous. Then Cudworth shouts over the noise of the Number One engine, "We have got to get on the ground or bail out… we are still high enough to bail out."

"What's the call?"

McCurdy looks at Cudworth, "We may need to belly in… or jump out."

He continued in a frustrated voice making a final decision, "Get the crew in crash positions… chute packs close by."

Just as he finished, Boxcar Control is heard in a clearer transmission over the radio, "Yellow Zero Eight the nearest field which is clear will be Dole airfield."

"Steer two five zero degrees for 25 miles, do you think you can make it?"

McCurdy responds quickly, "Roger… out."

"Aircraft having engine trouble and may have to bail out."

Cudworth looks at McCurdy and sternly asks, "Are we bailing out or belly in?"

In an angry tone he shouted, "We need to look for a open field to get in safely… and now!"

The aircraft position is northeast of Besancon, lots of open fields and low rolling hills outside the city boundary.

"I can barely hear Boxcar Control sir… I think I am hearing from Boxcar a confirmation for steering two five zero… they also want a confirmation on transition… they are cutting out," Lloyd shouts over the ever-increasing noise.

Lt. McCurdy ignoring or not hearing Lloyd directs over the Intercom, "Pilot to crew… crash positions… looking for a spot to belly in near Besancon… get in position now!"

The crew moves as quickly as possible to their assigned crash positions located forward of the bomb bay bulkhead and facing aft of the pilot's compartment.

McCurdy and Cudworth guide the aircraft just northeast of Besancon and then make a slow turn left just east of Besancon traveling over the eastern part of the city and towards farms and open fields. The ground is getting closer, power on Number One engine is straining and the noise is deafening inside the aircraft.

Looking around the area the cloud cover is low. Visibility is about five miles; there are open fields to belly in safely.

"Which one?" McCurdy asks.

Then Cudworth notices a field straight ahead and shouted, "We've got to take it down slowly… I think we can cut power for zero level landing."

"Look… that one just right of the farmhouse about two miles out."

"Yea… looks good… getting tired… it is getting harder to hold control," McCurdy responds in a loud shaky voice.

"My arms are going to fall off after we land… feels like I'm part of the plane." Cudworth adds.

McCurdy shouts, "We are losing altitude… can't get any lift… hold on!"

My Gal II "08" approaches above the U.S. Army Hospital in Besancon in a south-southeast direction; there are stunned looks of the medical staff walking outside the building looking up at the plane and noticing the loud distressed sounding engine. It is about five hundred feet above the roof. A B-26 with yellow markings from the 320th Bomb Group and a yellow number on the tail, "08" identification is clear; the sound is so loud it rattles the windows of the main building as the plane passes over.

A faint and steadily growing aircraft engine noise is heard north of the Jeannerod farmhouse south of Besancon. No plane in sight and then Monsieur Jeannerod, outside attending to some chores, notices the loud noise in the sky and then looking up towards the sound and coming out of some low clouds a B-26 heading right for his house. As the B-26 roars low overhead in a south-southeast direction over his head barely missing the roof, Monsieur Jeannerod notices the right engine out, propeller fixed, no smoke, and the yellow color markings. He has seen these color markings before from the Dijon-Longvic airfield. It looks like it is level and dropping in altitude for a belly landing, no landing gear down.

Looking north at an approaching B-26 low over the Jeannerod farmhouse, Monsieur Bussard, outside walking to his other farm building, notices a plane and a loud engine noise. His two children Simone and Paul are looking outside their large window on the north end from inside the farmhouse; they also notice the plane's approach. It appears to be headed straight for them; Monsieur Bussard and his children are frozen in disbelief and cannot move. They've seen a horrible amount of fighting since the war began and especially during September when the Allies drove out German forces in the area. The destruction passed them by but now it seems to be heading their way.

Struggling with a rapidly deteriorating control situation, Lt. McCurdy shouts to Cudworth, "Help me get over that fence on the rise ahead… power."

"No Room Tower… this is Rainbow Leader… approaching field… permission to land?"

"Remainder decoy flight and main force mission flight will follow, over." Rainbow Leader, Captain O'Mahony requests clearance to land.

Tower Control responds, "Roger Rainbow Leader… field is clear… approach from the north."

"Use standard approach for low level visibility… confirm visual."

"Initial approach at 2200 feet… descend to 1700 and start procedure turn."

"Final approach 1500 feet… altimeter is 726."

"Approach lights are on… wind speed at 5 miles per hour from north-northeast, gusting to 10 miles per hour."

Captain O'Mahony acknowledges and maneuvers his B-26 for landing, flaps and gear down gently slowing airspeed for landing, "Roger… wind speed 5 miles per hour from north-northeast… confirm visual."

"Riley, start the checklist for final approach, what's our speed?" O'Mahony concentrates on maneuvering "04" to a safe landing.

Lt. Riley responds, "Speed 172 mph."

O'Mahony directs, "Gear down... check warning indicator for down... check down from my view."

Riley verifies, "Roger... gear warning indicator down and locked."

"Flaps... one-quarter, no crosswind so far that I can tell from the wheel."

"Wind is 5 miles per hour gusting to 10." O'Mahony maneuvers "04" to approach and landing.

Riley confirms, "Roger... 5 miles per hour... feels calm to me just cold and dreary."

The plane gently descends on a straight path over the runway. The main landing gear makes contact on the runway with the usual bumps and rattles of the inside of the plane, and then the front nose gear touches down. The plane rides out the runway distance eventually slowing down to a safe taxi speed. The weather is about the same as it was during mission take off earlier with cold and some scattered ice on the runway; cloud cover is low with visibility from altitude at about five miles. O'Mahony maneuvers "04" to a parking spot to shut down; thoughts of the bomb run and how sloppy it seemed in execution cloud his thoughts.

"Lots of snow to blow around from the engines."

"The engineers need to clear the parking area when they can... gets hard on the gear to maneuver through the snow piles and drifts." O'Mahony looking around has a hard time parking "04" in the snow piles and drifts throughout the parking area. The plane finally stops and O'Mahony and Riley start the shut down checklist.

"This mission could have been executed better... too long between missions, we lose our edge."

"I'm embarrassed." O'Mahony frustrated with the overall mission performance pulls off his gloves throwing them into his lap commenting to his co-pilot Lt. Riley.

Riley returns the comment, "Yea... way too long since the last one... weather didn't help either."

"Damn... still cold, looks like its gonna snow again." O'Mahony responds, "Think so?"

Looking out through the windshield at the view of the airfield landscape and noticeable clouds, "Yea it does."

O'Mahony and Riley work through the shut down checklist. He wonders if "08" made it back to Dijon or to Dole for an emergency landing.

Both scan outside the windshield and watch the remaining B-26's landing with a few newly arrived on the ground taxiing to parking locations scattered around the runway. With the number of planes on this mission it will take about forty-five minutes to an hour to safely land all of the planes, then mission briefings with hot coffee and donuts. "The next mission order is probably already in the operations office and ready for crew and plane assignments." O'Mahony comments in a frustrated voice dreading mission planning for the next day.

Scanning through the checklist with Riley and finishing up O'Mahony asks, "Where's our ride?"

"Let's get out of this cold and get our mission briefing over with."

"Snuffy is not going to like my mission brief, we did not execute this well at all... not good."

"We need to stay sharp, being off because of weather is no excuse."

Then as an after thought and not meaning to have forgotten about the other aircraft on the mission he continues, "Did you hear any chatter on McCurdy in Zero Eight?"

Riley shakes his head, "No... they probably landed at Dole if they had engine problems."

"One engine with a full load and icy runways is a tough one... hope they dumped their heavy stuff."

"I thought I heard Boxcar give a steer for Dole... lots of static... not sure, but Dole is good."

"Yea... he probably made it to Dole for emergency landing." O'Mahony asks again. "Where is our ride?"

As soon as he asked where his ride was, a speeding Jeep approaches "04".

"There's Lt. Steier... looks like he is in a hurry."

"Crazy driver... look at him spin his wheels and weave side-to-side," Riley said.

"Hope he can stop... don't need to be overwhelmed with paperwork about a crazy lieutenant running into a B-26 with his Jeep."

Looking at each other, they chuckle and then gather their gear and move to the escape hatch.

Lt. Steier's driving skills are pretty good plowing through the slushy snow-covered flight line, he finally stopped skidding a bit in the slushy snow in front of "04" and waits for Captain O'Mahony to come out of the nose wheel well escape hatch. Hopping out of the Jeep he approaches "04" and waits, then as O'Mahony and Riley come out of the wheel well. "Sir... McCurdy went in east of Besancon... MP's and medics are on the scene."

"Major Smith doesn't know yet... well maybe... better get back to the squadron office as soon as you can."

O'Mahony worried about what happened responds, "OK... McCurdy contacted me just before he left formation... he said he had engine problems on his Number Two."

"Do you know what happened?"

Lt. Steier replied, "No sir I don't... get in let's get back."

Steier turns around in a slow trot slipping on every other step in the snow; he jumps in the drivers' side and puts the Jeep in gear. O'Mahony and Riley follow sloshing through snow, squeeze into the other side in the canvass covered Jeep; they head out of the parking area to the road back to the squadron area in Longecourt. Lt. Steier is slipping and sliding the Jeep through the snow and slush in a hurry as he heads out of the flight line area. The rest of the crew along with other plane crews get in the deuce-and-a-half GI trucks for transportation back to the squadron area for mission briefings. No one talks as they head back for the mission brief and to find out what Major Smith knows and if McCurdy's plane managed to land or belly in OK. Ken and Ed wonder how Nick is doing. They both overheard the radio chatter and were scared to ask Captain O'Mahony about what happened.

Major "Snuffy" Smith in the squadron operations office waits for O'Mahony and the rest of the mission aircraft to land and then get back from the flight line and mission brief. The squadrons' phone rings and he answers, "This is Major Smith, 441ˢᵗ Commanding Officer… may I help you?"

He hears an excited and fast talking French male voice trying desperately to ask for help or assistance. Major Smith finally figures out that there was a plane that came in by his farm and he or they need help.

He asks, "Do you have a tail number or names, monsieur?"

The voice on the other end answers with, "Yes, yellow and the number "08"… no names."

He tries to understand what he is actually asking for or telling him in broken English with intermittent French words and a heavy French ascent. As the French gentleman was talking, it sounded as if he was saying that some of the hospital ambulances and guards were arriving on the scene to help. The Frenchmen made a quick what seemed to be an apology, for what Major Smith couldn't figure out, and then a goodbye and thank you in French.

Major Smith would know each man personally on that plane; he has not been informed of any non-returns from mission yet. Just as he hangs up the phone, Squadron Operations Sergeant, Staff Sergeant Buijak, enters the office and hands him a note from Boxcar Control that McCurdy's plane went in east of Besancon.

He asked, "What's the status on this?"

"Survivors… aircraft condition?"

He shouts back at Buijak, "Call the medics and MP's for security of the crash site… got it… find out the status?"

"I just got a call from a nervous Frenchman about this… find out what's going on."

Buijak not used to Major Smith's shouting tone responds, "Yes sir… I'm on it… right away."

Just as Buijak leaves the room Captain O'Mahony walks in after arriving from the flight line not yet giving his post mission brief but wanting to know what happened to McCurdy's plane. Major Smith looks down at the note and says, "McCurdy went in near Besancon."

He hesitates still looking down at the floor of the office, "My French isn't too good, but from what the farmer told me on the phone a few minutes ago, it's a mess."

Looking up at Captain O'Mahony, "Sounded like the MP's and medics were arriving on the scene."

"I'm gonna drive up there to do what I can."

O'Mahony looking concerned, "Couldn't Fay or Francis go?" He immediately thought after he said it, he didn't volunteer. O'Mahony didn't like the idea of Major Smith going to the crash site. Snuffy knew everyone by first name on that plane and in the squadron. He was a schoolteacher before the war, a solid combat leader and between missions always protective and concerned for every man under his command

Smith shot back in an unfamiliar terse tone and in an assertive stance looking directly into his eyes regarding Francis and Fay, "Neither one of them is here."

He pulls back a bit and in a lighter tone says, "Besancon is only about 50 miles."

"I'll be back before dark."

Looking down at the floor with a blank stare he quietly gives a verbal order, "You're acting Commanding Officer while I'm gone, so stay close."

"OK… yes sir." O'Mahony quietly responds not knowing what to say or if he should say anything at all.

Major Smith puts the note in his pocket, slowly turns away from O'Mahony and leaves the office with his side arm, jacket, gloves and hat.

Heading out from the squadron office and into the cold and about to step into the drivers' seat of his Jeep, "Sir… Major Smith… wait!"

Staff Sergeant Buijak shouted as he ran out of the squadron office towards the Major's Jeep.

"Sir… got a last minute update from the hospital and MP's," Buijak hands a second note to Major Smith, it reads,

> *A B-26 yellow painted tail battle number "08" went directly over the U.S. Army Hospital-Besancon at about 1505*

He immediately thought that must have scared the hospital staff and patients half to death with the sudden loud noise and plane at a low pass overhead. The note continues,

> 46th General Hospital staff observed "08" pass over at approximately 500 feet. No fire, no smoke, no wheels down, right engine not running with fixed propeller Hospital is responding to the crash location—MP's securing area

"OK… thanks."

"Carry on sergeant."

"I'll be back later, O'Mahony is acting commanding officer."

Major Smith looks out of the windshield with a blank stare, not looking at Buijak, "Get all the information you can on this… OK?"

Buijak saluted, "Yes sir."

Smith returned the salute still looking forward through the windshield, started the Jeep and sped off through the snow-covered road out of the squadron area for the fifty-mile trip to Besancon. Buijak watched with concern as he left the area wondering what happened and if the medics got to the crew in time. Knowing Major Smith's camaraderie with everyone assigned to the squadron he ponders how this will affect his command, attitude, and relationships with the rest of us

The cloud cover is getting lower; it looks like it is going to start snowing again. No wind, just a bleak looking landscape around Longecourt as Major Smith leaves the immediate area heading south. The road is fairly clear where he finds the first road marker for the route to the east towards Besancon. He drives his Jeep cautiously on roads not totally clear with scattered icy patches and hard-packed snow. There is not a direct route to Besancon, only winding roads with turns left and right through small towns and villages. The MP's have the roads marked to direct anyone to the right unit location and village, town or major city. He approaches the sign with the *Red Cross"* and the notation *U.S Army Hospital—Besancon"* next left with a large black colored arrow pointing in that direction. Besancon is where the U.S. Army's 46th

General Hospital is located with plenty of medical staff and operating rooms to take care of any type of wounded or injured.

The weather is cold and lifeless with no wind except for wind passing around Major Smith's speeding Jeep. He sees more direction signs, following their direction to turn right or left. Then finally he spots the sign post on the east end of the village of Fontain just south of Besancon, *U.S. Army—46th General Hospital", "3 Miles/4.8 Kilometers"* with a large black arrow on the sign pointing to the direction requiring a left turn. Before turning and looking out over a dreary winter landscape he tries to locate a crash site, trees and buildings in the distance hide the view to open fields; he can't see a crash site. Turning left towards the Army hospital where he can get information and maybe see his crew, he thought they should be back at the hospital by now if the hospital ambulance got there just after the crash.

Traveling about one hundred yards he suddenly notices trucks, ambulances and people gathering in an open field off his right side and what looks like a wreckage about four hundred yards off in the distance. He slams on the brakes, turning around spinning his wheels on icy patches in the road and speeds towards the area making a left turn on a recently well-traveled road. It's strange that there seems to be no smoke or fire. Daylight is slipping away and it will get more difficult to look around the crash site

Arriving at the edge of a long fence he turned his Jeep to the north, left, and approaches the MP guarding the area.

The MP raises his right hand gesturing Major Smith to stop, "Sir… Halt."

"Can I see some ID please?"

Major Smith stops his Jeep next to the MP and pulls out his ID cards, and says to the MP guard in an authoritative voice, "I'm the Commanding Officer for the 441st Squadron, 320th Bomb Group… that's my crew and plane."

The MP guard, Sergeant Howe, replies, "Yes, sir… we have the area secure and the medics are… they are doing what they do best."

Looking toward the wreckage site and pointing broadly over the entire crash area, he says, "The wreckage is scattered around so watch your step… you may want to keep your Jeep here and walk over."

"Got it Sergeant… thanks." Major Smith acknowledged and asks another question, "Are there more trucks coming or ambulances?"

Sergeant Howe replies, "No sir… we have it covered with what's here now."

After a short pause he asks, "Can I do anything for you sir?"

Major Smith started to walk towards the activity at the crash site wondering what exactly is happening responds looking back at Sergeant Howe, "No… thanks again."

"Yes sir." Sergeant Howe replied and saluted. Major Smith returned the salute and continued his walk toward the scene where the trucks and ambulances are parked to talk with the medics and crew.

"Sergeant Buijak… can you get me today's mission operations order?"

"I am going to start my mission report… any word on "08" yet?" Captain O'Mahony asks while shuffling through mission notes taken in flight and the original mission planning documents.

"Yes sir… no word as of a few minutes ago, I'll track down what I can."

"Oh by the way… Major Hayward is on his way over, he is aware of "08"'s situation." Buijak acknowledges then turns around to get the remainder of the documents from O'Mahony's request and follow up on the status of "08" with the MP Company Headquarters in Besancon.

Just as Buijak turns to exit the office, Major Hayward enters around him with a look of concern on his face, "Captain… what's the status on "08"… and where is Major Smith?"

O'Mahony expecting his visit and anticipating his questions, "Sir, Major Smith went to the crash site southeast of Besancon… he said he would be back before dark."

"Regarding "08" status, we know the medics and MP's are on the scene."

"We have not seen a follow up report at this time, we are checking with the MP's and the hospital for status."

"Got it… keep me in the loop and let me know when you know," Major Hayward acknowledges.

"By the way, tell Snuffy that he is the Investigating Officer for this and his draft report is due to me by the end of the day tomorrow… 20 January, OK?"

"Oh… before I forget… there is no mission planned for tomorrow or the day after."

"Weatherman says it's going to snow, looks like a few days off for the group." Major Hayward quietly turns around and stops and looks back at O'Mahony, "These things don't get any easier in war."

"Find out what happened… and let me know how Snuffy's handling this… OK?"

"You've been there before… take it easy."

"Yes sir." O'Mahony acknowledges and waits for Major Hayward to depart the office area. Continuing to go over his thoughts about the mission he sits down by his typewriter and begins typing his mission report. He can't help thinking about what happened.

As Major Hayward exits the squadron offices, Sergeant's Ken Dixon and Ed Geronimos enter and Ken asks, "Sir… what happened to 08?"

O'Mahony looks up at Ken and Ed, "Sergeant… they went in east of Besancon."

"We are trying to find out what's going on… I really don't have any news for you," Captain O'Mahony responds with concern.

"I know you guys are best friends… but I don't have anything more to pass on."

"We'll let you know… get some rest and some coffee."

Ken and Ed looked at each other with a blank stare of great concern and Ken said. "Sir… we need to know when you know… please."

O'Mahony responded with a compassionate look standing up and placing his hand on Ken's shoulder, "Sergeant… we'll let you know."

"Get some rest and finish your mission briefs for the Intel guys… OK?"

"Yes sir." Ken and Ed turn around and headed out as if to finish up their briefings and back to the tent to wait. Instead, they both head out separately nervously wandering throughout the squadron, group and tent area not knowing what to think or do next. Can't think straight their minds clouded with the question of what happened. Is Nick in the hospital and is he OK?

It is getting dark and Major Smith finally gets back to the squadron office, it's been several hours. While Sergeant Buijak attempts to call the MP Company again, Major Smith walks in looking pale and cold staring at the floor as he enters the squadron office. Not greeting or looking at Buijak or O'Mahony but heading to that large comfortable soft leather chair in the office corner that others often use to relax in, it was a left over from the German occupation. Buijak follows him into the office waiting for a response on what he saw and what was the status of the crew

O'Mahony asks, "Major... what's the story?"

Major Smith is leaning back slumped into the chair and staring at the ceiling with a far off gaze not looking at either Buijak or O'Mahony. He looks emotionally spent.

Ken wandering around outside the squadron area, noticed Major Smith arriving in his Jeep. He ran and entered into the building. He walked past Buijak and in to the open office to listen in on what happened.

Major Smith started talking slowly and monotone. "Cold ride to Besancon... glad the signs were in place."

"I sort of forgot how to get there... no wind... dreary looking."

"I think it's going to snow tonight or tomorrow."

Then his voice started to quiver, "Mac (referring to McCurdy) must have had some hard control problems with the plane... it looked like he was trying to get in straight and clean."

"No flaps... gear up... but..."

He pauses taking a gulp then moving to sit up he looks down at the floor at his feet and with his right hand rubs his eyes to clear his emotions, "I couldn't recognize Mac... or Cudworth... the plane was ripped apart and both of them... weren't too far from the wreckage."

"Hill... Bentas... Tothammer... Rahl were thrown from the wreckage... didn't have a chance, it must have happened fast."

Ken listened; his lips began to quiver and tears starting to well up in his eyes. He took a deep breath as the tears started to stream down his cheeks. He thought of how Nick's family will react to what happened, how would they handle this? How can he handle this? This can't be real. His thoughts return to his time at the Sardinia base and the plane that Jeff was killed in and is numb trying to comprehend what just happened… not again. Disbelief, shock, sadness makes him sick to his stomach. Ken runs outside dropping to his hands and knees vomiting in the snow. He stops vomiting and sits in the snow leaning his back against the squadron office-building wall looking upward in disbelief and starts to cry uncontrollably.

Inside the office, Major Smith continues to talk about the detail not noticing that Ken suddenly left, "All his heavy stuff still in what was left of the fuselage… some scattered about… two bombs went out of the bomb bay, two stayed in."

"The two bombs that skidded out past the impact point headed towards a farmhouse and stopped just short of the outside wall… can't imagine the panic of the farmer's kids faces as two one-thousand pounders headed right at them."

"The medics said they might be there all night picking up the pieces… getting dark."

"I couldn't see well because it was getting dark… we had our headlights on to light up what…"

Captain O'Mahony trying to look into Smith's eyes, himself in shock trying to imagine the scene tells him, "Sir… you are the Investigating Officer by order of Major Hayward."

"He stopped by a while ago… you may want to go over to Group Headquarters to give him an update."

Major Smith pausing and feeling vulnerable and apprehensive for the rest of the squadron and all who knew the crew on "08" looks straight at O'Mahony with a glassy look in his eyes, "Yea… OK."

"Heavy as "08" was, no flaps and a windmillin' prop, those guys had as much chance as a one-legged man in a ass kickin' contest."

EPILOGUE

Prime Minister Sir Winston Churchill:
"Never in the field of human conflict has so much been
owed by so many to so few."

After the investigation was complete and the U.S. Army medics, MP's and engineers left the area having removed the remains of the crew and wreckage of "08", a cross was erected in memoriam to the crew at the impact spot by local French farmers who witnessed the event. Afterwards, the French respectfully gathered what they saw in overlooked pieces of remains of the crew and personal items and placed them in a box. They reverently buried it at the foot of the cross that became weathered and fragile over time.

After the funeral conducted near Dijon, each crewmember was interned at the Allied Cemetery at Epinal. The ceremony was cold but well attended.

The Final Investigating Officer Report dated 22 January 1945 found in official National Archive bomb group documentation is as follows:

DESCRIPTION OF ACCIDENT
(Brief narrative of accident—Statement of responsibility and
recommendations or action to prevent repetition)

At 1100 hours, 20 January 1945, I inspected the wreckage of Aircraft #43-34605 where it had crashed at a point approximately eight miles southeast of Besancon, France at about 1510 hours on 19 January 1945. The bodies of crewmembers had been removed but the wreckage had not been disturbed, although a blanket of eight inches of snow covered the aircraft and the scene of the accident

It was apparent that the aircraft approached from the direction of Besancon over which it had passed at a low altitude at about 1505 hours. The aircraft was headed southeast under a very low ceiling and was evidently in distress. It is assumed that it was aircraft #334605, which was sighted as it was positively identified as a B-26 type medium bomber carrying yellow markings

After passing over the crest of the hill about ¾ mile north of the point of impact, the aircraft barely cleared a farmhouse located on the southern slope of the hill. Two hundred yards below the farm house, the ship left its first visible mark on the ground where the cowling of the right engine had dug in. Debris was scattered in a southerly direction from this point for a distance of about a hundred yards to where the main concentration of wreckage came to stop

It was apparent that the aircraft struck the ground at a fairly steep angle on the right wing, nacelle, and lower right hand length of the fuselage. An examination of the engines and propellers revealed that the left engine was carrying power at the time of the crash while the right engine was obviously windmilling slowly but was not feathered. The position of landing gear units and the condition of the two recognizable flaps indicated that the ship came in clean. The bombs had not been salvoed but were in and near the wreckage. An investigation of the turret compartment revealed that no attempt had been made to jettison flak vests, helmets, ammunition, or other heavy objects

The disintegrated condition of the aircraft plus the snow coverage prevented further accurate evaluation of the evidence

Signature, Investigating Officer
Sidney P. Smith, Major, Air Corps
Signature, Deputy 320th Bomb Group Commander
Lawrence J. Hayward, Major, Air Corps

My Gal II Photo on 20 January 1945

The 46th General Hospital at the direction of its adjutant officer assigned the medical officer on the scene to complete, for the record, an investigation report in accordance with standard operating procedure. The following report was taken from the original document and had no attached diagram found in official National Archive bomb group documentation; it contains graphic descriptions, reader discretion is advised

DISPENSARY
46th GENERAL HOSPITAL (U.S.)
APO NO. 419 . S. ARMY EDS/hah

20 Jan 45

SUBJECT: Investigation of Death of the Crew in Airplane Crash

O: The Commanding Officer
441 Bombardment Sq.
320th Bomb Gp., A.A.F.
*APO **374**, US Army*

1. On 19 Jan 45 at 1800 hours, on orders of the Adjutant, the undersigned officer went to the scene of an airplane crash in the vicinity to investigate and report, bring in the bodies of those killed, and secure their personal effects

The following morning the scene of the crash was again visited in daylight in company with the Commanding Officer and three other officers of the unit to which the plane belonged

2. *The plane that crashed passed directly over the hospital at 1505 hours, 19 Jan 45, at very low altitude and apparently in difficulty. It crash landed directly after in open farm land about 1 mile south of the La Veze (8 miles S.E. of Besancon, France). The plane was a B-26 with the number 334-625/08 on the tail fin and was later identified as belonging to the 441 Bombardment Squadron, 320th Bomb Group, A.A.F. There was no local property damage*

3. *The plane came in over a farm house flying SSE parallel to and just E of a row of trees (see diagram), striking the ground 200 yards E of the house. The right engine, which it seems was stalled, struck first, digging a hole 1 foot deep and leaving a part of the cowling. The fuselage then apparently swung to the left, the left engine dropped out, the body broke apart thru the bomb compartment, the right wing was completely demolished along with the nose of the plane, the left wing turned over completely and came to rest pointing back along the course, the tail however remained upright but pointed almost directly ahead with severe damage to the right elevator. Two 1,000 lb. bombs remained in the center of the wreckage of the body but two others were thrown ahead an additional 125 yards. From the point of impact to where the tail came to rest was 100 yards There was no explosion or fire*

4. *The bodies of the entire crew of 6 were strewn along the course of the wreck (See numbers in diagram) death was instantaneous in all. The first body was found 20 yards beyond the point of impact, the second 10 yards further on and a little to the right, the next two were close together in a bit of detached wreckage of the body midway along the course, the co-pilot (1 Lt) strapped in his seat and wearing a throat microphone was found just before reaching the main mass of the wrecked body and wing, the pilot (2nd Lt), his head completely in shreds and both legs*

entirely amputated thru the thighs, lay in the midst of the main wreckage of the body of the plane. The crew, listed in the order their bodies were found proceeding in the direction the plane was traveling, along the course of the wreck, were as follows:

(1) *Hill, John C. S/Sgt., 18 071 305 (P)—Skull Crushed*
(2) *Rahl, Lloyd A. S/Sgt., 30 570 208 (P)—Skull Fractured*
(3) *Tothammer, Henry P. S/Sgt., 39838514 (P)—Skull Fractured*
(4) *Bentas, Nicholas (NMI) S/Sgt., 36564340 (C)—Concussion*
(5) *Cudworth, Elmer L. 1 Lt., 0 319 760—Skull Crushed*
(6) *McCurdy, Arthur L. 2nd Lt., 01 683 414—Entire skull crushed and in shreds, both legs completely amputated thru thighs, and right hand thru the palm*

Bodies #2, 3 & 4 were the only ones wearing identification tags; body #1, the only remaining one was identified by officers of his organization the following morning, who also checked the identity of the two lieutenants. A continuous guard had been posted by the local MP's at the site of the wreck shortly after the crash

5. The personal effects of each body, including 5 rings, and insignia of the officers, were removed and carefully listed separately. The following morning they were turned over to Major Walter P. Fay of their organization, together with copies of certificates of death for each. Receipt for the listed valuables was given by him

//Original Signed//
EDWARD D. SPAULDING
Lt. Col., Medical Corps
Investigating Officer

In early 1982 Dolly (Bentas) Cressy, Staff Sergeant Nick Bentas's sister, was contacted by mail, a letter with a return address from France. The letter was written in French, she immediately set out on an effort to get it translated. She noticed that there were references to her brother and the war that was recognizable even in French. As it turned out a dedicated group of boy scouts, led by Mr. Henri Gay, were determined to make a permanent memorial to her brother and his crew. They planned and then built the memorial. On April 10, 1983 a dedication ceremony took place. A permanent memorial was now in place to the American crew of "08" giving their lives for France's liberation and victory against tyranny. It is a constant reminder to all who see it to stop, thank and remember them for their sacrifice and courage. The letter writer was Mr. Henri Ducret. One item in particular that was found on January 19, 1945 and held in order to return it to family was an identification bracelet that belonged to Nick Bentas. It finally made its way back to family, Dolly (Bentas) Cressy and Matina (Bentas) Salens in 1986, thanks to Mr. Henri Ducret.

Memorial for "08"—Fontain, France

The final resting place for individual crew are as follows; Lieutenants' McCurdy, Cudworth, and Staff Sergeant Hill are buried at the Epinal American Cemetery Memorial in Lorraine, France. Staff Sergeant Tothammer is interned at a cemetery in Monterey, California, Staff Sergeant Rahl is interned at the Cedar Valley Cemetery, Arenac County Michigan and Staff Sergeant Bentas is interned at the White Chapel Cemetery World War II Memorial section Troy, Michigan.

For then, for now, for future generations… do not seize just the day, seize every second.

High Flight

Oh, I have slipped the surly bonds of earth
And danced the skies on laughter-silvered wings;
Sunwards I've climbed and joined the tumbling mirth
Of sun-split clouds—and done a thousand things
You have not dreamed of—wheeled and soared and swung
High in the sunlit silence. Hovering there
I've chased the shouting wind along and flung

My eager craft through footless halls of air
Up, up the long delirious burning blue
I've topped the wind-swept heights with easy grace
Where never lark, or even eagle, flew;
And, while with silent, lifting mind I've trod
The high untrespassed sanctity of space
Put out my hand, and touched the face of God

—*John Gillespie Magee, Jr*

ACKNOWLEDGEMENTS

Artwork:

The book cover artwork was completed by Jeff Putt of Jeff Putt Design (*jeff@jeffputt.com*), photo credit of the B-26 at sunset from (Mike Smith). "Martin B-26 Marauder Man Information at B26. COM." Mike Smith, n.d. Web. 18 Apr. 2004. *http://b26.com/*. Dr. Franz Reisdorf, Administrator for the 320th Bomb Group Association granted permission to use the squadron emblem for the 441st. The web site can be accessed at *http://320thbg.org/*. Other artwork cover photos from the Bentas/Cressy family photo album.

Documentation and Information:

A significant source that provided detailed operational information were the publications of aviation author Victor C. Tannehill who wrote extensively about the 320th Bomb Group and the B-26 Martin Marauder. The titles and publication information of his books are listed in the bibliography.

The 320th Bomb Group Association website maintained by families of members of the bomb group was a significant source of historical events. This site has archived bomb group information, stories, and photos of the group's activities during World War II. (Accessed at *http://320thbg.org/*)

An additional information and collaboration website that provided further insight into aircrew and pilots flying B-26's during World War II in the Pacific, European and Mediterranean Theaters of Operations was *http://www.b26.com/*.

The National Museum of World War II Aviation was instrumental in discussing and answering questions about B-26 engine and propeller operations. Their museum is one of the best World War II Aviation

Museums in the United States, and maybe the world. It is growing with more planned exhibits and aircraft. The web site is *http://www worldwariiaviation.org* . The museum tours are guided and include an additional side-tour at WESTPAC Restorations, their web site is *http://www.westpacrestorations.com*

Official documents obtained through the National Archives were reviewed to reveal missions where SSgt Nick Bentas was a crewmember. Documents included daily mission reports, aircraft accident reports/photos, medical evaluation reports, missing aircrew reports, and mission photos for pinpointing unit accuracy on targets. Knowledge of missions he participated on and the circumstances of each were obtained from personal journals, official reports and reactions during personal interviews.

Personal Contacts:

Henri Ducret (French citizen and a child during WWII)—Henri contacted my mother in 1982 regarding a memorial for the crew, much to her surprise. We corresponded at various times during the late 1980's and the 1990's. Since neither he nor I spoke or wrote each other's language, we found translators to write back and forth. Mr. Ducret provided some excellent detail of 19 January 1945 from eyewitnesses.

Gene Fulk (Technical Sergeant, USAAF retired, Engineer/Gunner with the 320th Bomb Group, 441st Squadron)—Gene was a good friend of Nick Bentas during his time in Sardinia, Corsica and France. He rotated back to the United States in January 1945 having completed 66 missions. I had the pleasure of meeting Gene at the Denver Colorado 320th Bomb Group 1998 reunion. He provided insight about my uncle's personality, off-duty activities and mission details. He provided additional photos that were unknown to our family. Gene passed away on March 18, 2005; he will be missed greatly by me.

Charles ("Chuck") O'Mahony (Captain, USAAF retired, Pilot with the 320th Bomb Group, 441st Squadron)—Chuck was of great help in providing detail on B-26 operations and missions presented on operations reports. He wrote the book *Blue Battlefields (1994)* which provided a personal perspective of his training, combat missions, photos and personal feelings. He also wrote several articles about his wartime experiences in several popular aviation magazine publications. Chuck passed away on May 12, 2012. He was a part of the "Greatest Generation" whom I honor and will never forget.

Jerry Raschke (Technical Sergeant, USAAF, Gunner, 320th Bomb Group, 441st Squadron & Captain, US Air Force Reserve retired)—Actual mission and off duty events were provided by Jerry in personal conversations and his personal journal entries detailing missions that he shared with Staff Sergeant Nick Bentas. His journals also bring out crew interactions during off duty time. He flew with Nick on four missions on the 19th, 23rd, and 30th of December 1944 and the 2nd of January 1945. Jerry has been a great help. We first met at the Denver Colorado 320th Bomb Group 1998 reunion and we continued corresponding through 2000. Searching for him on the Internet and hoping he may still be alive, I found him in August 2013. We talked and reconnected; he is in his 80's getting close to 90 years of age and active and working in his church.

Parker Rosenquist (Lt. Colonel, Pilot, USAF retired)—Parker is a friend of a friend and was glad to meet with him in October 2013. He flew twin-engine propeller cargo planes in Vietnam in the late 1960's on an aircraft that used the same engine type as the B-26, the Pratt & Whitney R-2800-43 Double Wasp Radial. These engines were manufactured and updated through the 1970's. Parker provided detailed information on aircraft handling during emergencies and on how difficult it is to handle a twin-engine aircraft on one engine. His career in the USAF was quite interesting and memorable; he served as a pilot for Air Force One during the Nixon, Ford, Carter and beginning of the Reagan administration. He flew for commercial airlines as a second career after his retirement from the US Air Force and is currently retired from his second career. His detailed information has been extremely helpful in schooling me on propeller aircraft operations.

Most notably and certainly not last in importance is my mother Daphne (Bentas) Cressy affectionately referred to as "Dolly", my Aunt Matina (Bentas) Salens, my grandfather and grandmother Costas and Edokia Bentas, and Ray Salens a younger friend in their Detroit neighborhood and future husband of my Aunt Matina. They provided personal insights to family interactions. My mother passed away on Father's Day June 20, 1993 and Ray Salens my "Uncle Ray" passed away after a long illness on May 2, 2009; my grandparents Costas and Edokia Bentas passed away in 1974 and 1967 respectively. May God provide them a rest in peace!

Notes:

Names used in the book were real personalities with exceptions and are contained in publically available documentation from the National Archives. Specific permissions were given by a few of the characters that I had personal contact with and include, Gene Fulk, Gerald Raschke and Chuck O'Mahony. They provided insight into the main character, other characters and their routine conversations that may have occurred. The 320th Bomb Group Association web site curator, Dr. Franz Reisdorf, gave permission to use whatever material on the site that would bring the story to life, including photos. Dr. Reisdorf is the son of a B-26 pilot Captain Benjamin Reisdorf 320th Bomb Group, 441st Squadron. Actual events depicted in this story were gleaned from observations found in listed bibliography sources, personal accounts in journals and official documents available to the public and obtained from the National Archives

Editing Assistance and Guidance:

The following individuals conducted review of the draft manuscript for grammar, facts, and content:

Lynn Cressy—My wife and trusted reviewer was instrumental in providing me with a check on what and where I was going with the story. She is a retired business teacher at the high school and college level with over 30 years of teaching experience.

Suzanne Boettcher—Is a close friend and wife of a fellow US Army officer, Fred Boettcher, Lieutenant Colonel, USA retired. Suzanne is a retired US Army civil servant with a senior GS rating. She served in various capacities preparing and publishing official US Army documents for senior field grade and general officers.

Galen Conrardy—Galen is a published author and retired high school English teacher with over 20 years of teaching experience. His book, *Growing Up with Roy, Memories of the 40's and 50's in Rural America"* chronicles his youth growing up in Colorado and Kansas. He attended the same high school as my wife Lynn. He is currently working on two additional book projects to be published at a later date.

BIBLIOGRAPHY

Books/Personal Journals/Poems:

Birdsall, Steve, illustrated by Greer, Don. *B-26 Marauder in Action, Aircraft No. 50,* Squadron/Signal Publications Inc., 1984.

Ethell, Jeffrey L. *Bombers of World War II*, Lowe & B. Hould Publishers, an imprint of Borders, Inc., Second Edition, 2001.

Havener, J. K. *The Martin B-26 Marauder*, Southern Heritage Press Second Edition, 1998.

Magee, John Gillespie, Jr. *High Flight,* poem written on 3 September 1941 during a Royal Air Force training mission over England.

O'Mahony, Charles J. (Captain, USAAF retired, Pilot with the 320th Bomb Group, 441st Squadron)—*Blue Battlefields,* Aviation USK, 1994.

Raschke, Gerald W. (Technical Sergeant, USAAF, Gunner, 320th Bomb Group, 441st Squadron & Captain, US Air Force Reserve retired)—Personal journal detailing missions that he shared with Staff Sergeant Nick Bentas, Self-published, 2005.

Roberts, William F. *Bonus Time—One Pilot's Story of World War II*, Xlibris Corporation, 2002.

Stapler, Hans-Heiri, illustrated by Greer, Don. *B-26 Marauder In Action No. 210*, Squadron/Signal Publications Inc., 2008.

Tannehill, Victor C. *Boomerang*, Boomerang Publishers 6164 West 83rd Way, Arvada, Colorado 80003, 1980.

Tannehill, Victor C. *Pilot's Flight Operating Instructions for the B-26 Martin Marauder*, Boomerang Publishers 6164 West 83rd Way, Arvada, Colorado 80003, 1981.

Tannehill, Victor C. *Saga of the 320th: A B-26 Marauder Group in WWII*, Boomerang Publishers 6164 West 83rd Way, Arvada, Colorado 80003, 984

Tannehill, Victor C. *First TACAF: First Tactical Air Force in WWII*, Boomerang Publishers 6164 West 83rd Way, Arvada, Colorado 80003, 998

Tannehill, Victor C. *The Martin Marauder B-26* Boomerang Publishers 6164 West 83rd Way, Arvada, Colorado 80003, 1997.

U.S. Government & Other Historical Sources:

National Archives World War II Official Documents, *320th Bomb Group Operational Records January 1, 1944 through January 31, 1945*, 2004.

Headquarters USAF, Office of Air Force History, *Air Force Combat Units of World War II* 1961.

Headquarter USAF, Office of Air Force History, *Combat Squadrons of the Air Force, World War II*, 1982.

Headquarters USAF, Historical Studies Branch, USAF Historical Division, *The Army Air Forces in World War II: Combat Chronology, 1941- 1945*, 1973.

Headquarters USAF, Historical Studies Branch, USAF Historical Division, Aerospace Studies Institute, Air University, Maxwell AFB,

Alabama, *Combat Crew Rotation—World War II and Korean War*, 968 *www.afhra.af.mil/shared/media/documents/AFD-08024-048.pdf*

Schwimmer, Marcus. *The Battle of the Bulge—Belgium MIA Project 2011- 2012*, A. Scott Foundation, Image of the Battle of the Bulge original source from Wikipedia. *http://www.ascottfoundation.org/ MIARecovery/ BotBMap.html*

Accessed Internet Sources:

320th Bomb Group Association web site *http://320thbg.org/b26_320th_aircraft.html*

B-26.COM web site *http://www.b26.com/*

B-26 Marauder Historical Society web site *http://B-26MHS.org*

Grid number format used during WWII, *Notes on the Modified British System of coordinates on the European Theater of Operations during WWII*, website with translator. *http://www.echodelta.net/mbs/eng-translator.php*

320TH BOMB GROUP HISTORY

320th Bomb Group Official History
(Copied from the Department of the Air Force history
and accessed from the 320th Bomb Group Association
web page, emphasis applied)

Constituted as 320th Bombardment Group (Medium) on 19 June 1942.

Activated on 23 June 1942. Trained with B-26 aircraft. Most of the group moved to North Africa via England, August-December 1942. Crews flew their planes over the South Atlantic route and arrived in North Africa, December 1942-January 1943. Began combat with Twelfth AF in April 1943 and operated from bases in Algeria, Tunisia, Sardinia, and Corsica until November 1944. During the period from April to July 1943, flew missions against enemy shipping in the approaches to Tunisia, attacked installations in Sardinia, participated in the reduction of Pantelleria, and supported the invasion of Sicily. Then bombed marshalling yards, bridges, airdromes, road junctions, viaducts, harbors, fuel dumps, defense positions, and other targets in Italy. The 320th Bomb Group supported forces at Salerno and knocked out targets to aid the seizure of Naples and the crossing of the Volturno River. Flew missions to Anzio and Cassino and engaged in interdictory operations in central Italy in preparation for the advance toward Rome. Received the French Croix de Guerre with Palm for action in preparation for and in support of Allied offensive operations in central Italy, April through June 1944. Received a *Distinguished Unit Commendation* (DUC) for a mission on 12 May 1944 when, in the face of an intense anti-aircraft barrage, the group bombed enemy troop concentrations near Fondi in support of Fifth Army's advance toward Rome. From June to November 1944 operations included interdictory missions in the Po Valley, support for the invasion of Southern France, and attacks on enemy communications in northern Italy. Moved to France in November 1944 and bombed bridges, rail lines, gun positions, barracks, supply points, ammunition dumps, and other targets in France and Germany until V-E Day. Received a DUC for operations on 15 March 1945 when the group bombed pillboxes, trenches, weapon pits, and roads within the Siegfried Line to enable a breakthrough by Seventh Army. Moved to Germany in June 1945 and participated in the disarmament program. Returned to the US, November and December.

Inactivated on 4 Dec 1945

ABOUT THE AUTHOR

Nick Cressy is the nephew of the main character; Staff Sergeant Nicholas Bentas is his mother's older brother. For over 25 years, he has researched facts and stories from members of the 320th Bomb Group, National Archive and other sources familiar with the bomb group's history in World War II in the European and Mediterranean Theaters of Operation.

Nick retired from the US Army as a full Colonel in December 2012 and enjoys World War II history, biking, and traveling locally (in Colorado) to enjoy the scenery and culture. He has undergraduate and graduate degrees in business management. Foreign countries visited during his lifetime include Canada, Mexico, France, Germany, Austria, and Switzerland. His military background began as an enlisted member of the U.S. Air Force trained in aircraft weapons and munitions loading from 1971 to 1975, briefly serving in the Michigan Air National Guard from 1977 to 1978. He received a direct commission in the U.S. Army (Reserve) Medical Service Corps serving from 1991 to his retirement in 2012. During his career, assignments included service in the states of Michigan, North Dakota, Colorado, Texas, Virginia and Hawaii. His overseas assignments included Vietnam, Thailand, Philippines, Bahrain, Kuwait and Afghanistan.

www.ingramcontent.com/pod-product-compliance
Lightning Source LLC
Chambersburg PA
CBHW052019070526
44584CB00016B/1820